FOREIGN INTERVENTIONS IN ETHNIC CONFLICTS

Global Security in a Changing World

Series Editor: *Professor Nana K. Poku, John Ferguson Professor, Department of Peace Studies, University of Bradford, UK*

Globalisation is changing the world dramatically, and a very public debate is taking place about the form, extent and significance of these changes. At the centre of this debate lie conflicting claims about the forces and processes shaping security. As a result, notions of inequality, poverty and the cultural realm of identity politics have all surfaced along side terrorism, environmental changes and bio-medical weapons as essential features of the contemporary global political landscape. In this sense, the debate on globalisation calls for a fundamental shift from a status quo political reality to one that dislodges states as the primary referent, and instead sees states as a means and not the end to various security issues, ranging from individual security to international terrorism. More importantly, centred at the cognitive stage of thought, it is also a move towards conceiving the concept of insecurity in terms of change.

The series attempts to address this imbalance by encouraging a robust and multi-disciplinary assessment of the asymmetrical nature of globalisation. Scholarship is sought from areas such as: global governance, poverty and insecurity, development, civil society, religion, terrorism and globalisation.

Other titles in this series:

Cocaine Trafficking in Latin America
EU and US Policy Responses
Sayaka Fukumi
ISBN 978-0-7546-7043-8

A Decade of Human Security
Global Governance and New Multilateralisms
Edited by Sandra J. MacLean, David R. Black and Timothy M. Shaw
ISBN 978-0-7546-4773-7

Non-Traditional Security in Asia
Dilemmas in Securitization
Edited by Mely Caballero-Anthony, Ralf Emmers and Amitav Acharya
ISBN 978-0-7546-4701-0

Foreign Interventions in Ethnic Conflicts

ROBERT NALBANDOV
University of St Andrews, UK

ASHGATE

Published by
Ashgate Publishing Limited
Wey Court East
Union Road
Farnham
Surrey, GU9 7PT
England

Ashgate Publishing Company
Suite 420
101 Cherry Street
Burlington
VT 05401-4405
USA

www.ashgate.com

British Library Cataloguing in Publication Data
Nalbandov, Robert.
Foreign interventions in ethnic conflicts. -- (Global security in a changing world)
1. Ethnic conflict. 2. Ethnic conflict--Case studies.
3. Conflict management--International cooperation.
4. Conflict management--International cooperation--Case studies. 5. Mediation, International. 6. Mediation, International--Case studies. 7. Security, International.
8. Security, International--Case studies.
I. Title II. Series
327.1'7-dc22

Library of Congress Cataloging-in-Publication Data
Nalbandov, Robert.
Foreign interventions in ethnic conflicts / by Robert Nalbandov.
p. cm. -- (Global security in a changing world)
Includes bibliographical references and index.
ISBN 978-0-7546-7862-5 (hardback) -- ISBN 978-0-7546-9693-3 (ebook)
1. Intervention (International law) 2. Ethnic conflict--Prevention--International cooperation. 3. Conflict management--International cooperation. 4. Armed conflict--International cooperation. 5. Security, International. I. Title.
JZ6368.N35 2009
341.5'84--dc22

2009026050

ISBN 9780754678625 (hbk)
ISBN 9780754696933 (ebk)

Mixed Sources
Product group from well-managed forests and other controlled sources
www.fsc.org Cert no. SGS-COC-2482
© 1996 Forest Stewardship Council
FSC

Printed and bound in Great Britain by
TJ International Ltd, Padstow, Cornwall

Contents

To my Mother

List of Maps

List of Tables

Acknowledgements

The book is the product of research at the School of International Relations, University of St. Andrews, Scotland, UK, with the generous grant of the Economic and Social Research Council (ESRS). I am enormously grateful to Dr. Erin Jenne for her rigorous support and friendly guidance during my research. I would like to extend my high appreciation and gratitude to Dr. Rick Fawn from the University of St. Andrews whose advice and comments during earlier versions of the Georgian chapter, as well as my overall activities at St. Andrews helped me a lot. I am grateful to the Munk Center for International Studies, University of Toronto, where I conducted the research for the Chadian and Somalian chapters. I also benefited from numerous conferences and round-tables where I presented different drafts of the book chapters and which allowed me to incorporate valuable comments of their participants. Finally, I would like to thank Irakli Machaidze and Dr. Basil Germond for helping me with the research on the legal documents and agreements in relation to the French interventions in Chad.

List of Abbreviations

AEF	Afrique Équatoriale Française (French Equatorial Africa)
ANL	Armée Nationale de Libération (National Liberation Army of Chad)
BET	Borkou-Ennedi-Tibesti province (Chad)
CDR	Conseil Démocratique Révolutionnaire (Democratic Revolutionary Council of Chad)
CIS	Commonwealth of Independent States
CSM	Conseil Suprême Militaire (Supreme Military Council of Chad)
FAN	Forces Armées du Nord (Northern Armed Forces)
FANT	Forces Armées Nationales du Tchad (National Armed Forces of Chad)
FAP	Forces Armées Peuple (People's Armed Forces)
FAR	Forces Armées Rwandaises (Rwandan Armed Forces)
FAT	Forces Armées Tchadienne (Chadian Armed Forces)
FLT	Front de Libération du Tchad (Liberation Front of Chad)
FROLINAT	Front de Libération Nationale du Tchad (National Liberation Front of Chad)
GUNT	Gouvernement d'Unité Nationale du Tchad (Government of National Unity of Chad)
HDM	Hisbia Digil Mirifle (Somalia)
HRFOR	Human Rights Field Operation in Rwanda
IAF	Inter-African Force
JCC	Joint Control Commission (Georgia)
MAD	Mutually Assured Destruction
MOD	Abbreviation of the Mareehaan, Ogaadeen and Dulbahante clans (Somalia)
MPS	Mouvement Patriotique du Salut (Patriotic Salvation Movement of Chad)
MRND	Mouvement Républicain National pour le Développement (National Republican Movement for Development of Rwanda)
NFD	The Northern Frontier District (Somalia)
NMOG	Neutral Military Observer Group (Rwanda)
NUF	National United Front (Somalia)
OAU	Organization of African Unity
OLS	Ordinary Least Squares
Parmehutu	Party for the Emancipation of the Hutu People
PKF	Peacekeeping Forces (CIS)

PPT	Parti Progressif Tchadien (Chadian Progressive Party)
RPF	Rwandan Patriotic Front
SDA	Somali Democratic Alliance
SDM	Somali Democratic Movement
SMP	Somali Patriotic Movement
SNM	Somali National Movement
SRC	Supreme Revolutionary Council (Somalia)
SSDF	Somali Salvation Democratic Front
SYL	Somali Youth Club
TNC	Transitional National Council (Somalia)
UDT	Union Démocratique Tchadien (Chadian Democratic Union)
UNAMIR	UN Assistance Mission in Rwanda
UNAR	Union Nationale Rwandaise (National Rwandese Union)
UNOSOM	UN Observer Mission in Somalia
UNT	Union Nationale Tchadienne (Chadian National Union)
USC	United Somali Congress
USP	United Somali Party

Introduction

The history of humankind is marked by constant struggle for existence, or conflict. Within states or between them, conflicts have always been principal driving forces for human evolution, contributing to development of peoples' thoughts, their ideas on reality, and their perceptions of the contemporary world.

When talking about the inter-state or intrastate wars, it is an agreed approach in contemporary conflict resolution and intervention literature to divide epistemological enquiry into post-WW II Cold War period and after the dissolution of the Soviet Union. The last decade of the 20th century and end of the Cold War, which shaped the relations within the international system of states for almost half a century, heralded a new era of democratization of the world but also proliferation of severe ethnic clashes within state territories between population groups having different identities. At this point, the ideological identity of conflicting groups was replaced or layered with religious and/or ethnic ones. Ethnicity and nationalism became key distinguishing features of groups representing country populations.

Important insights to the problem of successful resolution are contained in the character of participants of the process of conflict. Domestic actors do not engage in wars in complete vacuum: any processes significant enough to change a country's political and/or territorial settings would inevitably have a "butterfly effect" on its immediate surroundings and even far beyond. In essence, conflicts may run and end as a result of actions of the belligerents alone, or with participation of third parties. Although the warring factions can themselves, in principle, reach solutions to the disputes, outside interference, or third-party interventions, may play a critical role in shaping the course of domestic events. Outside actors may either aggravate or mitigate intrastate security dilemmas by skewing the local power balance towards the parties they support, or, in case of their neutrality, by favoring a common good of a larger regional and/or international community of states they represent.

Intra-state conflicts and the means of their resolution have been with the focus of international relations scholars and practitioners from diverse prospective and entry points – their participants; goals of belligerent groups; specific outcomes of the conflicts; regional and international environment in which the conflicts take place; consequences of civil wars and many more. While some investigate the endogenous nature of belligerents[1] and attempt to define conditions for the victory

1 Areguin-Toft, I. 2001. How the Weak Win Wars: A Theory of Asymmetric Conflict. *International Security*, 26(1), 93-128.

of domestic actors,[2] others contemplate on external players that affect the course of civil,[3] study of the effects of composition of third party interventions in the matter of conflict resolution,[4] successes or failures of negotiations,[5] the rules of the resolution process and the roles of post-conflict institutions in conflict management,[6] the ways in which civil wars end[7] and, finally, domestic and international factors contributing to specific conflict outcomes.[8]

With all the differences in approaches to the study of foreign interventions in domestic identity conflicts there is a general agreement to view successes of third party actions by the duration of peace established after interventions take place, which has become almost a commonplace in intervention and conflict discourse. The durable peace approach is widely used as a criterion for judgment about success of third party actions with different proxies of peace longevity. For instance, Hartzell (1999) and Licklider (1995) equate successful interventions with de facto peace lasting for at least five years.[9] Two years of successful peace-building after the ends of the wars are named by Doyle and Sambanis (2000) as an indicator of interventions' success,[10] while Regan (1998) applies a more rigid parameter for "success" of interventions: peace that lasts for at least six months.[11] Peace as the main outcome of interventions is also used in Carment and Rowlands' (1998) analysis of third-party interventions in civil wars.[12] For their part, Diehl et al. (1996) focus on successes of multilateral interventions, primarily, undertaken by the UN, in domestic conflicts from the point of view of successful peace-building.[13]

2 Mack, A. 1975. Why Big Nations Lose Small Wars: The Politics of Asymmetric Conflict. *World Politics*, 27(2), 175-200.

3 Snyder, J. and Jarvis, R. 1999. Civil War and the Security Dilemma, in *Civil Wars, Insecurity, and Intervention*, edited by B. Walter and J. Snyder. New York: Columbia University Press, 17-37.

4 Regan, P.M. 1996. Conditions of Successful Third-party Interventions in Intrastate Conflicts. *The Journal of Conflict Resolution*, 40(2), 336-359.

5 Walter, B.F. 1997. The Critical Barrier to Civil War Settlement. *International Organization*, 51(3), 335-364.

6 Hartzell, C.A. 1999. Explaining the Stability of Negotiated Settlements to Intrastate Wars. *The Journal of Conflict Resolution*, 43(1), 3-22.

7 Licklider, R. 1995. The Consequences of Negotiated Settlements in Civil Wards, 1945-1993. *The American Political Science Review*, 89(3), 681-690.

8 Henderson, E.A. and Singer, D.J. 2000. Civil War in the Post-Colonial World, 1946-92. *Journal of Peace Research*, 37(3), 275-299.

9 Hartzell, C.A. 1999, 14 and Licklider, R. 1995, 682.

10 Doyle, M. and Sambanis, N. 2000. International Peacebuilding: A Theoretical and Quantitative Analysis. *The American Political Science Review*, 94 (4), 779-801.

11 Regan, P.M. 1998. Choosing to Intervene: Outside Interventions in Internal Conflicts. *The Journal of Politics*, 60(3), 754-779.

12 Carment, D. and Rowlands, D. 1998. Three's Company: Evaluating Third-Party Intervention in Intrastate Conflict, *The Journal of Conflict Resolution*, 42(5), 572-599.

13 Diehl, P.F., Reifchneider, J. and Hensel, P.R. 1996. United Nations Intervention and Recurring Conflict. *International Organization*, 50(4), 683-700.

The quintessence of these research endeavors means that the interventions are considered successful as long as post-intervention peace in a target country lasts. Similarly, if the interveners fail to establish peace in war-torn countries, or the peace had not lasted long enough, they are said to be unsuccessful.

Using durable peace as the main factor variable for the outcome of interventions has a number of fallacies of theoretical and methodological nature. The main problem of this view is that it is void of the myriads of complexities of interveners and domestic players. Most importantly, this peace-centric approach does not take into account the real intentions of interveners and causes of interventions. Third parties may intervene in a target country as a response to a humanitarian crises resulting from civil war; they may even themselves start wars. Interveners may support belligerent groups by providing them open military and/or economic resources for prolonged hostilities or support by clandestine insurgencies. They may intervene alone or in coalition, be biased or neutral and/or impartial. The dimensions of success of all these different interest- and goal-driven interventions are all set up by the years of peace after their actions are over. Judging of intervention success by years of peace following the intervention brings in the "billiard ball"-like[14] view of interveners, that assumes that all "third parties intervene in intrastate conflicts to bring an end to the violence associated with the underlying dispute" and that they "do not intervene to exacerbate or prolong the fighting".[15] This means that all third parties are by definition equally peace-driven in their actions and that peace-making is their actual aim. However, when the matter concerns the real agendas of interveners and what they indeed wanted to achieve, this approach seems to be inadequate.

We may have conflicts where a third party directed its support to an ethnic group, which had eventually lost the war to its rival, thus ending the conflict and restoring peace in a target country. Duration of peace in this case would actually depend on how effectively and decisively the winner could triumph over the intervention-supported group thus making third-party actions unsuccessful. We may also have conflicts where interveners are not concerned with fate of the belligerents per se and resolution of conflicts in general, but, rather, aim at exercising their own power influence over the target country by keeping civil unrest longer. In these cases they would be more interested in continuation, rather than secession, of hostilities, and the longer peace deals last the less successful their actions would actually be.

Even if durability of peace is applied for a good reason and secession of hostilities is indeed the goal of the interveners, using such a protracted indicator as several years or even six months of peace after the end of wars gives us a distorted understanding of the phenomenon of intervention and is inconsistent with the actual situation on the ground in a post-conflict country. At the same time,

---

14 Wolfers, A. 1962. *Discord and Collaboration: Essays on International Politics*. Baltimore: The Johns Hopkins Press, 3-35.

15 Regan, P.M. 1998. Conditions of Successful Third Party Intervention in Intrastate Conflicts. *The Journal of Conflict Resolution*, 40(2), 340.

what may be a sufficient time for post-conflict settlement for one country's society may be not enough for others: domestic context matters, together with the wide array of goals and aspirations of third parties, the roles they play on international and regional arenas, interactions they have with other actors, composition of interveners themselves and the nature of the conflicting parties. Even more so, often outside efforts directed to ending conflicts become counterproductive to actual peace: interventions may either not end the conflict at all or provide temporal termination of hostilities, which are susceptible to resumption in a short time-span. Similarly, a ceasefire achieved through intervention may merely grant additional time to the belligerents during which they can marshal their forces for resumption of hostilities in future. All these differences make attempts to measure conflict resolution by a single constant parameter undesirably curtailed.

Apart from pure theorizing, the peace-centric line of reasoning has quite a strong normative and moral connotation. It is a universal truism that peace is better than war, the former leading to tremendous human suffering. If we assume that success of third party actions measured through long-lasting peace occurring after interventions, is good per se, and their failure, measured by resumption of hostilities after a certain time period, is bad per se, then the natural question arises, "How was this peace, or a good state of affairs established, in first place, and for whom was it good?" What if in order to reach long-lasting peace one ethnic group, being supported by a third party, had to completely wipe the other one out of the ethnic map of the country?

What makes peace-centrism even more problematic is its methodological failure to differentiate between *pro-pax* and *pro-bellum* third-parties by putting them in one melting pot of discourse. Years of peace as a result of peace-keeping and peace-building efforts of neutral and impartial interveners are equated in a statement of success along with extended non-resumption of wars achieved by biased third parties. In this line of reasoning the true nature of outside actors is evaded and restricted to mere counting years of peace.

Another methodological failure is its operationalization from the point of view of timescale of evaluating success. Even the most rigid criterion, such as a six-month period of peace after the intervention, proves unsatisfactory when considering different agendas of the interveners. A third-party intervention at some point in time aiming at reaching limited agendas (such as, for instance, providing support to the government against a rebellion, not completely crushing it) shall not be classified as failure when, five years after it had retreated the conflict scene, the government it had supported had been put down by the opposition if the aim of the interveners was not complete annihilation of the rival force. Also, interveners' preferences may change and, if they had intervened to provide support to the ruling government, they may decide not to do so another time when the same government is under threat, thus leading to the defeat of the previously aided side.

Intervention objectives vary depending on each specific case, hence the time-relevance of their success: a period enough for limited-scope and resources spec-ops operations would be highly unlikely a sufficient indicator for success of multi-faceted peace-building and state-reconstruction missions. A timescale approach may well be applied for humanitarian interventions; however, even in this case post-conflict development that follows their peacekeeping missions takes much longer time than six months or even five years. Consideration of immediate outcomes of interventions gives a better prospective on whether or not third parties were successful in their actions. A situation may change on the ground which falls outside of the interveners' powers to affect, and, depending on variations of specific objectives in time (for example, changes in mandates of third-party missions), fluctuating goals and corresponding actions of the same outside forces can be leading to interchanges of successes and failures.

The gap is clear: longevity of peace cannot be taken as a measure of considered success of interventions when peace is not their major objective. We cannot attribute the role of a mediator of peace agreement or an arbiter and an outside guarantors of peaceful settlements, as Walter (1997) argues,[16] to a third party whose objectives are not to end war, rather, to help one ethnic group win over another with no further commitment to long-lasting peace. Similarly, those interveners whose task is monitoring of the situation should not be held responsible for failure to stopping conflicts simply because it was not their objective: this is tantamount to blaming one's refrigerator for not being able to play your DVDs.

The way to solve this measurement quagmire is to not assume that peace equals success, but, rather, to view success of third party actions by actual fulfillment of their intervention objectives. Thus, to consider outside actors as successful would be possible if they managed to reach their intervention agendas and goals. If, on the contrary, they have failed to achieve their tasks, they should be viewed as unsuccessful. Judging about success of interventions through fulfillment of their tasks is quite a labor-intensive process since, unlike peace as a central dependent variable to success; objectives of third parties in each specific case shall be cross-referenced with actual end-state of their actions. To see what had been planned and what was achieved in reality and to evaluate the degree of fulfillment of objectives would require careful analysis of the intervention cases, their participants, courses of actions and outcomes. Such goal-oriented approach resembles the KPI (Key Performance Indicators) tool for measuring financial and non-financial performance of organizations to see how successfully they have developed within a certain period of time. The KPI defines goals and objectives and states the parameters of their successful implementation.[17] Unlike KPI method, which correlated planned

16 Walter, B.F. 1997. The Critical Barrier to Civil War Settlement. *International Organization*, 51(3), 335-364.

17 For the info on the KPI and Performance Measurement Systems see, among others, Parmenter, D. 2007. *Key Performance Indicators (KPI): Developing, Implementing, and Using Winning KPIs*. John Wiley and Sons, Inc., Hoboken, New Jersey; Smith, J. 2001. *The K.P.I. Book: The Ultimate Guide to Understanding the Key Performance Indicators of Your Business*. Insight Training and Development Limited; Eckerson, W.W. 2006. *Performance Dashboards: Measuring, Monitoring, and Managing Your Business*. John Wiley and

parameters with actual output indicators, the goal-oriented approach has a more stringent view on successes of interventions and measures them in binary absolute, or integer, values and not in fractions: either "yes" or "no".

The goal-oriented approach is neither free from its own fallacies, which are related to the nature of the phenomenon – goals and objective of the interveners – which may not necessarily be known to a researcher. The publicly stated objectives may (and, in some cases, would) differ from the ones pursued in the conflict fields. Interveners and their governments, which is usually the case with unilateral interveners, may have hidden agendas they endeavor to reach while presenting to their own constituencies and to the international community more peaceful intentions. However, this is a rewarding exercise since it would enrich the discourse on international security and conflict resolution at large, and foreign interventions in ethnic conflicts, in particular.

Form the point of view of participating actors, the success of peace-centric views is closely related to discussion on the nature of interveners, i.e. who the third parties are, and the nature of the warring parties, in defining likelihood of interventions' success. Here composition of external interventions plays an important, if not a decisive, role in their ability to reach and keep peace. Such an approach can also be applied and tested in goal-oriented approach with the relevant implications of their composition – being *unilateral* (i.e. undertaken by the leadership and being composed of one foreign state-actor) or *multilateral* (undertaken by the leadership and being composed of more than one foreign state-actor). Therefore, before answering the question "What makes the interveners to succeed?" the focus should be made on whether the postulates of the peace-centrism that outcomes of third party interventions in intrastate ethnic violence directly depend on their compositions is valid also in case of the goal-oriented approach. A transfer of the main hypothesis existing in the works of Regan and Licklider on third party intervention will help to unveil this intervention puzzle with substitution of peace by fulfillment of intervention objectives: ceteris paribus, multilateral interventions are more likely to be successful in reaching their agendas as goals in violent ethnic conflicts than unilateral interventions. Application of the similar hypothesis but from a different prospective would test the robustness of the commonly existing viewpoint of intervention multilateralism as a better tool for solving domestic political problems.

At the same time, composition of interveners as the main independent variable for success is alone insufficient for the in-depth theorizing on successes and failures of third-party actions exactly because of the differences between the conflicts and their participants. In order to define the factors contributing to the success of third party actions, it would be useful to employ combination of the traditional views that consider interveners' success in terms of their ability to bring peace to a target

---

Sons, Inc., Hoboken, New Jersey; Franceschini, F. 2007. *Management by Measurement: Designing Key Indicators and Performance Measurement Systems.* Springer-Verlag Berlin, Heidelberg.

country with the goal-oriented approach. This is done via studying the factors contributing to fulfillment of objectives from two levels of conflicts: the influence of other actors and/or its sub-systemic units on the course of conflicts and the nature and interaction between the sub-systemic units of the action-system; causes of conflict and how the hostilities actually ended; duration and level of casualties.

For this purpose, a revision of the current peace-centric stance to successes of third-party interventions, as well as existing datasets of foreign interventions in intrastate ethnic conflicts is required with subsequent development of a different data on the basis of the fulfillment of the interventions' objectives by the third parties. A large-N statistical regression analysis of success of third party actions in ethnic civil wars would help establish a correlation between the composition types of interveners (unilateral/multilateral as the main independent variable) and successes of their actions (the dependent variable). On the basis of the results received, in-depth case studies involving diverse participants, including the belligerents and interveners, are required to fine-tune the results of the regression analysis and to find additional factors that influence the ability of the interveners to pursue their objectives. Since the purpose of the case studies is to identify conditions that facilitate or impede third party interventions, the cases are selected on the basis of variations of extreme values of independent and dependent variables with the application of the Method of Structured and Focused Comparison:[18] the ethnic wars in Chad, Georgia, Rwanda and Somalia. The results from the case-studies, combined with the statistic analysis are further used to tease out the theoretical implications of third party interventions and to construct a theory that can be used to good effect by external actors in intervening in violent conflicts.

The book will proceed as follows: Chapter 1 presents a fit between the goal-oriented view into the existing scholarship on interventions' success and extends the framework of analysis on third party interventions. Chapter 2 delivers the results of the statistic analysis of successes and failures of interventions, and defines the variables that have primary importance for successful interventions. Chapters 3, 4, 5 and 6 present case-studies of the conflicts in Chad, Georgia, Somalia and Rwanda. Finally, Chapter 7 offers theoretical basis for the goal-oriented approach to successes of foreign interventions in ethnic conflicts.

18 George, A. 1979. Case Studies and Theory Development: The Method of Structured, Focused Comparison, in *Diplomacy: New Approaches in History, Theory and Policy*, edited by P.G. Lauren. New York: Free Press, 43-68.

Chapter 1
Theories of Third-party Intervention

Success of third parties largely depends on the perceptions of the belligerents of the enforceability power of the outcomes the interveners propose. The more the conflict parties respects externally imposed solutions, including sanctions, and who imposes them, the clearer they perceive threats for possible non-compliance with the options proposed by the third parties, the more they will believe that the opponents would have exactly same fears from the punitive actions of the interveners, and, thus, would better comply with the proposed outcome by trusting both their rivals and the external actors.

There is no unified approach either to the nature of the interveners affecting the end-state of conflicts or to the role of the composition of intervention forces that influences the durability of peace. While for some scholars neutrality of usually multilateral interveners contributes to their successes in the matter of resolving conflicts, for others individual interests of third parties make them more decisive in imposing solutions upon the belligerents. The quest for outcome- and objective-based theorizing on successes and failures of interveners starts with definitions of the roles they play, contribution of the compositional dichotomy to the ability of the interveners to successfully pursue their goals, and exploring local conditions in the target counties that either impede or facilitate interventions.

With all the complexities of outside actors, in enforcing their decisions upon the belligerents, third parties, at large, serve two roles – of an arbiter, a principal decision-maker and an imposer of its will, and a mediator, interested in no particular outcome but in a solution commonly acceptable to all the warring factions. In the first case not only does a third party offer a solution to the conflicting parties but it also enforces it through creation of necessary conditions for its acceptance. This is usually done by a force that the conflicting parties cannot withstand. Third-party further commits itself to keeping the outcome intact and, sometimes, even appoints the winner in the conflict. In doing so, the third party, according to Bloomfield (1995), "…can quite legitimately employ its own resources to bribe or threaten the disputing parties into agreement"[1] or any other outcome. An important aspect of interventions mentioned by Galtung (1965) is that, although the parties may or may not submit to arbitration voluntarily, "in either case they may agree to the solution only if they accept or have to agree".[2] The guarantee of acceptance of the solution

1 Bloomfield, D. 1995. Towards Complementarity in Conflict Management: Resolution and Settlement in Northern Ireland. *Journal of Peace Research*, 32(2), 152-153.

2 Galtung, J. 1965. Institutionalized Conflict Resolution: A Theoretical Paradigm. *Journal of Peace Research*, 2(4), 360.

is their bias and self-commitment to pursue its objectives "wholeheartedly". Even if a conflicting party is dissatisfied with the conflict outcome being imposed by the interveners, third parties will "...establish a hegemon by helping one side to win or by imposing direct rule by outsiders."[3]

The other role of a third party is of a neutral and/or impartial mediator with no vested interest in particular outcome of conflict. In the words of Galtung (1965), such interveners may "direct...antagonists towards the mutual acceptance of some point in the compatibility region. The task is not to decide on that point, only to indicate it, and serve as debate regulator so as to make the contestants better aware of the structure of the goal-space."[4] The guarantee of success of the interveners is their impartiality: that they will impose a without prejudice to any specific warring faction but will find a mutually acceptable solution. The third party may facilitate the negotiation process by offering "good offices", funding and hosting meetings and peace talks, and providing other relevant technical support.

In either of these roles, successes of third parties should be assessed on the basis of two different criteria. In case of a biased arbiter where the task of a third party is to enforce its own will, success should be evaluated by the belligerents' acceptance of this will. In case of a neutral mediator where the task is peace-keeping, peace-building and possible post-conflict rehabilitation, success should be defined in terms of years without war. In either of these cases presence of third parties in the conflicts alters cost calculations of the conflicting parties for the continuation of war and conveys the message to the belligerents that "the payoffs from cheating...no longer exceed the payoffs from faithfully executing its terms. Once cheating becomes difficult and costly, promises to cooperate gain credibility and cooperation becomes likely".[5] The interveners are "...either making the actual cost of fighting prohibitively high or by making the benefits of not fighting actually attractive. The successful intervention will result then from a cost-benefit calculation by the antagonists that leads to not fighting providing the highest expected outcome".[6]

The real problem is that even using this approach we cannot draw a clear line between what had been planned and what was achieved due to interveners' diverse aims and objectives. The criterion of stopping war and preserving longevity of peace of success cannot be applied even to a neutral and impartial intervener whose aims were mere monitoring of fulfillment of agreements: it is simply not meant for keeping durable peace.

3 Snyder, J. and Jarvis, R. 1999. Civil War and the Security Dilemma, in *Civil Wars, Insecurity, and Intervention*, edited by B. Walter and J. Snyder. New York: Columbia University Press, 27.

4 Galtung, J. 1965, 360.

5 Walter, B.E. 1997. The Critical Barriers to Civil War Settlement. *International Organization*, 51(3), 340.

6 Regan, P.M. 2002. *Civil Wars and Foreign Powers – Outside Intervention in Intrastate Conflict*. University of Michigan Press, 73.

Domestic Context of Interventions: Trust, Fear and Commitment

Enforceability of sanctions largely depends on the factor, which was not directly mentioned by Galtung, but which follows from his argument, and which is especially applicable in intra-state ethnic wars: trust of belligerents to the arrangements offered by the third parties. Trust, which, by a wide definition of Lawler et al. (1999), is "...an expectation that another will cooperate in a mixed-motive situation",[7] essentially signifies three psychologically explained types of believes: the belief by a belligerent group that it would be punished if it does not comply with the outcomes proposed by the intervener; that it would not be punished, abused or treated unfairly by the intervener if he does complies with the solution offered; and that its rivals would not cheat the intervener-imposed sanctions. Eventually trust builds up credibility of the intervention frameworks.

Key components to success of interventions – fear and trust of the belligerents to the outside actions – are inherent parts of the credible commitment theory of third party interventions, which originates from the "agent-principal" theories of economics. In the banking sector, for example, central banks commit themselves through banking supervision mechanisms to guarantee that in cases of insolvency of commercial banks, the depositors will "receive adequate compensation and [that] the system is insulated from the damage wrought by the ensuing contagion".[8] In doing so, central banks act as third parties in the relationships between the depositors, as principals, and the commercial banks, as agents, protecting the interests of the former and, in a broader sense, the stability of the banking system. Similarly, insurance markets are founded on this double commitment: that of the insurance agencies that they will honor the insurance claims made by their clients, and that of their clients' respecting the agreements and not cheating the insurance companies. Here, again, the central concept of the credible commitment is trust, which, in the words of Anderson et al. (1996), is "a belief that the counterpart will behave 'equitably' (in a manner that is 'fair' or which respects the interests of the trusting party)".[9]

In the field of resolution of ethnic conflicts, the credible commitment theory is applied to the majority-minority settings in the target countries and to the third parties acting as external guarantors of peace in civil wars. In conflicts in multi-ethnic states aggravated by "ethnically defined grievances, negative stereotypes, demographic threats, histories of ethnic domination, emotion-laden ethnic symbols, reciprocal fears of group extinction, de facto political anarchy, and the

---

7 Lawler, E.J., Ford, R. and Large, M.D. 1999. Unilateral Initiatives as a Conflict Resolution Strategy. *Social Psychology Quarterly*, 62(3), 242.

8 Hall, M.J.H. 1989. *Handbook of Banking Regulation and Supervision*. New York and London: Woodhead Faulkner, 75.

9 Anderson, E., Ross, W.T. Jr. and Weitz, B. 1996. *Commitment and Its Consequences*. American Agency System of Selling Insurance, INSEAD working paper, 96/42/MKT, 7.

political space and military means to act",[10] the minority ethnic groups need strong guarantees from state institutions against abuses of their interests, while majorities need similar guarantees from ethnic groups that they would not rebel against their rule. On the national level, in a normally functioning state with acting democratic constitutions, such guarantees are enshrined in public authorities, which keep interethnic tensions to minimum. The guarantees are absent or inefficient under the conditions of domestic anarchy resulting from state collapses, which bring ethnic security dilemmas into life. The situations with "…no central government exists to insure order, no police or judicial system remains to enforce contracts, and groups have divided into independent armed camps"[11] and subsequent security dilemmas are the milieus in which third-parties are most likely to operate during their actions, or which are caused directly by third parties.

Security dilemmas have serious implications for the third-parties' successes and failures since they directly influence the degree of fear and trust to outside actions. First described by Posen (1993), ethnic security dilemmas, resulting from state collapse and the incapability of weak or poorly functioning central governments to control their territories, pose the tasks of provision of their own security to the ethnic groups and make them resort to defensive actions.[12] Ethnic groups in trying to protect their members by replacing and substituting for the protector functions of the state, eventually acquire a state-like logic and its *modus operandi*. Under such "self-help" situations,[13] "…the groups emerging from an old empire must calculate their power relative to each other…and make a guess about their relative power in the future."[14] Self-assessment and assessment of others is done on the basis of the past experience of inter-group interactions and their subjective views on whether or not others bear threats to them. Ethnic groups become entrapped in their blurred views and distorted perceptions, by definition considering other as inherently evil. In preparing to defend their kin, or, in the words of Roe (1999) "…in trying to increase its societal security (strengthen its own identity), causes a reaction in a second society, which, in the end, decreases the first society's own societal security (weakens its identity)."[15] Ultimately, defense is considered to be less effective in protecting group identities, than offence, which becomes a preferred type of action making the "first-strike-wins" thinking prevail.

10 Kaufman, C. 1996. Possible and Impossible Solutions to Ethnic Civil War. *International Security*, 20(4), 175.

11 Walter, B.E. 1997, 338.

12 Posen, B.R. 1993. The Security Dilemma and Ethnic Conflict, in *Ethnic Conflict and International* Security, edited by M.E. Brown, Princeton University Press.

13 Kaufman, S. 1996. Spiraling to Ethnic War: Elites, Masses, and Moscow in Moldova's Civil War. *International Security*, 21(2), 108-138.

14 Posen, B.R. 1993, 110.

15 Roe, P. 1999. The Intrastate Security Dilemma: Ethnic Conflict as a Tragedy? *The Journal of Peace Research*, 36(2), 194.

From purely domestic point of view, groups mistrusting each other cannot find outside guarantors who, according to Fearon (1998), "...can credibly guarantee agreements between them...[and] ethnic majorities are unable to commit themselves not to exploit ethnic minorities".[16] From the point of view of credible commitment problem, security dilemmas contribute to rise of mutual perceptions of threats in ethnic groups coming from predatory intentions of others. Minorities fear that they would be tyrannized by the majorities, which are usually stronger and which enjoy overwhelming presence in state apparatus, including law-enforcement agencies and the military. Without their interests and rights effectively safeguarded by state authorities, a minority living in an anarchic state may at some point be faced with the dilemma whether to fight for a better life or continue living as before – in the same state. At the same time, majorities also worry that the minorities might find suitable moments, or "windows of opportunity" when the former cannot effectively control the situation and resort to nationalistic expressions wanting more benefits for their kin with possible ultimate of self-determination. The majority may, of course, use its comparative advantage in human capital, resources, technical factors, and, more importantly, military strength, to crush the minority completely in order to avoid any future upheavals.

Essentially, credible commitment problems exist by definition between the minority and majority in a state of regime transition and domestic anarchy, and their levels and severity are in direct correlation with the status of the minority/majority relations. The key solution to the this trust conundrum is how credibly the majority commits itself not to suppress the minority and offer its share of the country's benefits, and how credibly the minority commits not to pose any threat to majority and to stay within the state.

Reciprocal commitment to keep peace is quite difficult, since groups' leaders are appealing to perhaps the stronger cohesive force of ethnic solidarity – history. Stories, usually precipitated with negative episodes of ethnic interactions, are revived; fables and sagas of former grandeur, as well as suppression, are put in new contexts; own groups are over-glorified and over-stigmatized and others are depicted as evil. Not only do myths and legends enhance the creation of group-specific identities, but also they play an important role in ethnic mobilization. Lessons from the past are crucial in shaping the present mode of relations between ethnic groups and the interactions of their identities. Ethnic groups tend to assess potential threats coming from others "in terms of...cohesion and...past military records".[17] Past grievances, feelings of social deprivation and marginalization by others harden ingroup identities. As noted by Ross (2001), "In escalating intergroup conflicts key metaphors, such as the chosen traumas, serve both as a rallying point and as a way to make sense of events that evoke deep fears and

16 Fearon, J.D. 1998. Commitment Problems and the Spread of Ethnic Conflict, in *The International Spread of Ethnic Conflict*, edited by D.A. Lake and D. Rotchild. Princeton: Princeton University Press, 108.

17 Posen, B.R. 1993, 105.

threats to existence".[18] Group cohesion becomes "glued" by the memories of past oppression, which solidifies their identity.

Domestic anarchy further deepens the divide on "us" and "them" within ethnic groups and strengthens ingroup solidarity allowing for efficient mobilization when these groups' identities are threatened. In this line of reasoning Theiler (2003) claims that "…people distinguish their ingroups from outgroups in ways that they perceive favorably to reflect upon the ingroup and…negatively upon their outgroup…[T]hey continuously compare their ingroup to outgroups along dimensions that make their groups look good to them".[19] As a result, ethnic groups, create their own "…positive social identity [which]…refers to the part of an individual's self-image that relates to group membership…achieved through favorable evaluation of one's own group relative to other groups."[20] A crucial point of the ingroup cohesion is that its representatives tend to attribute more positive human characteristics – love, affection, loyalty, charity, brotherhood, family, gratitude – to their own kin and more negative ones – hatred, treachery, and greed – to the representatives of other ethnic communities, depicting them as less humane and by definition, hostile. Lake and Rotchild (1996) stressed the same point when talking about the roles historical background plays in relation to provoking ethnic conflict. According to them, "[p]olitical memories and myths can lead groups to form distorted images of others and see others as more hostile and aggressive than they really are".[21]

Such reasoning, leads to the creation of negative "ethnic stereotypes"[22] – historically justified set of characteristics that differentiate one group from others, which are transmitted through generations and further disrupt the interactions between ethnic communities. While developing in some groups the sense of moral superiority, stereotyping leads to increasing feelings of deprivation and grief in others. A group, thus, becomes a bank of emotions, a repository of common heritage, which is positively related towards own kin and negative to all the rest.

Depending on whom the third-parties support or even if they are neutral and/or impartial, ingroup solidarity may become a significant factor in ability of the former to reach intervention goals. The higher ingroup ethnic mobilization level, the more committed the group representatives are to fight for their cause, which

18 Ross, M.H. 2001. Psychocultural Interpretations and Dramas: Identity Dynamics in Ethnic Conflict. *Political Psychology*, 22(1), 167.

19 Theiler, T. 2003. Societal Security and Social Psychology. *Review of International Studies*, 29, 261.

20 Levin, S., Sidanius, J., Rabinowitz, J.L. and Federico, C. 1998. Ethnic Identity, Legitimizing Ideologies, and Social Status: A Matter of Ideological Asymmetry. *Political Psychology*, 19(2), 374.

21 Lake, D.A. and Rothchild, D. 1996. Containing Fear: The Origins and Management of Ethnic Conflict. *International Security*, 21(2), 55.

22 Jost, J.T. and Banaji, M.R. 1994. The Role of Stereotyping in System-justification and the Production of False Consciousness. *British Journal of Social Psychology*, 33, 1-27.

makes the actions of the third-party aiding that group more effective and less costly – a "wholehearted" action and backing from whom the third parties support contribute to their successes by creating favorable receptive grounds, cutting their operational costs and providing large community support. On the other hand, ethic cohesion increases domestic resistance to the third parties helping the opposing groups. This is also true in case of neutral interveners, since they would face equally strong resistance on the part of all the belligerents if their ingroup cohesion is strong. Such cases make interveners' neutral and impartial actions even more difficult since, in order to achieve positive reception of their solutions, they have to mollify not only the present grievances of the belligerents, but also to smooth their past stigmas. Likewise, if the mobilization level is low in the warring factions, depending on direction of a third-party support, this may correspondingly facilitate or hinder the pursuit of third-party agendas.

A key feature of Fearon's commitment problem theory is its focus on domestic variables without the participation of any external actors. Although "the commitment problem can be eliminated if there is some powerful third party willing and able to commit to intervene if the minority does not respect political commitments to the minority",[23] this is highly problematic due to the high costs of entry that external players will be hesitant to bear. However, impartial and neutral third parties may still play a significant role in decreasing mistrust and acting as outside sponsors of domestic peace. According to Walter (1997), third parties "...can change the level of fear and insecurity that accompanies treaty implementation and thus facilitate settlement...[They] can guarantee that groups will be protected, terms will be fulfilled, and promises will be kept".[24] Here a third party resolves the commitment problem by providing external security to the belligerents and credibly committing itself to punish any "defector" of the ceasefire. By supplying correct information about actions of the conflicting parties, controlling arms, safeguarding agreements, and offering credible "carrots and sticks" to ethnic groups, impartial outside interveners can significantly reduce mutual fears and uncertainties, which are the basis of security dilemmas. For this, the commitment of an outside intervener should satisfy the three conditions: it must be biased with own stakes in solving the conflict; it "must be willing to use force if necessary, and its military capabilities must be sufficient to punish whichever side violates the treaty;...[and] an intervener state should be able to signal resolve".[25]

For biased interveners, credible commitment problems represent the nutritious ground for pursuing their interests. Playing on the fears and expectations of the belligerents, or themselves causing commitment problems, third parties contribute to further destabilization of the situation in the target country and hinder possible peace arrangements between the belligerents that would otherwise disrupt their intervention goals, which eventually allows them to shape the outcome of the

23 Fearon, J.D. 1998, 108.

24 Walter, B.F. 1997, 340.

25 Walter, B.F. 1997.

conflict in accordance to their best interests. Here we are dealing with another type of credibility – perceptions of the threats and punishment for defection.

Unilateral versus Multilateral Interveners

The problem with this approach to external guarantors of domestic peace is its general focus on the phenomenon of commitment of interveners per se and does not make distinction between types of interveners. Without due attention given to the added value of the composition of interveners in their ability to fulfill their plans or even to keep peace, the research on solving or furthering security dilemma and credible commitment problems would be highly incomplete and deprived of the actors' complexities. Attempts to position the unilateral/multilateral compositional dichotomy in evaluating successes or failures of third parties have been ongoing within the peace-centric framework, producing diverse opinions and outcomes in relation to the role of third parties' composition in the matter of keeping peace.

There is a general agreement that multilateral interveners, exactly because of their multilateralism and neutrality, are more successful in keeping peace longer that single third parties. Neutrality of intervention associated with the concepts of goals, compositions and activities of intervening forces predisposes the warring sides to accept external involvement. With this regard, multilateral interveners are more likely to contribute to a lasting peace than unilateral actions.[26] Multilateral interventions, especially those conducted by and on behalf of the intergovernmental organizations, such as the UN, provide for the "international enforcement [that] can help solve commitment and cooperation problems by imposing order or by directly implementing peace agreements or raising the costs of defection from them".[27] Although the UN involvement, according to Doyle and Sambanis (2000), "…signals international interest in ending the conflict and offers needed assistance to the parties",[28] its actions should be backed by major international actors, both operationally and functionally. From the point of view of durable peace, multidimensional involvement, i.e. composite intervention strategies including peace-keeping, peace-building and post-conflict reconstruction, would "contribute both to reduced violence…and… institutional and political reform, elections, and democratization".[29]

Stability of peaceful settlements is positively related to deployment of international peacekeepers. Almost 70 per cent of the agreements concluded with the mediation of the international organizations have been lived longer, according to Fortna (2004). With intervention success measured as the risk of peace failing in particular time periods, "[t]raditional [UN] peacekeeping missions and observer

26 Regan, P.M. 2002.

27 Doyle, M. and Sambanis, N. 2000. International Peacebuilding: A Theoretical and Quantitative Analysis. *The American Political Science Review*, 94 (4), 781.

28 Doyle, M. and Sambanis, N. 2000, 785.

29 Doyle, M. and Sambanis, N. 2000, 791.

missions have been the most successful, reducing the risk of war"[30] substantially. In general, interventions followed by peacekeeper missions substantially decreased the risk of resumption of conflicts – by more than a half. At the same time, non-UN missions have a larger effect on the duration of peace than UN involvement. The outcome of conflicts is also important for the post-war stability: peace is maintained longer if there it had been achieved as a result of a decisive victory of any warring group. The victory would help third parties save their resources and would decrease the chances for renewed hostilities organized by the losing side.

Multilateral interveners, in contrast to a sole actor, which "tends to favor one side or the other in the conflict," foster "a solution that meets the interests of the disputants as well as the international community". They enjoy a increased trust of the belligerents; higher degree of acceptability of the options proposed by the third parties; and, by the nature of their composition, ensure consideration of interests of major actors in the international arena. In addition, interventions undertake by the UN provide a "better guarantee than unilateral…action that the interests [e.g. major powers or other states in the same geographic area] will be respected".[31]

At the same time, peace-centrism contains a number of quite strong reservations concerning the role of the multilateral organization, notably, the UN, in the matter of conflict resolution. The UN capacities and its political will as an intergovernmental organization are limited to the capacities pledged and offered by its member-states. The UN involvement usually happens "only after [disputes] have passed some high threshold of severity" saving the lives of its peacekeepers but not the people in the target countries. The UN also "tends to be quick to leave" the conflict scene: due to its limited resources, the UN has limited objectives, and, once hostilities are over, the presence of the UN missions end unless further extended in their mandate, which is also subject to lengthy negotiations within the Security Council. A final objection to UN involvement is that it offers artificial solutions: while conflicts may end in a number of ways, including decisive victory of one side, the UN "actions may halt that process and lead to an impasse that only delays, rather than prevents the renewal of hostilities".[32] Contrary to the UN, regional multilateral interveners are more operationally successful than UN interventions. Analysis of Carment and Hill (2001) concludes that, being indirectly affected by intra-national conflicts, for example, by the flow of refugees, political instability, and close economic ties with a conflict-affected country, "regional organizations perform favorably in stopping the violence when compared with both individual states and the UN".[33]

---

30 Fortna, V.P. 2004. Does Peacekeeping Keep Peace? International Intervention and the Duration of Peace After Civil War. *International Studies Quarterly*, 48, 283.

31 Diehl, P.F., Reifschneider, J. and Hensel, P.R. 1996. United Nations Intervention and Recurrent Conflict. *International Organization*, 50(4), 687-688.

32 Diehl, P.F., Reifschneider, J. and Hensel, P.R. 1996, 688.

33 Carment, D. and Harvey, F. 2001. *Using Force to Prevent Ethnic Violence*: *An Evaluation of Theory and Evidence*. Westport, Connecticut, London: Preager Studies on Ethnic and National Identities in Politics. Praeger, 129.

From a purely operational prospective another downside of the multilateral interventions is the lengthy period between decision-making, forging coalition of "likeminded states" and actual deployment of troops. Member-states of international coalitions face domestic opposition to their participation in an intervention, thus producing Putnam's "Janus-faced" model of the "two-level games".[34] The more state actors are involved, the more the chances of free-riding or escaping from responsibility. The states may pledge to allocate certain number of troops and military equipment for the intervention out of the wish of having prestige on the international arena and staying in the "club of good states", they may never fulfill their promises. The state-participants of multilateral initiatives would have their own domestic interest actors and veto-groups, which may be in opposition to the ruling regime of their own governments and challenge international involvement of their country from considerations of domestic power games.

Such deliberations of states may also include a rational component, i.e. high costs of participation in the intervention coalition. According to Carment and Rowlands (1998), the expenditures of external involvement are differentiated by the following two types: the costs undertaken by interveners themselves and the costs associated with the solutions imposed by third parties: "All strategies involve risk to the intervener. Doing nothing may precipitate undesirable outcomes. Forceful intervention may lead to further escalation and unnecessary costs for the intervener".[35] Besides, inadequate intervention (for instance, low-intervention in high-risk environment) may turn out to be even more costly for the intervener and, eventually, for the belligerents. Interveners make their calculations of possible implications, benefits as well as associated costs in economic and human terms, and if the benefits are higher than the costs, they decide to intervene.

When applying the compositional differences of the third parties in the goal-oriented approach, the hypothesis of multilateral interveners being more successful than unilateral ones, has a number of assumptions pertinent to the factor of composition of interveners. First, irrespective of the recipients of external support – be it the target government or the challenger-ethnic group – any outcome of interventions "...require[s] the stamp of institutional legitimacy upon which long-term measures depend".[36] In order to be sustainable, any end of the conflict – peace agreement, defeat or a stalemate – needs some sort of legal frameworks, upon which institutionalization of the conflict outcomes would depend. The more parties are involved, the more legitimate the option offered to the belligerents would seem, even if this is not their best-possible option. Here multilateral interventions provide the institutionalized legitimacy of more than one party to the outcomes of conflict, even if the peace and conflict resolution are not immediate objectives of interveners.

34 Putnam, R.D. 1998. Diplomacy and Domestic Politics: The Logic of Two-Level Game. *International Organization*, 42(3), 427-460.

35 Carment, D. and Rowlands, D. 1998. Three's Company: Evaluating Third-Party Intervention in Intrastate Conflict. *The Journal of Conflict Resolution*, 42(5), 576.

36 Carment, D. and Harvey, F. 2001, 129.

The second assumption being closely connected with the notion of institutional legitimacy is impartiality of actions of the multilateral interveners, which minimizes the incentives for defection from the ceasefire by the belligerents and increases the level of their credibility in the eyes of the conflicting parties. The warring factions should clearly know that, if they disarm or demobilize, the intervener will not impose a victory on either side. Of course, the states participating in multinational coalitions may have their own interests and stakes in particular outcomes of the interventions. However, their self-interests would be "neutralized" by the presence of other states: functional impartiality of multinational interventions balances the interests of the different actors which they are composed of. On the contrary, when states intervene unilaterally, the guarantees they offer to conflict participants in relation to outcomes are shaped in accordance with their interests and stances toward the different groups, which negatively influences their levels of credibility. State interests, quite volatile for a single state, would affect the courses of intervention less in multilateral organizations. Being characterized by a higher degree of path-dependence in their policies than individual states, multilateral organizations are more resistant to dramatic change of political visions would inevitably lead to transformation of the basic institutional pillars upon which they are based and which require consent of the majority, if not all, of the member-states.

Even if multilateral interveners are not impartial in their action, or may seem so by acting against one side of the conflict in imposing their will, the third assumption supporting the hypothesis advocates for the shared operational bias in their actions. In ethnic wars, when sometimes the best possible outcome for one side is the worst one for the other, "[m]utually preferable settlements are unattainable because large, well-armed groups are aware that they can make greater gains by holding out and support provided to one side will be opposed by the other".[37] Acting against one group would by definition mean supporting its rival, which would further deplete the sense of legitimacy of third party actions. From this point of view, what distinguishes multilateral interventions is their common biased, which is diffused among their members: the will of the one is juxtaposed by the will of the many, which is difficult to oppose, not because of their punitive capacities but out of the consent of a larger international community of states.

The fourth assumption is a higher degree of transparency of multilateral interventions in comparison with the unilateral ones. Once an intervener becomes a major player in an ethnic conflict, it can easily hide from the international public movements of its troops, their numbers, strategies and types of military equipment used on the ground and influence public opinion through using different tools, including mass media. Hence, its actions are more clandestine and may include undercover operations, supplies of arms and unregulated economic support. When such an intervention is conducted by more than one state, and, ideally under "the leadership of international command…[it] entails the active placement of personnel

37 Carment, D. and Rowlands, D. 1998, 580.

on the ground [which] are not involved in supplies/re-supplies of arms".[38] This is also because of the role of a role of neutral observers that multilateral interveners usually play, which allows them to spare their troops from possible clashes with the belligerents. Transparency of actions and intentions builds up their credibility and makes the threat of use of force and promises of rewards more effective. Eventually, transparency of third party actions externally mitigates security dilemmas by decreasing of uncertainty and fears of the belligerents in relation to the interveners' moves.

At the same time, it is important to mention that the factor of composition of the third party actions alone may not completely account for their successes or failures: conflicts differ much in their geographic locations, compositions of the belligerents, domestic power games, and interests of neighboring countries. Any of these factors or their various combinations may have quite significant effect on the course of interventions and their ability to achieve planned results. Country- and intervention-specific factors directly influence the outcomes of third party actions by contributing to or decrease the likelihood their success. The focus can be made on various domestic variables: conflict condition before entry of the third party; nature of the conflict (on ethnic, religious, or communal grounds); power balance among local actors; geographic locations of warring parties and their proximity to the territories of possible interveners; administrative-political division of target countries; economic resources that sustain belligerent groups, and many more.

The conflict condition prior to the intervention plays an important role in the overall success of third-parties actions. Four options are possible: an ongoing war, a decisive victory of one side, a military stalemate and a negotiated settlement. Depending on the situation on the ground and the conflict participants (the warring parties and who supports them), the interveners would face variety of different obstacles and supporting factors for their actions.

The first possible scenario is an ongoing war, where the outcome would much depend on whom the third parties support. Interveners may assist either the minority opposition (usually being the opposition – the weaker side), or majority (usually being the government – a stronger participant), or be neutral and assist no one. By supporting the weaker groups, interveners increase their domestic power standing by bringing in own resources, thus, equalizing the power balance with the stronger factions. This may lead to extended conflicts and increased chances for the weaker to sustain military operations against the target governments, but would also affect third-party casualties and increase the chances of the stronger side's seeking support from outside and bringing in other external actors. If, however, the interveners help the majority, they bear less costs by spending fewer resources that they would otherwise have had they supported the weaker side. They may also achieve their own goals more easily by supporting the side that already enjoys military advantage over its rival. Aiding the government would also contribute to ending the conflict quicker by decreasing the expected utility of the weaker

38 Regan, P.M. 2002.

group and may make them more tractable. If interveners are neutral and impartial without backing any belligerent sides, the situation may put them in the midst of a cross-fire between the rival factions. The less third parties become operationally involved in actual hostilities the less their damage.

A stalemate is another environment operationally quite similar to the active warfare. In such "no-peace/no-war" situations, "neither combatant is able to make noteworthy advances on the battlefield due to the strength of the opposing side, and neither side believes that the situation will improve in the near future".[39] However, from the point of view of successful intervention, this may be considered a better-favored situation: while the parties may have exhausted their military capacities as a result of the conflicts, they remain still aware of each other's belligerent potential, which, in principle, can be used at any time and against any intervener. Although stalemates may offer a needed respite to the populations, they also allow the belligerents to marshal their resources and recruit more forces for renewed hostilities, thus making the interveners face increased military confrontation on the grounds. Thus, third parties may choose to engage in active negotiations with the belligerents and suffer less from war-related damage.

A stalemate or an active warfare can end up with possible conclusion of a ceasefire agreement between the belligerents achieved by themselves alone or with the help of external mediators. Here the outcomes of conflict resolution are based on cooperative efforts of the warring parties, which, according to Bloomfield, "...solve the conflict...by jointly finding their own integrative solution, thereby becoming their own guarantors of the agreement".[40] With the outside assistance, usually in a form of "good offices", neutral and impartial third parties have more chances to succeed in forging peace deals than biased ones since the vitality of such agreements would depend much on the trust of the belligerents to interveners acting as external guarantors of peace.

Finally, it is an evident or already existing decisive victory of any of the conflict parties that might meet the interveners in the target countries. According to Licklider (1995), military victory of one side means that "an opposition will have great difficulty in starting a civil war...A negotiated settlement to a civil war is likely to result in veto groups that will not surrender power to social change whose impact on them is uncertain; but a military victory will destroy the power of such groups, making renewed conflict more difficult and allowing the government to act as it pleases".[41] The fact of a decisive military victory assures the winner that the looser will not resume hostilities due to the damage inflicted to its military power. Even if the loser tries to restore its fighting potential over time, the winner is likely to do the same, so it would be still more optimal for the winner to maintain

39 Walter, B.E. 1997, 347.

40 Bloomfield, D. 1995. Towards Complementarity in Conflict Management: Resolution and Settlement in Northern Ireland. *Journal of Peace Research*, 32(2), 152.

41 Licklider, R. 1995. The Consequences of Negotiated Settlements in Civil Wards, 1945-1993. *The American Political Science Review*, 89(3), 685.

its military advantage gained as a result of its victory. In this case, interventions in support of the majority groups (the stronger) would have higher likelihood of success, whereas providing support to the weaker ones would prolong the conflicts and increase own damage of the interveners. Neural third parties, on their part, would nothing left but to confirm the victory of the winner and to engage in peace-building activities, if they wish so.

From the additional domestic variables, the nature of and relationships between belligerents also plays an important role in the interveners' pursuit of their objectives. This is especially true in relation to the peace-making agendas of third parties, which might be harder to implement in identity conflicts than in the conflicts on ideological grounds. The analyses done by Fortna (2004) revealed that the resolution of identity conflicts may be harder to maintain than in ideological confrontations.[42] Also, according to Licklider (1995), ethnic and religious identity wars had higher likelihood of resumption than other conflicts.[43] These conclusions were, however, not supported by Dubey (2002)[44] and Hartzel et al. (2001),[45] who found no significant difference between the nature of participants of conflicts and successful intervention with peacekeeping agendas.

Low rate of casualties is said to be another determinant of successful interventions. The bloodier the conflict the higher the likelihood of its resumption and, as a consequence, the actions of the interveners would face with more hostilities on the ground.[46] In other words, the more people arc killed on both sides the more the belligerents want to avenge the death of their kin. This leads to persistence of conflicts and increases violence, which makes it harder for third parties to operate. A higher rate of casualties means comparative advantage for the majority, which can absorb higher losses on the battlefield and be prepared to wage longer wars. On the other hand, a higher death toll in all the sides may mean less opposition to the interveners since the parties would be weary of fights and more inclined to accept an imposed or offered solution coming from outside.

Geographic location of ethnic groups and their administrative separation may also incite foreign interventions and be a favorable or negative factor in the matter of fulfillment of their objectives. Apart from economic and political marginalization that ethnic groups may feel living on the "edge" of development – on the country's outskirts, where central administrative control is usually weak, borders represent ideal grounds for external support. This argument is strengthened by the possible

42 Fortna, V.P. 2004, 283.

43 Licklider, R. 1995.

44 Dubey, A. 2002. *Domestic Institutions and the Duration of Civil War Settlements*. Paper to the Annual Meeting of the International Studies Association, New Orleans.

45 Hartzell, C., Hoddie, M. and Rothchild, D. 2001. Stabilizing the Peace After Civil War. *International Organization*, 55(1), 183-208.

46 Dubey, A. 2002. *Domestic Institutions and the Duration of Civil War Settlements*. Paper to: the Annual Meeting of the International Studies Association, New Orleans; Doyle, M. and Sambanis, N. 2000, 799-801.

existence of external and bordering ethnic kin living in neighboring countries, which increase movements of populations, goods and economic and military support and make them less controlled by central governments. The factor of ethnic kin living in the neighboring countries provides strong incentives for the states to intervene on behalf of their blood brethren. Intervening in countries with ethnic groups living in these encapsulated enclaves, or "ethnic islands",[47] makes third parties' easily and promptly provide military and/or economic assistance to bordering regions.[48] Interventions become, thus, less costly, quick and more effective.

Willingness of third parties to engage in ethnic conflicts is said to be strengthened by administrative separation of ethnic groups into autonomies, which would allow interveners to institutionalize outcomes of their actions. Cornell (1999, 2002) and Hartzel (1999) consider that autonomies contribute to consolidation and mobilization on ethnic grounds and ignite conflicts,[49] while for the third parties ethnic autonomies act as an attractive force for finding legitimate grounds for their actions on the basis of the national self-determination principle.

Finally, domestic capacities prove to be are important factors in defining future successes or failures of third party actions. Natural resources, or "lootables" (oil, gas, minerals, gold, diamonds, as well as other income-related variables, such as sea access and transit roads) sustain war-related activities of the belligerents,[50] provide strong incentives for third party interventions, and are important predictors for lasting peace settlements. If the belligerents possess substantial resources for military activities, the conflicts will last longer and will be more difficult to solve.

---

47 Posen, B.R. 1993.

48 Walter, B.E. 1997.

49 Cornell, S.E. 1999. The Devaluation of The Concept of Autonomy: National Minorities in The Former Soviet Union. *Central Asian* Survey, 18(2), 185-196; Cornell, S.E. 2002. Autonomy as a Source of Conflict: Caucasian Conflicts in Theoretical Perspective. *World Politics*, 54(2), 245-276; Hartzell, C.A. 1999. Explaining the Stability of Negotiated Settlements to Intrastate Wars. *The Journal of Conflict Resolution*, 43(1), 3-22.

50 Collier, P. and Hoeffler, A. 2000. Greed and Grievance in Civil War. *CSAE WPS/2002-01* [Online]. Available at: http://www.csae.ox.ac.uk/workingpapers/pdfs/2002-01text.pdf [accessed: May 6, 2009]; Elbadawi, I. and Sambanis, N. 2001. How Much War Will We See? Estimating the Incidence of Civil War in 161 Countries. *World Bank Policy Research Working Paper* [Online]. Available at: http://siteresources.worldbank.org/INTKNOWLEDGEFORCHANGE/Resources/491519-1199818447826/multi0page2533.pdf [accessed: May 6, 2009]; Dubey, A. 2002. *Domestic Institutions and the Duration of Civil War Settlements*. Paper to: the Annual Meeting of the International Studies Association, New Orleans; Ross, M. 2006. Mineral Wealth and Equitable Development, *Equity and Development*, World Bank Development Report, Background Papers [Online]. Available at: http://siteresources.worldbank.org/INTWDR2006/Resources/477383-1118673432908/Mineral_Wealth_and_Equitable_Development.pdf [accessed: May 6, 2009]; Doyle, M. and Sambanis, N. 2000. International Peacebuilding: A Theoretical and Quantitative Analysis. *The American Political Science Review*, 94 (4), 779-802.

In foreign interventions, these resources could either contribute to success of third party actions or act against it depending on whom the interveners help: third parties would benefit from purely mercantile viewpoint by supporting the factions that have larger and more important natural resources at their disposition.

Chapter 2
Quantitative Analysis of Foreign Interventions in Ethnic Conflicts

Intervention is a complex phenomenon. It includes any action of a state in relation to another country ranging from purely military operations to economic aid or sanctions. Interventions can be limited to sending monitoring groups to conflict-affected countries, or providing economic aid to or imposing sanctions upon the belligerent groups. Third parties may act openly by sending regular troops to target countries to participate in military actions or conduct secret spec-ops missions. Intervention may also involve official mediation or arbitration efforts by single actors and/or multinational institutions or clandestine military and/or economic support to warring parties.

Due to the diverse and, sometimes, vague nature of involvement of one state in the internal affairs of another, it is necessary to clearly define what an intervention is and what it is not. Notwithstanding the considerable scholarship on intervention embracing wide spheres and areas of actions, there is no general and universally accepted definition of intervention. The literature is abundant with different sorts of interventions: military operations, propaganda, economic aid, diplomatic negotiations, multidimensional interventions involving all of the above, unilateral and multilateral interventions. Perhaps the broadest definition of intervention is offered by Rosenau (1969): "modifications of the behavior of persons and groups in the target nation that would not have occurred if the intervening nation had not engaged in interventionary activities".[1] Such a view is unsatisfactory due lack of falsifiability by putting every step of a foreign actor vis-à-vis a target state as an intervention. It becomes clear when viewing the notion of intervention from the pivots of Complex Interdependence theory, developed by Keohane and Nye (1977),[2] where alteration of behavior of a state toward its counterpart, depending on the level of their interactions and connectivity, puts the latter in either vulnerable or sensitive position and forces it to modify its own domestic settings. This way nearly every action of a state causing subsequent reciprocal reaction in another can be regarded as intervention.

In the same line of reasoning, if we take the definition of intervention as actions of an external actor aimed at influencing domestic affairs of another state,

1 Rosenau, J.N. 1969. Intervention as a Scientific Concept. *The Journal of Conflict Resolution*, 13(2), 159.

2 Keohane, R.O. and Nye, J. 1977. *Power and Interdependence: World Politics in Transition*. Boston, Little and Brown.

then inaction, or absence of any external influence, can still be considered as an intervention. Absence of actions from outside also influences domestic conflicts where, for instance, a party would have lost had it not have been supported from outside. The problem of this broad definition of intervention is that nearly each and every instance of actions by a state outside of its territorial borders in the affairs of another state can be considered an intervention. If everything is intervention, then the term loses its meaning. Therefore, a parsimonious and restrictive definition of external intervention is needed.

The following wording of intervention combining the definitions of Licklider (1995) and Regan (2002)[3] on third-party actions presents interventions as narrowly as possible, and yet not less precisely: A convention-breaking military and/or economic interference in the domestic affairs of a foreign country aimed at altering the internal balance of power by targeting either the authority structures and capacities of the government, the challenger or providing no support to any warring party. Here, interventions have three types of limitations: geographic, operative and connotation: they should occur on a limited territory, have narrow modus operandi in their actions and a clear direction of their actions.

In the statistic analysis presented below, with the purpose of evaluation of the *ceteris paribus* impact of third party composition on the success of fulfillment of their objective, actions of interveners are presented as a dummy independent variable: multilateral if undertaken either under joint command of an international/regional organization, or when multiple actors jointly pursue common goals and take actions in the same direction; and unilateral – interventions of a single outside its own state.

Since the test hypothesis argues about a higher degree of success of multilateral interveners than unilateral ones, at the stage of regression analysis the independent variable will not differentiate between various types of multiple actors, such as interventions undertaken by more than one state, or the interventions under the aegis of a multinational or regional organization. Here the task is to see the pure compositional effect of the binary nature of interveners on the ability to reach their goals. The substantive issues of actor differences in multilateral coalitions are presented later in case studies.

The dependent variable – success of intervention – shall be also be rediscovered. For the purposes of goal-oriented approach to interventions, time limitations in measuring successes or failures have to be abandoned. Neither five or two years, or even six months of durable peace can fully explain whether the interveners managed to reach their objectives successfully or not, where the fulcrum is the notion of success. Thus, an intervention can be considered as successful if it managed to reach its intervention agendas and aims and unsuccessful if it failed to

3 For the definitions of intervention see Licklider, R. 1995. The Consequences of Negotiated Settlements in Civil Wards, 1945-1993. *The American Political Science Review*, 89(3), 681-690 and Regan, P.M. 2002. *Civil Wars and Foreign Powers – Outside Intervention in Intrastate Conflict*. University of Michigan Press, 2002.

do so. This view would give us a limited, parsimonious and yet complete picture of what the interveners were planning to achieve by their actions and what they had actually achieved. In order to isolate the factors that yield successful interventions and measuring the success of interventions, the actual outcome of each case of intervention – the dependent variable – must be cross-checked against intervention agendas and aims.

In doing so time-relative notion of success are substituted by end-points of interventions. This can be done by reflecting on the following two tiers of evaluation of successes and failures. First, since the dependent variable is fulfillment of intervention objectives, their successes or failures shall be defined once interveners had exited the conflict scene having reached their goals or failed to do so. For example, a neutral third party may intervene to end hostilities in a conflict-affected state, and if the peace was achieved, this can be considered a successful intervention. Or, if a party intervened with the purpose of helping a minority group in its fight against the majority, and that group had eventually turned up to be a winner, this shall also be considered a successful intervention.

At the same time, goals and objectives of interveners may change in time depending on numerous factors: the nature of the environment they operate in, their own domestic political situation and international reaction to their actions, to name a few. This is a usual case with multinational interventions, who have their objectives and operational tasks embedded in their mandates, which are not written in stone – they can be changed, amended, extended to include other geographic coverage or aims or even be replaced completely. With a unilateral actor reshaping foreign policy interests being reflected in its intervention can happen, for example, as a result of changes in its government when the opposition faction, ones in power, may not approve actions of state abroad. In their operations interveners may be more successful in fulfilling some of their respectful mandates while be less successful in others. Therefore, due to such a non-rigid nature of their mandates fluid nature of tasks, a so-called "freeze pane" view shall be adopted where third party actions are evaluated at each end-point in intervention agendas.

Statistic regression of successes and failures of interventions services two purposes: it would help, first, identify the impact of the independent variable of composition of third parties (multilateral versus unilateral) on the success of their intervention agendas. This would define, in a sense, "pure" relationship between the independent and dependent variables. At the same time, it is necessary to mention that, apart from the composition variable of interventions, there are other factors, either belonging to the domestic environments of target countries or the arrangements at the international system level that have intervening effects over the overall course of fulfillment of intervention agendas. Without holding these effects constant, we cannot establish the true relationships between the type of intervention and the success of the intervention.

Control variables transferred from the peace-centric approach include the direction of third party support, intervention tools and power factors in interventions included in the present dataset to test their robustness in the goal-oriented approach to interventions. In addition to those variables that deal primarily with domestic factors influencing the courses and results of interventions, the international political climate and interactions among the states on the systemic level have also taken into account. For the purpose of assessing the effect of the international system on domestic rivalry in conflict-affected countries, an additional variable – proximity of conflicts to the end of the Cold War – was introduced to see whether the end of the bipolar confrontation in the international system had an influence on the outcomes of sub-systemic ethnic wars. The full list of control variables is presented below with their relevant assumptions.

Control variable 1: the recipient of third party support. As far as the relations with the belligerents are concerned, a third party has essentially three choices: to aid the target, support the challenger or be neutral. Current view on interventions in civil wars holds that the neutral intervening force ahs positive effects on the de facto peace and its duration. When no warring parties receive outside support this denotes neutrality of interveners in relation to the belligerents, even though third parties may actually be interested in a certain conflict outcome out of their own best interests. It was also noticeable that when represented by a coalition of states, multilateral interventions enjoy a higher degree of neutrality being better received by domestic warring parties: their shared operational bias and the presence of more than one state in an intervention force contributes to perceptions of absence of biased actions in the eyes of the belligerents. The probit analysis tests the relevance of the recipient of third party support on the probability of intervention success in the goal-measurement framework.

Control variable 2: type of interventions. The peace-centrism postulates that military, economic or mixed interventions can bring different results to the conflict settings. For example, according to Regan's study, the combination of military aid with financial support increases the chances that interveners will reach sustainable peace in civil wars.[4] In other words, when military victory is backed up by economic aid (as economic and military actions of African countries, Sweden and Ireland under the aegis of the UN aimed at restoring order in Zaire in 1960-1965 and preventing the country from breaking apart), this combined help contributes to achieving victory over the side that has no such complex assistance. In addition, interventions should also be tailored to the context of each particular conflict. For example, long-fought conflicts that cause significant destruction that may require more emphasis on economic and political development, while in shorter conflicts military interventions alone may suffice. Such joint strategies would mean that interveners are ready to commit themselves not only to a relatively short-term militarily presence, but also to much longer economic assistance, which itself increases the trust of the belligerents who receive external support.

Control variable 3: the relative powers of the interveners. This variable has been adopted from previous research on third-party interventions, which posits that the presence of a superpower both in absolute (the UN, global superpowers,

4 Regan, P.M. 2002.

such as US and USSR) and relative terms (regional superpowers: France in its African interventions) alone or together with other countries is positively related to fulfillment of the intervention's aims.[5] Although it would be quite logical to assume that a stronger state would be more successful in military operations and provision of economic support to any of the conflict parties, the power variable will contribute to the understanding of success of interventions and help determine whether the power alone is a sufficient precondition for success of third parties within the goal-oriented premises. Probit analysis is to determine the effect of presence and absence of superpower factor in both unilateral and multilateral interventions separately: whether a powerful actor gives the multilateral interventions a greater probability for success than when there is a relative parity among the coalition members and whether a single superpower is more likely to fulfill its goals then a sole non-superpower intervener.

Control Variable 4: the closeness of interventions to the end of the Cold War (+/- 5 years from the moment of dissolution of the Soviet Union, i.e. from 1986 to 1995). The peace-centric approach states that proximity of conflicts to the Cold War increased the likelihood of foreign interventions.[6] The underlining assumption is that the end of the bipolar world and absence of ideological rivalry between the US and USSR, which enjoyed a certain degree of cooperation during the Cold War, is negatively related to the success of interventions. At the same time, during the Cold War interventions in ethnic confrontations tended to be fueled with ideology (such as the USSR and Cuban support of Ethiopian Government during the Ogaadeen conflict in 1977-1978; Belgian intervention in Zaire during the Katanga conflict in 1960-1965),[7] where belligerents and interveners alike used their respective ideological affiliations to apply for outside assistance and to intervene.

During the Cold War, conflicts at the systemic level were brought down to the domestic rivalry in the allied states where the belligerent groups sharing conflicting ideologies acted as pawns of superpower rivalry (also known as "proxy wars"). On the contrary, the proliferation of non-state actors after the end of Cold War led to an increase in the numbers of low- and medium-intensity conflicts in the countries that could no longer be restrained by their former patrons, which can also explain the lower success rate of all interventions at this time.

In sum, the quantitative analysis tested the degree of success of multilateral versus unilateral interventions vis-à-vis their actual outcomes, further identifying

5 Fortna, V.P. 2004. Does Peacekeeping Keep Peace? International Intervention and the Duration of Peace After Civil War. *International Studies Quarterly*, 48, 269-292; Paul F. Diehl, Reifchneider, J. and Hensel. P.R. 1996. United Nations Intervention and Recurring Conflict. *International Organization*, 50(4), 683-700; Regan, P.M. 2002.

6 Regan, P.M. 1998. Choosing to Intervene: Outside Interventions in Internal Conflicts. *The Journal of Politics*, 60(3), 754-779.

7 For more examples see Jenne, E.K., Saideman, S.M. and Lowe, W. 2007. Separatism as a Bargaining Posture: The Role of Leverage in Minority Radicalization. *Journal of Peace Research*, 44(5), 539-558.

causal factors that determine their success or failure in reaching their target agendas. For this purpose a new dataset was created, which exemplifies goal-oriented approach in the study of interventions in ethnic civil wars. A number of sources and datasets containing durability of peace as the dependent variable, as well as the analysis of policy- and ethnicity-related think-tanks and sources, have been consulting during selection of cases and defining successes and failures of interveners with the purpose of finding intervention agendas of third parties and how these agendas correspond to the actual outcomes of the interventions.

Sources used in building the current dataset include: The "Correlates of War Intrastate War Data, 1816-1997 (v3.0)" dataset with 35 ethnic conflicts from 1946 to 1997. The number of cases is quite small due to restrictive approach to the definition of ethnic conflict employed by COW, particularly the threshold of 1000 casualties per year and a five-year period from the moment of secession of hostilities; "Intervention Data" by Patrick Regan, Binghamton University; Database of the Conflict Early Warning Systems (CEWS) research project of the International Social Science Council; the Uppsala University Conflict Data Program (developed together with the PRIO) and the Conflict Termination Dataset; case-studies produced by the "Beyond Intractability Project Version II"; essays and surveys of the European Centre for Conflict Prevention; "Conflict Histories" data and "CrisisWatch" searchable database of the International Crisis Group; Federal Research Division of the Library of Congress; Encyclopedia of the Nations; Global Issues. The data on the UN interventions has been taken from the UN Department of Peacekeeping Operations. For defining aims of some interventions the United Nations Treaty Collection Series was consulted.

The dataset includes 107 instances of interventions in 50 conflicts that happened after the end of the WW II (i.e. from 1948 till 2003). For the purposes of dataset, the cases have been selected which fit into the following definition of intrastate ethnic wars: a sustained military conflict between geographically contiguous ethnic groups, one being the central government (the target), and the other(s) – the challenger(s), with at least 1,000 battle-death per year, the outcome of which is either reshaped administrative-political territorial arrangement of the country or altered power balance between these ethnic groups. This classification is based on Licklider's description of an intra-national conflict[8] and includes considerations of the aspirations of conflicting parties in relation to the actual end of conflicts.

In addition to de facto resolved conflicts, there are also eight ongoing civil wars (Burma vs. Karens, 1948-present; Philippines vs. MIM and MNLF, 1970-present; Mauritania (Western Sahara Independence Movement), 1975-present; Morocco (Western Sahara Independence Movement), 1975-present; Sri Lanka vs. Tamil Insurgency, 1982-present; Somalia, 1991-present; DRC vs. Ituri, 1999-present; Sudan (Darfur), 2003-present), which were also included in data. The Russian intervention in Georgian in 2008 has not been added in the dataset; however, it has been used as a control case during the case-study.

8 Licklider, R. 1995, 682.

Probit Analysis of Interventions

The dataset of interventions includes the following categories: *Conflict* (name of the conflict and/or conflicting parties); *Dates* (dates of the beginning and end of conflict); *Intervener* (a foreign actor intervening in the domestic affairs of a target country). The independent variable is *Composition* (composition of the intervening force: "0" for unilateral (codified as "U") and "1" for multilateral interveners (codified as "M"). Since success of interventions is viewed as the fulfillment of the interveners' agendas, their indicators can take only binary values, i.e. either "yes" or "no", and cannot be expressed in relative terms (i.e. there cannot be "slightly more successful" or "slightly less successful" interventions). Thus, the independent variable *Success* also represents a categorical, or a "dummy" variable with "1" as success of intervention and "0" as failure.

Other control variables include *Type* (operational characteristics of interventions): "0" for military interventions (codified as "Mil"); "1" for economic support or sanctions against the belligerents (codified as "Eco"); and "2" – mixed interventions, including military and economic components (codified as "Mix"); *Support* (direction of intervention actions): "0" when the third party supports the opposition (codified as "O"); "1" when it supports the target government (codified as "G"); and "2" when it supports neither side and is operationally neutral (codified as "N"); *Power* (relative capabilities of actors and third parties: "0" for the interveners having relative parity with the warring parties (codified as "Parity"); and "1" when one of the interveners is a major regional power (codified as "Power"); and *System* (condition of the international system): "1" for the conflicts started within a ten-year period after the end of the Cold War – from 1985 to 1995 (codified as "Hectic") and "0" for the conflicts started before 1985 or after 1995 (codified as "Stabile").

Large-N probit analysis using the "R 2.2.0" software package was used to determine the impact of composition of intervention on the probability of their success. Because the dependent variable is a binary response, using an OLS (Ordinary Least Squares) model would be inappropriate. Instead, the probit transformation was employed to estimate the probability of attaining an outcome $a=1$ (success). In general, the probability $Y(a)$ of a specific intervention outcome a (where a = {success, failure}) is a continuous variable that can take any value between "1" or "0." In the given model, a value close to "0" means that $a=1$ (intervention success) is very unlikely, and a value close to "1" means that $a=1$ (success) is very likely.[9] Thus, the probability of success of interventions $\{a=1\}$ can be expressed as a function of the set of factor variables of interest, $\mathbf{X}=\{X^1,\ldots,X^p\}$: $P\{a=1|\mathbf{X}\}=f(\mathbf{X})$. The probit model can also estimate the difference in the probability of success when moving from unilateral to multilateral types, while holding the value of the intervening variables constant at their means or typical values.

---

9 Pampel, F.C. 2000. *Logistic Regression: A Primer*, Sage Publications 2000; Series: Quantitative Applications in the Social Sciences, 2.

Table 2.1 Intervention dataset

Conflict	Dates	Intervener	Type	Support	Power	System	Composition	Success
Burma vs. Karens	1948-present	China	Mil	O	Power	Stabile	U	No
Zaire vs. Katanga	1960-1965	Belgium	Mil	G	Power	Stabile	U	No
		UN	Mix	G	Power	Stabile	M	Yes
		Algeria	Mil	O	Parity	Stabile	U	No
		Egypt	Mil	O	Parity	Stabile	U	No
		Belgium	Mix	G	Power	Stabile	U	Yes
Ethiopia, Ogaaden I	1960-1964	Somalia	Mil	O	Parity	Stabile	U	No
Iraq, Kurdish rebellion I	1961-1966	Syria	Mil	G	Parity	Stabile	U	No
Eritrean War	1962-1991	Cuba	Mil	O	Parity	Stabile	M	No
		USSR	Mil	O	Power	Stabile	M	No
		US	Mix	G	Power	Stabile	M	No
		Cuba	Mil	G	Parity	Stabile	M	Yes
		USSR	Mix	G	Power	Stabile	M	Yes
		Sudan	Mil	O	Parity	Stabile	M	No
Cyprus	1963-1964	UK	Mil	N	Power	Stabile	U	No
		Greece	Mil	G	Parity	Stabile	U	No
		Turkey	Mil	O	Parity	Stabile	U	No
		UN	Mil	N	Power	Stabile	M	Yes
Chad Civil War I	1966-1971	France	Mil	G	Power	Stabile	U	Yes
		Libya	Mil	O	Parity	Stabile	U	No
Iraq, Kurdish rebellion II	1968-1970	Iran	Mil	O	Parity	Stabile	U	Yes

Table 2.1 continued Intervention dataset

Conflict	Dates	Intervener	Type	Support	Power	System	Composition	Success
Oman, Dhofar Rebellion	1970-1975							
		UK	Mil	G	Power	Stabile	M	Yes
		Iran	Mil	G	Parity	Stabile	M	Yes
		Jordan	Mil	G	Parity	Stabile	M	Yes
		YPR Yemen	Mil	O	Parity	Stabile	U	No
PLO-Jordan War	1970-1971							
		Syria	Mil	O	Parity	Stabile	U	No
South Africa, African Nationalist Struggle	1970-1994							
		UN	Eco	O	Power	Stabile	M	Yes
		US	Eco	O	Power	Stabile	M	Yes
		UK	Eco	O	Power	Stabile	M	Yes
		USSR	Mil	O	Power	Stabile	U	Yes
Pakistan vs. Bengalis	1971							
		India	Mil	O	Parity	Stabile	U	Yes
Uganda, Obotes Overthrow	1971-1972							
		Tanzania	Mil	G	Parity	Stabile	U	No
Burundi vs. Hutu	1972							
		Zaire	Mil	G	Parity	Stabile	U	Yes
Philippines vs. MNLF	1972-present							
		US	Mil	G	Power	Stabile	U	Yes
Rhodesia	1971-1979							
		Cuba	Mil	O	Parity	Stabile	U	Yes
		South Africa	Mix	G	Parity	Stabile	U	No
		UN	Eco	O	Power	Stabile	M	Yes
Pakistan vs. Baluchi Rebels	1973-1977							
		Afghanistan	Mil	O	Parity	Stabile	U	No
		Iran	Mix	G	Parity	Stabile	U	Yes

Table 2.1 continued Intervention dataset

Conflict	Dates	Intervener	Type	Support	Power	System	Composition	Success
Cyprus	1974							
		Turkey	Mil	O	Parity	Stabile	U	No
		Greece	Mil	G	Parity	Stabile	U	No
		UN	Mil	N	Power	Stabile	M	Yes
Iraq, Kurdish rebellion III	1974-1975							
		Iran	Mil	O	Parity	Stabile	U	No
Mauritania, Western Sahara Independence Movement	1975-present							
		France	Mil	G	Power	Stabile	U	No
		Morocco	Mil	G	Parity	Stabile	U	No
		Algeria	Mil	O	Parity	Stabile	U	No
		Saudi Arabia	Eco	G	Parity	Stabile	U	No
Morocco, Western Sahara Independence Movement	1975-present							
		Mauritania	Mil	G	Parity	Stabile	U	No
		Algeria	Mil	O	Parity	Stabile	U	No
		Libya	Mil	O	Parity	Stabile	U	No
Ethiopia, Ogaaden II	1977-1978							
		Somalia	Mil	O	Parity	Stabile	U	No
		Cuba	Mil	G	Parity	Stabile	U	Yes
		USSR	Mil	G	Power	Stabile	U	Yes
Zaire, Shaba Crisis I (FLNC)	1977							
		Angola	Mil	O	Parity	Stabile	U	No
		Morocco	Mil	G	Parity	Stabile	M	Yes
		Belgium	Mil	G	Power	Stabile	M	Yes
		France	Mil	G	Power	Stabile	M	Yes
		USA	Mil	G	Power	Stabile	M	Yes
		Egypt	Mil	G	Parity	Stabile	M	Yes

Table 2.1 continued Intervention dataset

Conflict	Dates	Intervener	Type	Support	Power	System	Composition	Success
Zaire, Shaba Crisis II (FLNC)	1978-1979							
		Zambia	Mil	O	Parity	Stabile	U	No
		Morocco	Mil	G	Parity	Stabile	M	Yes
		Belgium	Mil	G	Power	Stabile	M	Yes
		France	Mil	G	Power	Stabile	M	Yes
		USA	Mil	G	Power	Stabile	M	Yes
		Senegal	Mil	G	Parity	Stabile	M	Yes
		Togo	Mil	G	Parity	Stabile	M	Yes
		Gabon	Mil	G	Parity	Stabile	M	Yes
		Ivory Coast	Mil	G	Parity	Stabile	M	Yes
Chad Civil War II	1978-1982							
		Libya	Mil	O	Parity	Stabile	U	Yes
		France	Mix	G	Power	Stabile	U	No
		Congo	Mil	N	Parity	Stabile	M	No
		Zaire	Mil	N	Parity	Stabile	M	No
		OAU	Mil	N	Power	Stabile	M	No
		Libya	Mil	O	Parity	Stabile	U	Yes
Iran, Kurdish rebellion	1978-1979							
		Iraq	Mil	G	Parity	Stabile	U	Yes
Uganda I	1980-1986							
		US	Mix	O	Power	Stabile	U	No
		ROK Korea	Mil	G	Parity	Stabile	U	No
Somalia	1982-1991							
		Ethiopia	Mix	O	Parity	Stabile	U	No
		US	Mix	G	Power	Stabile	U	Yes
		US	Mix	O	Power	Stabile	U	No
Sri Lanka vs. Tamil	1982-present							
		India	Mix	G	Parity	Stabile	U	No
		Norway	Eco	O	Parity	Stabile	U	No
		UK	Eco	O	Power	Stabile	U	No

Table 2.1 continued Intervention dataset

Conflict	Dates	Intervener	Type	Support	Power	System	Composition	Success
Chad Civil War III	1983-1987							
		France	Mix	G	Power	Stabile	U	Yes
		Libya	Mil	O	Parity	Stabile	U	No
		Zaire	Mil	G	Parity	Stabile	U	No
Iraq, Kurdish rebellion	1985-2003							
		Iran	Mil	O	Parity	Hectic	U	No
		US	Mil	O	Power	Hectic	U	Yes
		UN	Mix	O	Power	Hectic	M	Yes
Liberia I	1989-1990							
		ECOMOG	Mil	G	Power	Hectic	M	Yes
Chad Civil War IV	1989-2003							
		France	Mil	G	Power	Hectic	U	Yes
Rwanda vs. Tutsi I	1990-1993							
		France	Mil	G	Power	Hectic	U	Yes
		UN	Mil	N	Power	Hectic	M	Yes
Rwanda vs. Tutsi II	1994-1996							
		UN	Mil	N	Power	Hectic	M	Yes
		France	Mil	N	Power	Hectic	U	Yes
Niger	1990-1995							
		Liberia	Mil	O	Parity	Hectic	U	No
Mali	1990-1995							
		Liberia	Mil	O	Parity	Hectic	U	No
		UN	Eco	G	Power	Hectic	M	Yes
Georgia vs. Abkhaz	1991-1993							
		Russia	Mix	O	Power	Hectic	U	No
		CIS	Mil	N	Power	Hectic	M	No
Georgia vs. South Ossetia	1991-1992							
		Russia	Mix	O	Power	Hectic	U	No
		CIS	Mil	N	Power	Hectic	M	No

Table 2.1 continued Intervention dataset

Conflict	Dates	Intervener	Type	Support	Power	System	Composition	Success
Azerbaijan vs. Nagorno-Karabakh	1991-1994							
		Armenia	Mil	O	Parity	Hectic	U	No
		Turkey	Mil	G	Power	Hectic	U	No
Somali	1991-present							
		US	Mix	N	Power	Hectic	U	No
		UN	Mix	N	Power	Hectic	M	Yes
		UN	Mix	N	Power	Hectic	M	No
Croatia vs. Serbs	1991-1993							
		UN	Mil	N	Power	Hectic	M	Yes
		Yugoslavia	Mil	O	Parity	Hectic	U	No
Bosnia/ Herzegovina vs. Serbs	1992-1994							
		Yugoslavia	Mil	O	Parity	Hectic	U	No
		UN	Mil	N	Power	Hectic	M	Yes
		NATO	Mil	G	Power	Hectic	M	Yes
Moldova vs. Transdniestria	1990-1994							
		Russia	Mix	O	Power	Hectic	U	No
Liberia II	1992-1997							
		ECOMOG	Mil	G	Power	Hectic	M	Yes
		UN	Mix	N	Power	Hectic	M	Yes
Indonesia vs. East Timor	1999-2002							
		UN	Mix	N	Power	Stabile	M	Yes
DRC	1998-2002							
		Rwanda	Mil	O	Parity	Stabile	U	No
		Burundi	Mil	O	Parity	Stabile	U	No
		Uganda	Mil	O	Parity	Stabile	U	No
		Zimbabwe	Mil	G	Parity	Stabile	M	Yes
		Angola	Mil	G	Parity	Stabile	M	Yes
		Namibia	Mil	G	Parity	Stabile	M	Yes

Table 2.1 continued Intervention dataset

Conflict	Dates	Intervener	Type	Support	Power	System	Composition	Success
		Chad	Mil	G	Parity	Stabile	M	Yes
		Libya	Mil	G	Parity	Stabile	M	Yes
		Sudan	Mil	G	Parity	Stabile	M	Yes
		UN	Mil	N	Power		M	Yes
DRC-Ituri	1999-present							
		Uganda	Mil	O	Parity	Stabile	U	No
		Rwanda	Mil	O	Parity	Stabile	U	No
		France	Mil	N	Power	Stabile	U	No
		UN	Mil	N	Power	Stabile	M	Yes
Kosovo	1998-2002							
		Serbia	Mil	G	Parity	Stabile	U	No
		NATO	Mil	N	Power	Stabile	M	Yes
		UN	Mix	N	Power	Stabile	M	Yes
Sudan II (SPLA)	1983-2003							
		US	Eco	N	Power	Stabile	U	Yes
Sudan III (Darfur)								
		OAU	Mil	N	Power	Stabile	M	No

The optimal model of intervention success given below has been received through the forward-backward stepwise search method,[10] which features the unconstrained model (including the full set **X** of independent variables), and then tests whether any of these control variables are insignificant and can be removed from the model. The first variable to be removed will have the least impact on the overall model. As a result of this analysis, only the most "important" variables have been kept in the model – in other words, those variables that have higher values than others.

10 Field, A. 2000. *Discovering Statistics using SPSS for Windows: Advanced Techniques for the Beginner*. London: Sage Publications, 169.

Multilateral versus Unilateral Interventions

In order to find out whether the initial working hypothesis on highest likelihood of success of multilateral interventions is true, a generic model is presented, which included all the variables predicted to have effects on the outcome of interventions. This helped to further "purify" the model by eliminating variables with uncertain influence on the dependent variable. In the end, the "R" selected the simplest model that represents the "best-fit" for explaining the success of interventions. The predicted probability of success, given a specific values of the independent variables, is calculated by computing the cumulative distribution function of the normal distribution at the predicted value of the latent variable, $P(Y(x)=1|x=\mathbf{X}) = \Phi\ (intercept + ax_1 + bx_2 + \ldots + zx_p)$, where $x_{1\ldots p}$ are the independent variables, and $a\ldots z$ are their corresponding coefficients in the underlying linear model.

As a result of the probit analysis, the multilateral character of interventions appeared to play a very significant role in their overall success. Although all multilateral interventions in the dataset account for only 1/3 of the total number of cases of interventions, the rate of success of these interventions is, in fact, quite high. The data revealed that these interventions have been successful in 27 cases, or almost 84 per cent. Unilateral actions enjoy a much lower rate of success: only ¼ of the total number of unilateral interveners (19 out of 75 cases) managed to reach their initially planned goals. The probit analysis revealed quite a significant increase of probability of success when moving from unilateral to multilateral interventions, making them more successful in pursuit of their tasks. It established that, if taken separately, multilateral interventions increase the odds of success (Pr (success = 1) Type =T) = Φ (intercept + T · 1,6740) (with "0" for unilateral and "1" for multilateral interventions) by approximately 60 per cent as compared to unilateral foreign actions.

Probit Analysis – A Pure Impact

Unilateral interventions: $\Phi\ (-0.6640 + 0) = \Phi\ (-0.6640) = 25.33\%$
Multilateral interventions: $\Phi\ (-0.6640 + 1.6740) = \Phi\ (+1.01) = 84.37\%$

At this point, on the basis of initial results not yet supported by the case-studies, the advantages of multilateral interventions can be explained by a number of factors, which are related to the degree of institutionalization of their commitment to fulfill intervention tasks. Whenever multilateral interveners act, they do so either on under the aegis of an international organization or without such an entity. In the latter case such interventions are multinational, which means that they are organized by more than one state to carry out joint tasks. In either case we are talking about an institutional approach to interventions, which, on the one hand, sets frameworks for actions at the outset, and, on the other, provides fewer incentives for "logrolling" and acting unilaterally. When interventions are organized on behalf of an international or regional organization or are mandated by such an entity, there are certain rules, norms, moral and operational standards and best practices that the members of these institutions have to obey. In cases where the interveners are acting together without the backing of an international organization, there are also rules and standards set by bilateral and/or multilateral agreements and memoranda that the states entering into multilateral coalition have to sign. These rules delineate aims, operational scenarios and who-is-doing-what strategies. In the third and final case, interveners act alone, unilaterally, and the rules of engagement are set at the discretion of the sole intervener. For instance, out of the total 33 multilateral interventions conducted from the period of 1948 until 2003, 79 per cent was undertaken under the aegis of multinational organizations, such as UN, NATO, and ECOWAS. Only 5 failed to achieve their goals, and the remaining 21, or over 80 per cent have been overall successful in reaching their targeted goals.

So, why is the institutional approach to interventions so important to their success? Because rules and frameworks attach a perception of legitimacy to the activities of the interveners. Legitimacy is needed in all four levels of third party intervention: at interveners' homes, within interveners' coalitions, in a larger international context, and in the target states. By acceding to the intervention arrangements, the governments of the member-states can legitimately justify to the domestic constituencies as well as numerous veto players the military and economic efforts of their country connected with its participation in the coalition. Internally to the third party coalition, greater the number of rules guiding such interventions, the lower the odds of free-riding and predatory behavior by any member of coalition, and the longer the coalition can stay intact to internal and external pressure. Legitimacy is also needed for the larger international community of states to politically support the actions of the interveners. Externally, through intervention mandates and/or otherwise institutionalized legal documents, which are the embodiment of institutionalized rules, domestic warring groups clearly see what the interveners can do and what they cannot.

Legitimacy contributes to perception of trust to the interventions that their actions and options offered will be respected and fosters the sense legitimacy of these options. Such multi-party legitimacy is a fundamental difference between unilateral and multilateral interventions that contributes to the success of the latter by internationalizing and institutionalizing the conflict outcomes. When intervening, the multilateral third party coalition through its mandate commits itself to legitimize the outcomes of the conflict. In ethnic conflicts, when interventions are undertaken by multinational organizations, such commitment denotes agreement by the international community to legally recognize either secession (a new independent state, like Eritrea or East Timor), reintegration (a pre-war status quo in Liberia in 1989-1990) or concessions from the target state (a power-sharing arrangements, such as in Mali in 1990-1995). The responsibility for offering and recognizing such outcomes are equally shared by the members of the coalition, thus decreasing possible bias of any of its members in favor of one side of the conflict. In contrast, if an intervention is undertaken by one party, its commitment, and, as a consequence, legitimacy depends on the actions of that party only.

Another explanation of the success of multilateral interventions as opposed to unilateral ones can be found in an increased level of transparency attached to their operations. Rules and standards set up in the intervention mandates of multilateral interventions make the member-states accountable for their actions not only to their own domestic constituencies, but also to other countries and their public, which participate in the interventions. Not only are the activities of multilateral interventions more transparent, but all the resources and technical means they use are subject to international scrutiny. Whether the intervention is undertaken under the aegis of an international or regional organization or by a coalition of states without organizational support, every milestone of intervention is subject to economic and political oversight by other members of the organization issuing intervention mandate. The prescribed modus of actions is also under continual review of the coalition members. This is because, for example, human rights violations (if any) or one-sided support to certain belligerent group of one member-state tarnish the image of all members.

Transparency of interventions is also a vital element of trust of the warring factions to the third parties: multilateral interveners tend to have more open agendas, which are reflected in overt intervention actions, such as movement of troops, allocation more resources and intervention goals, which are embodied in their mandates available to everyone. Such modus operandi is positively received by nearly all the belligerents who want to know what is going on in their own country, what capacities the interveners have and, more importantly, that no state will cheat the others within the coalition and act in support to their rivals. Unilateral actions, on the contrary, conducted by even highly democratic states, do not have the same degree of transparency. Of course, there can be a domestic review process and international oversight of certain degree, but there still would be more frivolity in their actions.

The higher degree of success of multilateral interveners is closely associated with another assumption underlying the work hypothesis – functional impartiality of multilateral interveners, which follows directly from the notion of institutionalization of interventions. Multilateral interventions tend to be more functionally impartial than their unilateral counterparts and, thus, more trusted by and acceptable to the combatant parties. Whatever the preferences of the countries participating in intervention coalition are, they may be opposed by the preferences of others. Individual state's interests may range from the desire to act as pure peacemakers, to secure their image of a significant actor on international arena to mercantilist aspirations. There also would be states joining interventions coalitions out of with wish to help the belligerent groups in the target countries with whom they have ethnic links. In a coalition, the individual preferences of member-states become institutionalized in a sense that even if that member manages to make the coalition follow its own strategies, its preferences in options to be offered to the belligerents would thus become preferences of everybody in the coalition.

This way the notion of functional impartiality directly contributes to the build-up of trust by the belligerents who would believe that they would not be punished discriminatively by any biased coalition member.

Another factor supporting the working hypothesis is shared operational bias, which makes multilateral third parties more successful than sole actors. The problem of all interventions is that the options they offer or the ways their goals are implemented must be accepted or, at least, not opposed by the warring parties. Quite often interventions cannot satisfy aspirations of all warring factions, which in ethnic conflicts usually have clashing interests, unless they all concur on the matter of ending conflicts in mutually acceptable ways. Even if the interveners are neutral and impartial, their actions, undertaken with the purpose of implementation of their mandates, might be perceived as biased if the interveners are not helping them to win their war aims. Given the collective nature of multilateral interventions, views and preferences of their members would be melted and molded into a joint interest and aspirations, where the bias (if any), becomes impersonalized and shared by all. When interventions are undertaken by international organizations, the bias is institutionalized through its mandates and conventions, which increases the credibility of the interveners' commitment in the eyes of the belligerents. Shared operational bias may also be better for the belligerents and used by them as a good face-saving exercise. Even if a warring faction believes that it has fallen victim of discrimination, it must see that the decision to act was taken not by one state alone, but by the whole group of states. In this sense, emotionally it may be even better for a loser group to become the victim of the many than the victim of one: defeats in battlefields and on political grounds can be easier justified and explained to their domestic supporters if incurred and imposed by an organization rather than a single state.

Intervening Factors for Intervention Success

Due to a whole range of endogenous and exogenous nature that affect outcomes of interventions, the composition of the intervention force alone cannot entirely account for their successes or failures. Apart from revealing a higher probability of success of multilateral versus unilateral actions of interveners, the probit analysis included additional control variables that have an intervening effect on the overall success of the third parties' abilities to reach their target agendas. These factor variables were brought to the model after evaluating the effect of the main independent variable on the dependent one. It appeared that introduction of these variables had diverse effects on the efficiency of all types of interventions. The probit analysis of the overall model including all the variables is presented below.

The model reveals high significance of the three variables – Composition, Power and Time. The remaining factor variables – Support and Type, turned out to have low significance for the model. These insignificant variables were further eliminated by the stepwise search method due to their negligible impact on success of interventions.

Table 2.2 Combined probit model of third party interventions

Deviance residuals:

Min	1Q	Median	3Q	Max
-2.0114	-0.5309	-0.2715	0.5371	2.0145

Coefficients:

	Estimate	Std. error	z value	Pr(>|z|)	
(Intercept)	-1.1195	0.2677	-4.181	2.9e-05	***
Factor(Composition)1	1.6185	0.5182	3.124	0.001787	**
Factor(Power)1	1.6373	0.4382	3.736	0.000187	***
Factor(Time)1	-0.6774	0.3777	-1.794	0.072852	.
Factor(Support)1	0.5978	0.3562	1.678	0.093279	.
Factor(Support)2	-0.7478	0.5680	-1.317	0.187945	
Factor(Type)1	-0.0928	0.6965	-0.133	0.894001	
Factor(Type)2	-0.5220	0.4259	-1.226	0.220307	

Note: Signif. codes: 0 '***' 0.001 '**' 0.01 '*' 0.05 '.' 0.1 ' ' 1.

With regards to the Support variable, finding that intervention neutrality or its support to the government is unrelated to intervention success contradicts the arguments of a number of scholars who believe neutrality to be a positive factor in reaching peace. For instance, Diehl et al. (1996) largely attributed the success of the UN interventions to their neutrality, which fosters "a solution that meets the interests of the disputants as well as the international community".[11] Neutrality is thus thought to engender trust on the part of the parties in conflict that the interveners are committed to the general goals of peacekeeping rather than self-aggrandizement. Similarly, Regan (2002) stressed the greater likelihood of success of multilateral than unilateral interventions exactly due to the neutrality of the former. Neutral interveners get the warring sides to accept their involvement: operationally, their troops "are not engaged in partisan combat but play a neutral role in preventing an outbreak or spread of fighting".[12] Success of neutral multinational interventions was also noted by Doyle and Sambanis (2000), who claimed that "international enforcement can help solve commitment and coordination problems by imposing order or by directly implementing peace agreements or raising the costs of defection from them".[13]

11 Diehl, P.F., Reifschneider, J. and Hensel, P.R. 1996.

12 Regan, P.M. 2002, 102.

13 Doyle, M.W. and Sambanis, N. 2000. International Peacebuilding: A Theoretical and Quantitative Analysis. *American Political Science Review*, 94(4), 781.

However, when the success of intervention is measured not by the peace-centric approach, i.e. presence or absence of de facto peace in a target country and its longevity, but by success of implementation of their agendas by third parties and is specifically applied to ethnic conflicts and not all the civil wars, in general, none of the three characteristics of direction of third party support turns out to play a significant role. This is especially true in the case of neutral unilateral interventions – a solitary intervener is rarely neutral but rather pursues its own vital national interests in the conflict; it therefore faces difficulty in persuading the belligerents of its neutrality. A multilateral force, however, is by its very nature more neutral; however, its neutrality may not yield a mutually acceptable outcome for all the belligerent sides.

The complexities of interethnic interactions, apart from purely numeric characteristics of the roles of factor variables, show that in many instances, it does matter whom the third parties support. In fact, when forceful external imposition of the options by the interveners is the only preferred or available option to achieve intervention goals, the domestic power balance is an intervening variable that has to be taken into account in the logistic regression. Support to minorities or majorities, challenger or target government all involve operation of third parties in the context of domestic power settings. The main problem here is that the government may not necessarily be the strongest out of all the belligerent groups: governments can be dominated my minorities who have higher representation in administrative and political structures but lower membership in law and order agencies, including the army and police. On the other hand, opposition may as well be represented by the majority groups who are stronger than their ruling minorities (as it was during the Rwandan "Social Revolution" in 1959). Therefore, not statutory but comparative belligerent capacities shall be taken into account. Also, in some cases third parties may provide support to the government or the opposition factions but limit them to insignificant inputs. In such cases de-jure support to any side has to be cross-referenced with the de facto aid that group had actually received to see how the participation of the interveners contributed to their successes. All these peculiarities cannot be expressed by the statistic model, especially within a uniform peace-centric approach.

By supporting weaker groups, interveners improve their domestic power standing by joining their own resources and, thus, equalize the situation with the stronger ones. This may lead to an extended conflict and increased chances for the challengers to sustain military operations against the target government. If, however, the interveners help the stronger side, they spend fewer resources that they would have had they supported the weaker side. They may also achieve their own goals more easily by supporting the side that already enjoys military advantage over its rival. Finally, such support of a third party will contribute to ending the conflicts quicker by decreasing the expected utility of the weaker group out of acting against the government, being usually stronger.

Although the probit analysis shows that for the interventions to be successful in their tasks, it does not matter whom they should support, because of the nature of the independent variable – unilateral and multilateral composition of interventions – the interaction between intervention composition and direction of support does matter for intervention success in ethnic conflicts, which cannot be presented by the statistic model. Notwithstanding the fact that variable Support was excluded from the model, it still had higher parameters than Type and stands close to the main significant variables. In order to assess the effects of this interaction, in-depth case studies are needed to see whether the nature of the recipient of third party support is relevant to successful pursuit of intervention agendas by different types of interveners.

The logistical regression analysis also showed that the combination of military and economic strategies (a total of 20 mixed interventions, or 19 per cent) is not a significant predictor of intervention success in ethnic strife. This finding, too, goes contrary to the peace-centric viewpoint on conflict resolution. Mixed strategies, according to Regan (2002), would produce a higher probability of success when the latter is viewed by the number of years of peace.[14] The type of aid provided by the third parties to the belligerents would be an important factor in considering the success of interventions from the point of view of durable peace. However, when the goal-based approach is applied, they are insignificant in the matter of resolving conflicts.

The reason why mixed strategies appeared to have an significant role in peace is because they are, indeed, required for long-term settlement of conflicts. For instance, five years is quite a long period of time for the target country to restore its normal functioning and provision of state services, with or without interveners. Economic assistance also helps people in many ways: to recover the losses of property and other assets, to sustain minimum living standards, to create work places, to pay salaries, pensions, compensations, and, in general, to revive human dignities. It helps overcome the feeling of being underdeveloped, being neglected and discriminated, which may lead to renewed conflicts, where "they" (other ethnic groups) are blamed in "our" economic troubles. When effects of interventions are measured by the number of peaceful years, the more economic aid follows military support, the easier it will be for a country to recover from conflict. In simpler terms, military aid helps in bringing peace, while economic aid helps in keeping it. That is why peace-centric view highly appreciates mixed strategies for interventions.

Insignificance of this variable in the general model has another explanation, too. The military and economic components are not always easy to distinguish when judging about success of interventions from the point of view of their initial goals. For instance, training troops of a belligerent group can be considered both as military aid and as improvement of economic standing of that group (like the Indian support for Tamil insurgents in Sri Lanka or the training of the Chadian military by the French officers), since the recipient party could spend the money allocated for its military needs on other purposes.

14 Regan, P.M. 2002.

When the goal-based approach is employed, immediate observation of the success of interventions comes into light. The long-term effects of mixed actions are difficult to determine: while the impact of military side of interventions is usually easier and straight-forward to observe, it takes time for economic interventions to have a significant impact on the success of interventions (as was the case with the UN and Belgian interventions in the conflict in Zaire in 1960-1965). Interveners' goals may also change during the period of intervention – they may start with peace-enforcement by their military followed by peace-building and state-reconstruction activities, which would eventually require more economic resources than military force. In this case, success of each specific type of aid shall be evaluated immediately after the end of each specific phase, which means more fluid nature of intervention goals and the means to achieve them.

The Optimal Model

The probit analysis of the remaining variables – Composition, Power and Time – is presented below:

Table 2.3 Optimal probit model of third party interventions

	Estimate	Std. Error	z value	Pr(>|z|)	
(Intercept)	-0.9526	0.2186	-4.359	1.31e-05	***
Factor(Composition)1	1.1524	0.3595	3.205	0.001350	**
Factor(Power)1	1.3728	0.3644	3.768	0.000165	***
Factor(CW)1	-0.7180	0.3513	-2.044	0.040951	*

Note: Signif. codes: 0 '***' 0.001 '**' 0.01 '*' 0.05 '.' 0.1 ' ' 1.

The reduced model received as a result of the stepwise method includes the main independent variable Composition and the control variables Power and Time. Although presence of these control variables decreased slightly the coefficient of the independent variable, the influence of these variables over the predicted probability of success of interventions, in general, continues to confirm overall prediction that multilateral interventions are more successful than unilateral ones. However, it is interesting to note that these intervening variables have different impacts on the probability of success depending on their composition.

The next table reveals that, in general, the presence of a superpower in all types of intervention has a positive effect on their success. The model above defines unilateral interventions undertaken by a country with relative power party vis-à-vis belligerents as the least successful, whereas the highest rate of success is enjoyed by multilateral coalition containing a superpower. Presence of superior military – either in international or regional terms – capable of destruction of the

Table 2.4 Probabilities of intervention success with a power factor

	Unilateral	Multilateral
Superpower	48.62%	87.70%
No superpower	14.55%	55.57%

capacities of the belligerents increases the chances for success both for multilateral and unilateral interventions. A powerful intervener will not only present a credible threat of defeat to the side it is opposing, but can also be a trust-worthy guarantor of peace and/or victory of any party to the conflict. Once such a powerful actor enters the scene, further developments in the conflict largely depend on the interests of an intervener and the policy it decides to implement in the conflict.

With the high effect the Power factor has in the matter of achieving success of interventions, is still more important for unilateral interventions than multilateral ones: the success of unilateral actions almost doubles (from 25.33 per cent to 48.62 per cent) if an intervening state is a superpower versus a state with relative power parity with a target country, whereas it is almost insignificant in multilateral interventions – only a 3 per cent increase (from 84.37 per cent to 87.70 per cent). At the same time, without superpower factor, multilateral interveners prove to be nearly four times as successful as unilateral ones. Non-superpower interveners are likely to achieve success in only 14.55 per cent of interventions whereas more than half of the instances of the multilateral coalitions without superpower states within their ranks were successful.

Several factors may account for overall success of a "superpower" on the success of interventions. From a pure operational perspective, superpowers enjoy military superiority, allowing them to perform their intervention tasks better and quicker than countries having relative parity with the warring factions. Especially in multilateral interventions, superpowers usually have higher stakes when

Table 2.5 Probabilities of intervention success with a power and Cold War factors

Cold War Period

	Unilateral	Multilateral
Superpower	66.28%	94.21%
No superpower	17.04%	57.92%

Five years before and after the end of Cold War

	Unilateral	Multilateral
Superpower	38.29%	80.36%
No superpower	4.74%	30.21%

intervening: apart from military victories, there is an issue of superpower prestige in the world arena. Other participants of the coalition may also have "psychological" assurances that if a superpower decides to act, it will use its resources decisively to achieve success because its reputation as a world power is at stake.

The final variable, *Time*, or proximity of conflicts to the decade commencing the dissolution of the bipolar system, is also an important predictor of intervention success, confirming higher chances for efficiency of multiple third parties during the period of superpower rivalry. While multilateral interventions proved still more successful than unilateral actions, the probability of success of intervention was higher for all types during the period of bipolar world than after the end of US-USSR confrontation.

Out of all the types of interventions, the most efficient are joint actions with a superpower presence in a multilateral coalition undertaken during the bipolar period: 94.21 per cent compared to initial 84 per cent (a 10 per cent increase in efficiency). The Cold War period also positively affected the remaining types of interventions: unilateral with and without superpower presence and multilateral interventions without a superpower. It is interesting to note that the value of the Cold War factor in all unilateral interventions is relatively equal: the rate of success of unilateral parity interventions undertaken during the Cold War as opposed to at the end of the war almost doubles (from 4.74 per cent to 17.04 per cent). The situation is roughly the same with unilateral superpower interventions, which see quite a significant increase in success – a 28 per cent (from 38.29 per cent to 66.28 per cent) in overall success rate. This was also true for the multilateral interventions: when undertaken during the Cold War, even regardless of presence of a superpower within its ranks, they were all more successful if compared with similar interventions five years before and after the end of the bipolar rivalry. Likelihood of success of all multilateral interventions increased during the Cold War: by 27.71 per cent without a superpower and by 13.85 per cent with a superpower.

Higher probability of success of interventions during the Cold War era and after the end of the Communist system can be explained first, by viewing interactions between states at the systemic level and within them at the sub-systemic levels, and, second, by the nature of intra-state ethnic relationships. The bipolar world was characterized not only by ideological rivalry between superpowers, but also by a form of "contained cooperation", where each of them feared annihilation from its rival in the event of a major conflict. Systemic security dilemma culminated in the MAD (Mutually Assured Destruction) strategy, which advocated for total nuclear war and, at the same time, acted as a restraint on the superpowers in usage of nuclear weapons. One of the first who drew the attention to this phenomenon was Miller (1992), who noted that during the Cold War ideologically dissimilar superpowers cooperated in international security arena and jointly managed regional conflicts.[15] This idea is also supported by a Russian Cold War historian

15 Miller, B. 1992. Explaining Great Power Cooperation in Conflict Management. *World Politics*, 45(1), 1-46.

Bogaturov (2006), who claimed that during "1960s confrontational stability was characterized by activation of a dialogue between the USSR and the USA, détente of their position on the issue of arms control and international situation in Europe on the background of high level of conflict in regional sub-systems..."[16]

The post-Cold War world was divided into the two areas of influence for the two hegemons, which, while refraining from direct collision, tested their muscles on other countries trying to spread their influences. The rivalry between the two superpowers from the systemic level was transferred onto the domestic settings of their satellite and "no man's" countries by taking the form of civil strife. The superpowers provided economic and/or military assistance to the faction who would pledge their loyalty to the ideological camp of their patrons (such as, for example, the "Scientific Socialism" project of Barre in Somalia) and avoiding direct confrontations between each other at any costs (the Cuban Missile Crisis is a perfect example of escape from the global war). Both the US and the USSR refrained from direct military actions against each other out of fear of total world collapse in case of nuclear war, which was inevitable taken the capacities of these countries.

Last years of the 1980s shook the reign of bipolarity, the collapse of which cascaded with Gorbachev's Glasnost and Perestroika leading to the systemic anarchy and appearance of new independent states with their domestic rivalries and made the cooperation at the systemic level more difficult. The new Russia was preoccupied with its own internal problems of economic decline, political instability and territorial conflicts, while the US was facing *terra incognita* of "fresh" international relations with plethora of opportunities, as well as threats.

From a sub-systemic viewpoint, domestic anarchy conditioned relationships between ethnic groups in the newly created countries who were left without their foreign benefactors. Ethnic conflicts (re)emerged, reanimated by suddenly materialized primordial hatred, which found no ideological bounds to be constrained. Collapse of the Communist bloc, which decreased economic support to satellite states equally from the former superpowers, paved the way to a deep financial crisis in many countries, breakdown of main elements of domestic order, political disintegration and rising nationalism. The shaky situation was also reflected on the ability of the interveners to successfully implement their intervention agendas. Third parties intervening after the end of Cold War had, generally, an overall low rate of success: both unilateral and multilateral interventions tended to be less successful in the face of domestic forces that had been unleashed by systemic collapse. After fermentation of the international system was more or less over (a ten-year period is considered as sufficient enough for re-setting the system), cooperation on the international arena increased. Although interventions remained after 1995, they were all more successful in comparison to those undertaken during the period of reshaping of the international system. International cooperation made the states

16 Bogaturov, A.D. (ed.) 2006. *Sistemnaya Istoriya Mejdunarodnix Otnoshenii* [The System History of International Relations]. M.: Kulturnaya Revoluciya, 278-279.

more dependent on each other through wide participation in international political and economic institutions. Globalization also contributed to universalization of democratic values. Although the states, especially superpowers, continue to muscle in domestic affairs of other countries, increased order on the international system level left fewer political interstices unfilled, and the former hegemons become more stabilized in their interests and aspirations.

Conclusions

The probit model correctly predicted the success of 31 multilateral interventions out of 41 (75.61 per cent) and the failure of 51 unilateral interventions out of 66 cases (77.27 per cent). The total validity rate of the model is 76.64 per cent – it altogether correctly predicted 82 cases out of 107. The statistic regression has revealed several sets of relationships that require theoretical explanation. It has confirmed the work hypothesis advocating for the greater success of multilateral interventions as opposed to unilateral ones. Interventions undertaken by coalition of states were proved to be more successful in reaching their goals then were the actions of single states. The degree of power wielded by the third party had a significant effect on the interveners' ability to reach their agendas. The presence of a superpower in unilateral interventions confers substantial advantage to the interveners, although it has less significant value in multiple third parties. Finally, rivalry and cooperation between the world superpowers before and after the end of the Cold War is positively related to success of all interventions, while the period of transition was associated with a low rate of success.

The probit model essentially showed that multilateral interventions were more successful than unilateral interventions notwithstanding their substance and the type of support they provided. The regression analysis also revealed that interveners were equally successful no matter whom they supported – the target government or the challenger, or when they were neutral. Altogether, interventions have the highest probability of success in an international climate of cooperation between the world superpowers, when undertaken by a coalition of states, by a country with absolute and relative power superiority vis-à-vis the target government, and those under the aegis of an international/regional organization. The least successful were interventions of a single state with rough power parity with the belligerents that were undertaken around the time of the end of the Cold War.

With the purpose of defining causal factors that contribute to or impede the success of interventions, in-depth case studies were conducted. The cases have been selected from the list of the conflicts and interventions used for the quantitative study. The first two instances interventions to be studied are those that were correctly predicted by the probit analysis: with successful multilateral interventions and unsuccessful unilateral interventions to see what factors facilitate the fulfillment of the intervention agendas. The remaining two cases have been selected from the list of incorrectly predicted interventions: with successful unilateral and unsuccessful multilateral intervention to see what factors impede the fulfillment of the intervention agendas. This will allow to further theoretical premises of successes and failures of interventions and to refine the framework of analysis with addition of the intervening factors salient for successful third party operations. Incorrectly predicted cases will contribute to falsifiability of the goal-based approach and would give the account of the instances in which the theory of third party commitment would not work.

In selection of the cases two criteria have been applied: variations of the high and low level of independent and dependent variables to further theorize on the successes of interventions and in-case similarities between the conflicts to keep important intervening factors constant, such as the nature of the intervener, history, geography, political settings, economic conditions, post-imperial experience, etc. These criteria produced the following cases: successful unilateral and successful multilateral interventions in the conflict in Rwanda; unsuccessful unilateral and unsuccessful multilateral interventions in the conflict between Georgia and Abkhazia; successful and unsuccessful unilateral interventions in long-lasting conflict in Chad; and successful and unsuccessful multilateral interventions in Somalia.

These cases of intervention have many things in common. The most remarkable commonality between them is the characteristics of target countries, timeframes of interventions and the nature of the interveners themselves. Notwithstanding the geographic, historical and cultural differences between the African and European countries, all the target countries during times when interventions had been conducted were more or less "failed states": states suffering from domestic anarchy with no or extremely week central governments, no "legitimate authority to make collective decisions" and chronic inability "to provide reasonable public services" through malfunctioning administrative resources.[17] By the time of interventions Rwanda, Chad, Somalia and equally Georgia were all experiencing large-scale civil war, in some cases instigated or supported by the third parties themselves. Weak economies, identity differences (culture, religion, ethnicity, and geography) also contributed to state failure in these cases.

Historical backgrounds of the conflicts were also similar: all the countries share colonial past history. The conflicts within the territories of the cases all happened shortly after the countries gained their independence from their patron-states and were experiencing a dangerous mix of upheaval of national pride, historical stigmatization and a devastated economy.

From the point of view of the timing of interventions, the conflicts in Rwanda, Somalia, and Georgia all happened after the dissolution of the bipolar system and during the decade of systemic chaos, when the old rivalry was gone without building up new patterns of relations between the two superpowers. The outlier

17 Failed States Index, Fund for Peace [Online]. Available at: http://www.fundforpeace.org/web/index.php?option=com_content&task=view&id=102&Itemid=151 [accessed: May 7, 2009].

case in this respect is Chad, where the interventions of third parties started long before the end of Cold War. However, even in this case the final resolution of the conflict – when Libya was made to return the Aouzou Strip to Chad by the decision of the International Court of Justice in 1994 – coincided with the end of the Soviet Union.

The conflicts studies were also similar in the nature of the third parties that intervened. In nearly all these conflicts (except for the US intervention in Somalia) the interveners had historical ties with the target countries. Also, in majority of the conflicts interventions were conducted by the same actors at least twice with diverse or equal degree of success. By having similar actors intervening in same conflicts allowed, first, to keep the nature of the intervener constant and to keep the attention away from the factors pertinent to actor-specific divergences, and, second, to see what makes the same actor succeed and fail under the same country environment. At the same time, the is in-case broad variance with regards to the composition of third parties: unilateral interventions (France and Libya in Chad, Russia in Georgia); unilateral intervention with a multinational agency mandate (France in Rwanda); a coalition of multilateral forces (US in Somalia); formally multilateral but essentially force (Russia in CIS peacekeeper troops); and, finally, multilateral organizational interventions (UNAMIR, UNOSOM).

Chapter 3

Chad (1966-1987): Muscling in for Control

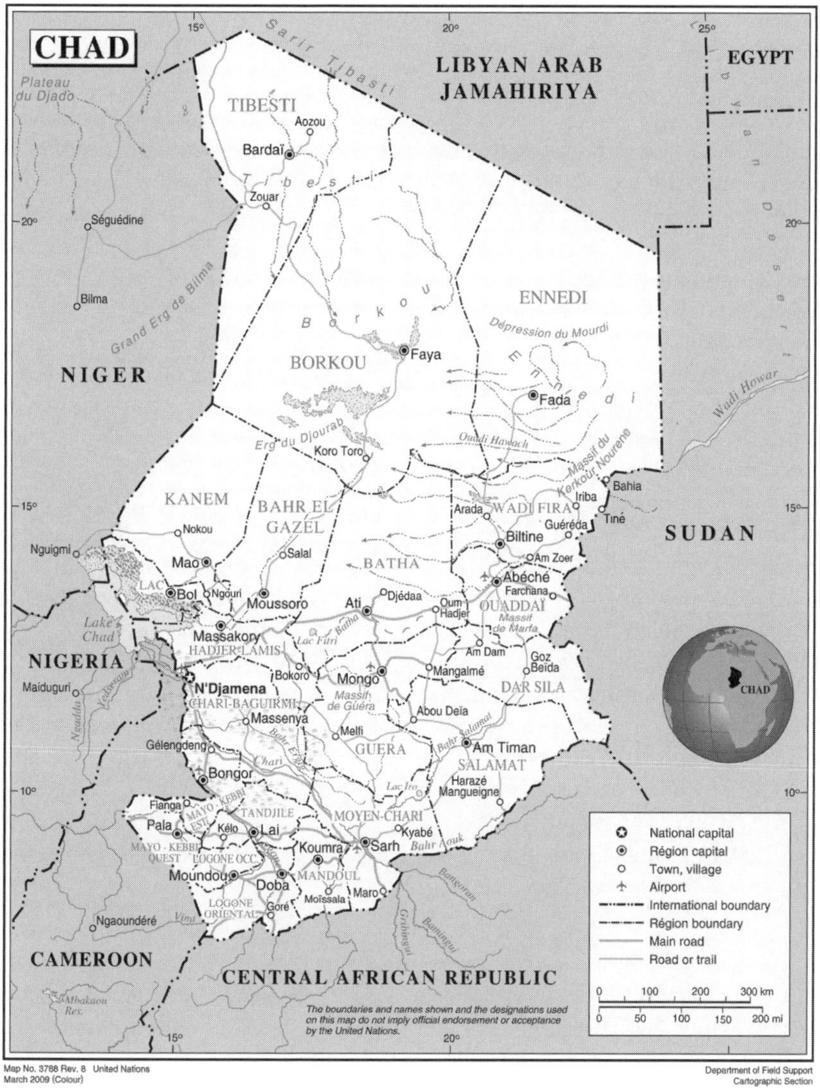

Map 3.1 Map of Chad

Source: Reprinted with permission of the UN Cartographic Section.

The conflict in Chad stands out from similar ethnic conflicts in Africa and elsewhere in many respects. Although not as intense and violent as other cases of ethnic strife, the Chadian civil war has been known as one of the most protracted civil conflicts in the post-WW II era. Nearly two generations of Chadians were born and lived their lives through constant threat of numerous rebellions, coups, instability, economic hardships and interventions.

Conflict Background

Like the majority of Northern-central African countries, Chad had been a French Colonial possession – a status that determined its most post-colonial political developments. Although in most parts deprived of valuable resources, such as oil, gas, gold, gems, etc., Chad is well-situated along the major trans-Saharan cross-roads, which made for development of trade, crafts, as well as trafficking of slaves. Ethnic, environmental and religious fragmentation is a distinctive feature of the Chadian society. The country is divided into the Northern, Central and Southern parts having about 200 ethnic groups[1] speaking over 100 different languages.[2]

In 1916 Chad joined the French Equatorial Africa together with three French colonies to the South – Ubangi-Chari, Moyen-Congo, and Gabon. In 1920 the country became a separate French colony. The French rule in Chad was characterized by strong favoritism towards Southerner Christians over the Northerner Muslims and the settlers over the pagan nomads. Social and political segmentation of the Chadian society that happened exactly along these geographic and religious lines was at the heart of nearly all subsequent internal conflicts. As Azevedo and Nnadozie (1998) described, "[T]he French administration reinforced polarization between North and South through the constant use of contrasting terminology: *chrétien* (Christian) versus *musulman* (Muslim); *sudiste* (Southerner) versus *nordiste* (Northerner)…"[3] Subsequently, this geographic and religious stratification created political-economic regionalization gaps in the country: the underdeveloped North (called by the French as "Tchade Inutile") lagged behind the industrially advanced and better-educated South ("Tchade Utile"). As a result, it was the southerners who, after the independence of Chad, occupied the best administrative positions and enjoyed political and economic dominance over the rest of the country.

1 Chapelle, J. 1980. *Le Peuple Tchadien*. Paris: Hartman, reprint in *World Almanac* (1993). New York: Press Publication Company, 741.

2 Morrison, D.G., Mitchell, R.C. and Paden, J.N. 1989. *Understanding Black Africa: Data and Analysis of Social Change and Nation-Building*. New York: Paragon House and Irvington, 412.

3 Azevedo, M. and Nnadozie, E.U. 1998. *Chad: A Nation in Search of its Future*. Westview Press, 38.

De-colonization process itself was painful for the Chadian society: it left the country with an essentially traditional and import-oriented economy; an insignificant industrial sector; a cotton-dominated agriculture; and a rather inadequate infrastructure. Economic hardships were aggravated by the turbulence arising from local politics, fragmentation of the population into separate and sometimes conflicting groups along ethnic, religious and regional lines. This population divide led to creation geographically and ethnically oriented political parties after the end of WW II: the PPT (Parti Progressif Tchadien – Chadian Progressive Party), representing Southern interests, and the UDT (Union Démocratique Tchadien – Chadian Democratic Union), which was an influential local branch of De Gaulle's Rassemblement du Peuple Français. By the time of independence of the country in August 1960, the PPT and the South dominated the Chadian politics.

On August 11, 1960, Françoise Tombalbaye of PPT became the first president of Chad. Faced with the daunting task of consolidating the divided society, Tombalbaye used substantial French support by employing the French advisers in many governmental posts and allowing France to control most of the nation's financial operations. This way France continued to remain its "statutory" patron. Not only did the Chadians, according to Thompson and Adloff (1981), "continue… to look upon France as their natural protector and source of aid,"[4] but also France itself viewed Chad as an essential component of its prestige and external security. This relationship was reflected in numerous agreements signed between France and nearly all the Chadian governments.

For example, on the basis of the bilateral "Assistance Agreement" signed in August 1960, France undertook the responsibility to "provide it [Chad] with the assistance it requires to achieve the goals of economic and social advancement… [by] carrying out studies, supplying equipment, sending experts and technicians, training personnel and granting financial aid."[5] Within the frameworks of the multilateral "Agreement and Conventions to Maintain Order in African Malagasy States" signed between France and Chad, as well as Madagascar, Congo, Gabon, Cote d'Ivoire and Niger and covering 1966-1967,[6] France could intervene both indirectly and directly to uphold domestic law and order in the countries in question. While the indirect help included provision of logistics and communication support,

---

4 Thompson, V. and Adloff, R. 1981. *Conflict in Chad, Research Series – Institute of International Studies, #45* (University of California, Berkley), 12.

5 Assistance Agreement between the French Republic and the Republic of Chad [Online]. 1960. United Nations Treaty Collection. Available at: http://treaties.un.org/doc/Publication/UNTS/Volume%20821/volume-821-I-11745-English.pdf [accessed: May 13, 2009].

6 Accords et Conventions de Maintien de l'Ordre dans les etats Africains et Malgashes [Agreement and Conventions to Maintain Order in African Malagasy States] 1966-1967. United Nations Treaty Collection. [Online]. Available at: http://www.rue89.com/2008/02/03/laccord-secret-qui-lie-la-france-au-tchad [accessed: May 13, 2009].

direct assistance envisaged the French interventions on behalf of the presidents of these countries. During the French military operations, "the national forces [of the countries] although remaining under the authority of their direct command, temporarily and locally are included into the French command for the duration of the operations." The French government was also entitled to "to use its forces for keeping order in one State…maintained in another State." Another agreement – on technical military assistance – allowed Chad to seek the French assistance in establishing their interior forces – *Gendarmerie* and National Army. Article 5 of this agreement made the Chadian government bound on seeking "assistance exclusively from the French Republic in respect of the maintenance and further provision of equipment and supplies for its armed forces."[7] All these provisions, including more than 20 agreements and treaties were directed at normalizing the relations with the new country and a former colony and making it a deserving member of the international community.

Soon, however, Tombalbaye's "one-man-only" rule antagonized majority of the population and gave birth to the powerful opposition within the other ethnic and clan groups. Tombalbaye was from a southern Sara group and allotted the majority of the administrative positions to his clan kin and Southerners, in general, thus squandering his legitimacy through repressive tactics and regional favoritism. Heavy-handed policies against other groups exacerbated their grievances, and the Northern Muslim religious leaders and warlords, each with ethnic-based agendas and supporters, began to openly challenge Tombalbaye's regime. The opposition increasingly used traditional loyalties and enmities to condemn the ruling Southerners and to gain popular support among their own supporters. Popular dissatisfaction steadily grew; alleged or real coups were uncovered, and the government increased oppression of all the layers of population, even including president's own Sara group.

One of the very first rebellion originated in the Northern parts of Chad in 1966 and further developed into a major political actor in ensuing domestic conflicts – the FLT (Front de Libération du Tchad – Liberation Front of Chad). The FLT was later renamed into FROLINAT (Front de Libération Nationale du Tchad – National Liberation Front of Chad) with a strong military component. Although FROLINAT united people dissatisfied with Tombalbaye, it suffered from the lack of common political will and vision, absence of a specific and concrete political platform and only vague plans for future governance. Its political goals and objectives were too broad, too ambiguous and ambitious. Another weak point of the FROLINAR, as Nolutshungu (1996) notes, was that it "…had always been highly regionalized in its

---

7 Agreement Concerning Technical Military Assistance between the French Republic and the Republic of Chad [Online]. 1960. United Nations Treaty Collection. Available at: http://treaties.un.org/doc/Publication/UNTS/Volume%20821/volume-821-I-11741-English.pdf [accessed: May 13, 2009].

command structure, and its regional wings were of different ethnic composition."[8] Ethnic fragmentation among its members was worsened by diversities in personal loyalties and uneven access of various clans to the top political leadership and their differential treatment. This patchy nature of the rebellion significantly affected successes and failures of the future foreign interventions in Chad.

Three major military groups with separate agendas constructed the core of FROLINAT: the FLA (First Liberation Army), which later became the "Volcan Army", was led by Abba Siddick and was largely composed of ethnic Arabs. Its internal rival was the Second Liberation Army, or the FAN (Forces Armées du Nord – Northern Armed Forces), probably the most influential and enjoying strong Libyan support, was led by Hissène Habré (a Gorane) and Goukouni Oueddi (the son of a *derdei*, the Chadian spiritual leader exiled by Tombalbaye in Libya). The Third Liberation army mainly operated in the west-central Kanem district, and did not represent more or less a significant actor.

The only consolidating point for FROLINAT was that, while originating in the Muslim Toubou region of BET (Borkou-Ennedi-Tibesti) province and including in its ranks predominantly Muslims, it never actually wanted to secede from the rest of country. On the contrary, it had a very centric position and advocated for a unified Chad. However, this wish to keep the country intact and homogenous was quite rational: according to Nolutshungu (1996), there was "little for FROLINAT to gain from pulling out of the Republic the least prosperous and economically least promising North, and certainly not when it had a realistic chance of taking the whole country."[9] Secession of a less developed Northern region would place it victim to the interests of Libya, which, since the very arrival of Quadaffi to power, wanted to annex Northern Chad. Such Libyan aspirations were well-known to FROLINAT leaders, who, if seceded, would find themselves as regional heads under the Libyan.

French and Libyan Interventions

Gradually FROLINAT was gaining significant territorial control in the North by advancing in the BET and the Wadai provinces. The Chadian army stationed there was mainly composed of the Southerners who were viewed as aliens to the local population sympathetic to FROLINAT, which was fighting on its own territory. Unable to cope with the increasing dissatisfaction in the North, Tombalbaye invited France to stop the rebellion advances. France promptly responded by sending an expeditionary force, the aim of which was "to make possible the reinstallation of the Chadian administration in the BET"[10] – a mission narrowed geographically

8 Nolutshungu, S.C. 1996. *Limits of Anarchy: Intervention and State Formation in Chad*. University Press of Virginia, 97.

9 Nolutshungu, S.C. 1996, 61.

10 Nolutshungu, S.C. 1996, 71.

and operationally. The primary aim of the intervention was short-term salvaging the Chadian postcolonial government from internal political turbulence. Neither Tombalbaye nor the French had the ultimate goal to completely crush the revolt: the former feared mass retaliation from the Northern provinces, and the later were not prepared to get engaged in a costly and lengthy war.

The intervention occurred in two stages: the first phase began in August 1968 and lasted for three months. This time, the French sent only a limited number of troops, which, by the end of intervention, amounted to 2,000 French marines. After a series of military clashes with the rebels, the French succeeded in retaking the government outposts in the North, held under siege by FROLINAT since March. The second phase began in April 1969 and was considerably larger in terms of personnel and resources. The intervention was officially ended in June 1971, however around 1,200 French military personnel continued to remain in Chad to train the national army – the FAT (Forces Armées Tchadienne – the Chadian Armed Forces), which was about twice as big as the French contingent – altogether about 2,700 infantry and air force.[11]

The result of the French intervention was suppression of the revolt in the central and eastern parts of the country, curbing the threat from the BET, in general, and Tibesti, in particular. FROLINAT's early gains in the North had been reversed, its southwards advances thwarted and it was unable to re-capture most of the previously occupied regions. Participation in direct clashes with FROLINAT on the side of the FAT also raised the battle morale of its soldiers and gave them the feeling of being backed up by a regional power-stae. In sum, the French, according to Nolutshungu (1996), "progressively weakened FROLINAT's influence in this region and permanently deprived the Center-East of its leading role in the rebellion."[12] Looses on the battlefields also seriously disorganized FROLINAT internally. Internal divide within its political structures grew even deeper and made the whole movement feeble and more susceptible to outside pressure.

After the intervention France insisted upon conducting administrative reforms aiming at decentralization of the state authority and a shift to provincial officials and traditional community leaders. In doing so, France was promoting its own completely rational objective: being aware that the rebellion was far from being over, France feared of further worsening of the situation in Northern Chad, which might lead to another call from Tombalbaye for intervention. Aspired to the idea of democratic governance as a precondition for civil peace, France advocated for the power-sharing mechanisms in Chad that would foster national reconciliation, increase the quality of public administration and improve relations between Northern and Southern parts of Chad with the purpose of satisfaction of the diverse viewpoints of population in order to prevent future discontent and possible renewal of rebellion.

11 Nolutshungu, S.C. 1996, 69.

12 Nolutshungu, S.C. 1996, 63.

Following the French recommendations, the central authorities started negotiations with the local chiefs; managed to improve local tax collection practices and released some of the political prisoners. Unfortunately, these reforms turned out to be visionary, and failed to address fundamental problems of the Chadian society – regionalization, poor economy and political instability. Nothing had been done to improve domestic political climate and one-party dominance: Tombalbaye effectively remained the sole ruler of Chad. Dissatisfaction grew also in the FAT, which was feeling a sense of pride due to its recent successful operations against FROLINAT and which wanted to play an active role in the political life of the country. Tombalbaye, for his part, feared the growth of the political power in the army, and started reshuffling in the army ranks and arresting the most intractable military officers on suspicion of organizing coups. The army revolved and on April 13, 1975 Tombalbaye was killed during the mutiny. General Félix Malloum, another southerner with strong kinship ties to the North and a former government critic imprisoned by Tombalbaye, became the second President of the country.

Malloum formed the CSM (Conseil Suprême Militaire – Supreme Military Council), bringing in northerners in large number, which marked the beginning of the subsequent shift from the Southern to Northern political dominance of the country. Soon the CSM became largely Muslim having more representatives from Northern and eastern Chad. By having independence of Chad from any outside influence, especially from that pro-Tombalbaye France, as its top priority, the new government, as Nolutshungu stresses, became increasingly "militar[istic]…, with only a few civilians occupying fairly minor ministerial positions."[13]

Like his predecessor, Malloum strengthened the ties with France in the "Agreement on Cultural Co-Operation between the Government of the French Republic and the Government of the Republic of Chad" signed on March 6, 1976. The Agreement envisaged cooperation between the two countries in the field of education and research, technical education; mutual recognition of diplomas issued by Chad and France; fostering cultural exchanges and training courses; establishment of libraries, research centers, cultural facilities.[14] Another treaty – "Agreement on Technical Military Cooperation between the Government of the French Republic and the Government of the Republic of Chad" signed on March 6, 1976. According to this agreement, France was responsible for "…provision of the French military personnel required for organizing the military forces of Chad and their training". French personnel will stay for a fixed period determined by France, which allowed France to withdraw them by its own discretion. In accordance with Article 4, the French forces were to abstain from participation in "operations during wartime nor in maintenance or enforcing law and order."

---

13 Nolutshungu, S.C. 1996, 94.

14 Agreement on Cultural Co-Operation between the Government of the French Republic and the Government of the Republic of Chad. 1976. United Nations Treaty Collection. [Online]. Available at: http://untreaty.un.org/unts/1_60000/30/16/00058760.pdf [accessed: May 13, 2009].

France also undertook the responsibility to provide military equipment and logistic support to the Chadian military and to train its officers at its military educational institutions.[15]

Notwithstanding French political, military and economic backing, the problems with the Malloum's government soon surfaced. The fact is that the majority of the Chadians were not that much supportive of Malloum – he was not a prominent leader even during his opposition times and did not enjoy mass public support – they were merely against Tombalbaye. Being neither a potent reformer nor a skilled administrator, CSM leadership was unable to retain its authority, legitimacy, and popularity it had from the first days of the coup and largely failed to transform its initial gains into a longer-term political stability. Gradually Malloum's governance resembled that of his predecessor: he seized control of all branches of government and banned almost all political activities, including suspension of the National Union of Chadian Workers and prohibition of strikes.

Under such circumstances, FROLINAT became the organization which united the opposition against CSM. Feeling considerable liberty in their actions with no large French military around, FROLINAT successfully managed to reestablish alternative administrations in outlying areas to compete with N'Djamena, the capital of the country. In the meantime, in the aftermath of defeats in 1968-1971, the rebel movement itself split as a result of internal chronic rivalry between Goukouni and Habré. The former, being generally receptive to Libyan interests, did not want FROLINAT to fight on two fronts: against N'Djamena and against Libya, who had its own stakes in the domestic political developments in Chad.

Relations between Chad and Libya resembled the one between amiable yet antagonistic neighbors. The strained nature of their interactions was born out of the centuries of ethnic, religious, and commercial interactions. The countries shared the same colonial past – Chad being a colony of France and Libya – of Italy, and the rivalry between the colonial powers framed the relations between their former satellites. After Libya became independent in 1969, its new leader Quadaffi reclaimed the Aouzou Strip, a 100,000-square-kilometer portion of Northern Chad known for its uranium resources, once given by France to Italy by their treaty of 1935. The Libyan presence did not trouble Goukouni much: for him the top priority was defeating the central government, and then possibly ousting Libya from Aouzou. In contrast to him, Habré objected to cooperation with Libya whom he considered an occupier.

Another significant rift within FAN happened when Habré kidnapped a German and two French citizens and subsequently murdered a French security forces officer who came to negotiate a ransom. While Goukouni wanted to free the hostages fearing retaliation from the Europeans, Habré insisted on keeping

15 Agreement on Technical Military Cooperation between the Government of the French Republic and the Government of the Republic of Chad. 1976. United Nations Treaty Collection. [Online]. Available at: http://untreaty.un.org/unts/1_60000/30/17/00058811.pdf [accessed: May 13, 2009].

them as long as possible to re-negotiate ransom. Finally, the French managed to release the hostages after holding direct talks with Habré, which outraged Malloum as the country's leader. He first ordered the remaining French forces to go home as revenge for their alleged connections with the rebellion but, because of the continuing volatile situation in the country he still retained several hundreds of the French soldiers, and renegotiated a series of military accords to ensure emergency aid.

Urged on by African heads of states and the French advisers to provide for power-sharing political arrangements that would prevent future instability from arising, Malloum attempted to bring Habré and Goukouni into the government. However, they soon clashed with each other, and, later, with Malloum. While Habré's troops engaged Malloum's forces in the North, Goukouni defeated them in the central parts of the country and threatened N'Djamena. To shore up his position, Malloum offered a formal alliance to Habré, which was embodied in the Fundamental Charter, forming the coalition government in August 1978. Malloum became President and Habré Prime Minister of the new government.

The attempted collation government, however, failed to resolve the conflict now brought into the national forum. Feeling marginalized in the new government Goukouni, was now against Malloum and Habré alike. Composed of three armies and with a new name – FAP (Forces Armées Peuple – People's Armed Forces), his military force had its objective to overthrow the coalition regime of the governmental FAT/FAN. By 1978 FAP got hold of the Southern provinces and in April approached N'Djamena.

The situation became explosive not only for Malloum, who was faced with the prospect of losing power completely in case of successful actions of FAP, but also for the French. They were afraid that the growing strength of FAP, as a Muslim force with the backing of Libya, might challenge the commonly accepted view that Africa was under French political, economic, linguistic, religious and cultural influence. They were highly suspicious of the links between FAP and Libya and that the latter might exploit this situation in which the central government was weak and the opposition was growing stronger every day for its own benefit. The French were also afraid that the advances of FAP would jeopardize their secure access to the uranium resources of Niger, which were vital for France's nuclear *force de frappe*.

The second French intervention in April-May 1978 in support of the government was a small-scale short-term rapid airlift of 1700 troops with battle aircrafts. France created a buffer zone around the capital and heavily bombarded the advancing rebel troops. These actions beaconed to the opposition that the government – even composed of former enemies – enjoyed strong support of France, which was committed to retain its influence the country by keeping the ruling regime in power. As was the case in their first intervention, the French refrained from deep engagement into the Chadian politics and had no aim of completely defeating FAP. Nor were they prepared to act as external guarantors of peace and state-building between various Chadian warring factions.

As a result, the French confined their presence in N'Djamena and used their limited resources to achieve limited goals. The French intervention dissuaded FAP from further attacks on the government forces and the capital, and pushed the rebels back northwards, to the province of Ati. These French actions revealed an important modus that appeared in all remaining French interventions in Chad: persistent conformity with the recipient of their aid – the government. A decade after their first operation in 1968 France continued assisting the country's leadership in staying in power, even though this government now included the actor France had fought against and with whom it had uneasy relations due to the hostage problem – Habré. Ultimately, for France, it was not so important who was actually in power in Chad: it still provided military aid to the central government, which was, besides, the stronger group.

After the victory the Malloum/Habré coalition, at first glance, seemed to manage consolidation of its power on the basis of apparent similarities between the interests of its leaders. Both of them opposed the Libyan role in Chad. They, too, managed to reach consent in rejection of the idea of a federal form of government that would aggravate existing ethnic divisions. At first, they shared a common vision on a secular state, where Arabic would be given same status as French, thus keeping Muslim aspirations of the North, backed up by Libya, to a minimum. Finally, Malloum and Habré equally argued for a strong state-controlled economy. The problems within the coalition government started, however, when Habré, among other things, demanded that more governmental positions be given to the Northerners, and the usage of the Arabic language instead of French in radio broadcasting. He also refused to surrender the FAN forces loyal to him under FAT's control, and insisted on using them as his personal guards, which led to the situation with "de-jure two armies in…[a] city of barely quarter of a million souls, one belonging to the president and the other to the prime minister, both armed by France."[16]

The tension further heated up when an exchange of anti-Malloum and anti-Habré pamphlets led to clashes between college students supporting rival factions. The final push towards another civil war, now between Malloum and Habré, was the seizure of passports of three of Habré's ministers at the airport, which triggered escalating provocations. The major fighting, known as the First Battle for N'Djamena, occurred on February 12, 1979. Interestingly enough, the French contingent remained neutral and had not taken a major part in the conflict between the two governmental factions any one of which would form another government with a new president, to the idea of supporting of which France had never objected so far.

At the same time the French were tacitly favoring Habré, notwithstanding his kidnapping of the French civilians and assassination of the French officer. There was only one occasion when the French pilots, contracted by FAT, attacked FAN, but Habré managed to thwart their air raids by threatening retaliation against

16 Nolutshungu, S.C. 1996, 106.

French civilians. This was, one of the most decisive factors in their confrontation: as Azevedo and Nnadozie claim (1998), "Had the French not forced the Chadian government to stop air raids against enemy positions in February 1979, Malloum's troops would have prevailed on the ground."[17] Thus, although the French remained formally neutral, protecting only "...the central bank, the airport (where its base was), the urban telephone system (there were scarcely any telephones in African quarters), and the Israeli-built international hotel...,"[18] their operational inaction ultimately led to the collapse of Malloum's CSM.

Demoralized from the abandonment of their French supporters, FAT retreated from the capital. This was followed by mutual retaliations between the retreating Southerners and the advancing Northerners. During the battle of N'Djamena about 1,000 people were killed and more than 80,000 fled the capital. In ten days, Goukouni's FAP, on its part, seized the opportunity given by the resulting chaos and entered the capital. By March 1979 the struggle led to de facto partition of Chad: FAN controlled the North, the capital was under Goukouni, and Malloum's troops occupied the five Southern prefectures.

Clashes between Muslims and Christian Southerners shifted the conflict from the North into the South and led to numerous reconciliation efforts by foreign governments. Four peace conferences with the mediation of neighboring states, primarily, Niger, were held from March to August 1979. However, their effectiveness was limited – as ascertained by Thompson and Adloff (1981), the belligerent "...leaders...wanted more power than they could acquire through a coalition administration and...believed that they had the strength to seize it."[19] Although deployment of a peace-keeping force was envisaged by all these conferences, and some (800 Nigerians, for instance) have indeed been dispatched, according to Nolutshungu (1996), "they were neither an effective substitute for a police force nor able to disarm the contending factions. They were...too few to dissuade a determined aggressor nor to decide the outcome of any battle between the indigenous armed political groups – and even less able to impose Nigeria's choice of leader of the Chadians."[20] Under such circumstances, the Nigerian peacekeepers could not offer credible third party guarantees of peace in return for their observance of a peace agreement.

The most important of these conferences was the last one, held in Lagos in August 1979, which managed to include all the parties and political and military movements in Chad. Apart from stressing the need for demilitarization, the release of prisoners, amnesty, neutrality in radio broadcasting, and introduction of a peacekeeping force, the participants agreed on forming the GUNT (Gouvernement d'Unité Nationale du Tchad – Government of National Unity of Chad), which would reconcile the belligerent forces. Distribution of cabinet posts was regionally

17 Azevedo, M. and Nnadozie, E.U. 1998, 53.

18 Nolutshungu, S.C. 1996. 114.

19 Thompson, V. and Adloff, R. 1981, 91.

20 Nolutshungu, S.C., 124.

balanced. As a power-sharing mechanism, GUNT tried to incorporate all leaders: Goukouni was the country's president, Kamougue (a Southerner and the leader of the Third Liberation army) – vice president, and Habré – minister of defense.

From the very start, GUNT suffered from the problems similar to those of CSM. Its leaders mistrusted each other failing it to achieve political cohesion. Politically, apart from Habré, all the leading roles in the new government were given to pro-Libyan people, thus antagonizing Habré – one of the main figures of anti-Libyan movement. On a personal level, the rift between Goukouni and Habré during the early years of FROLINAT continued in GUNT. After installation of the new government, Goukouni and Habré maintained separate spheres of influence and occupied separate parts of N'Djamena. GUNT was also inefficient in implementing power divisions of Lagos: as Thompson and Adloff (1981) noted, "...none of the key provisions of...[Lagos] had been carried out, the cabinet had met only once, the Southern prisoners had not been liberated, and none of the African peace-keeping forces had yet arrived in Chad."[21]

The confrontation between the two leaders led to another civil war that started in March 1980 and lasted for nine months without much change in the standings of the combatants. In December 1980, the Second Battle for N'Djamena took place. In addition to FAP and FAN, Kamougue's Southern Third Liberation Army also reached the suburbs of the capital, but was pushed back suffering heavy losses. Almost entire civilian population of N'Djamena had left the city. Even when 600 Congolese peacekeepers had finally arrived, together with the present French troops, they were completely inefficient in bringing peace in the city divided into several sectors controlled by opposing factions. Fearing that he might lose the war, Goukouni called for Libya to intervene.

Libyan Intervention

A number of factors translated into long-time Libyan interests in Chad. The quest for dominance over Chad was for Libya a mix of rational calculus and historical support to the Muslim North. On the one hand, there was a reported cache of minerals in the Aouzou Strip, including uranium that Libya wanted to get hold of. At the same time, once being a colony, Libya wanted to liberate itself from its past in a very peculiar way – it wanted to become a colonial power itself and to colonize Chad. Following this reasoning, Nolutshungu (1996) claimed that, similar to France, Libya was interested in establishing "[a]t most, a pro-Libyan government, similar in ideology and willing to accept the fait accompli of Libyan incorporation of the Aouzou Strip would be desirable; better still, it should unite with Libya and be led by men in whom Quadaffi had confidence."[22] Alongside such interests stood the desire of Libya to reduce the European presence in Africa

21 Thompson, V. and Adloff, R. 1981, 97.

22 Nolutshungu, S.C. 1996, 147.

and project Islamic influence into the Sahel lacing Chad and Sudan. Thus, by weakening Chad's ties with the West and reducing African dependence on the Western nation-state system, Quadaffi hoped to fulfill his dream of a unified Muslim North Africa. Since the Chadian post-colonial government, highly dependent on France both economically and militarily, was not consistent with this picture, Quadaffi established alliances with several opposition leaders, including Goukouni, Siddick, Ahmat Acyl (a Chadian of Arab descent and head of CDR (Conseil Démocratique Révolutionnaire – Democratic Revolutionary Council)), and Kamougué – all those who could foster his interests once in the Chadian government and shape their policies in accordance with Quadaffi's views.

In June 1980 Goukouni's GUNT and Libya signed the "Treaty of friendship and alliance" between Libya and Chad signed in June 15, 1980,[23] which allowed Chadian government to call upon Libya, should the independence, territorial integrity, or internal security of the country be jeopardized. The Treaty defined Chad and Libya as "two fraternal people" with "common destiny and common objectives and aspirations" united by "the deep-rooted spiritual, economic, human and cultural ties." In accordance with Article 1 of the Treaty, "The two Parties shall defend each other if either Party or both Parties are exposed to direct or indirect foreign aggression" and that "any aggression against one Party [shall] constitute aggression against the other." Libya also pledged to make its economic, material and cultural resources available for the economic and military reconstruction of Chad. For its part, Chad committed itself "not to permit the presence of any foreign base or colonialist, imperialist troops in its national territory" and had "the right to call upon the Socialist People's Libyan Arab Jamahiriya for assistance in the event of a threat to its independence, territorial integrity or internal security."

Through this Treaty Libya claimed to support GUNT, which was, according to the Lagos Agreement, the legitimate government of the country. Using this treaty agreement as a pretext, Libyan troops entered Chad in November 1980 at the invitation of Goukouni. Altogether, around 7,000-9,000 Libyan troops with tanks and self-propelled artillery, plus 4,500-5,000 soldiers from the Islamic Legion, rapidly occupied the posts in the Northern and Central Chad.

The result of the Libyan intervention was landslide success in suppressing FAN and bringing GUNT to power. Starting from Northern Chad, the united front of the GUNT and the Libya-backed Islamic Legion gained control of N'Djamena on December 15, 1980. The results of the Libyan intervention were devastating for FAN, which lost nearly all its major battles. In one month, FAN was defeated, and Habré was forced to flee to Sudan and reorganize his forces in Abéché, the fourth largest city in Chad. As a concession for their support, in January 1981 Libya made Goukouni agree to the merger of the two countries. This was soon, however,

23 Treaty of Friendship and Alliance between the Socialist People's Libyan Arab Jamahiriya and the Republic of Chad. 1980. United Nations Treaty Collection. [Online]. Available at: http://untreaty.un.org/unts/60001_120000/5/23/00009133.pdf [accessed: May 13, 2009].

disavowed by GUNT after pressure from France and a number of African states who were unreceptive to and even feared such Libyan "enlargement".

Apart from gaining quite tangible benefits for itself in the form of institutionalizing their presence in the country and continuous control over the Aouzou Strip, the Libyan intervention also helped normalize the internal situation in Chad. According to Nolutshungu (1996), Libya's "…presence helped to restrain clashes among GUNT factions, facilitated the withdrawal of forces from the capital and their redeployment elsewhere, and the disarmament of civilians. The Libyan troops were deployed where they were most needed, and…held back the advantage of Habré's rapidly constituted forces…" Libya was also concerned with popular support way beyond traditional spheres of its influence in the North and in doing so "had brought money, thus giving a stimulus to economic life…"[24]

As in 1979, the French abstained from intervention and made no efforts whatsoever to support Habré and to fight the Libyans. Most probably they did not want to escalate the conflict into an inter-state war with Libya. However, just in case the French increased their contingent in the Central African Republic, which should have acted as a show of force to the Libyans and a credible signal from France that it would intervene had Libya made any substantial moves infringing upon the Chadian statehood. In response, Libya threatened to impose oil embargo on Chad. Eventually, under pressure from the OAU and upon the request of Goukouni, who feared he might lose the country completely to Libya, Quadaffi withdrew his forces from N'Djamena in November 1981.

Several reasons can explain such behavior of Libya who so promptly left the conflict scene, economic considerations, probably, being most plausible. Libya simply could not sustain the cost of a widening of its intervention to cover the whole country. Its southward advances were quite quick and did not consider a large-scale permanent occupation connected with higher costs of Libyan presence. Also, in majority of the areas of Chad, except for its Northern part, Libya enjoyed little popular support – its troops were even more alien to the Southern Sara than were their Muslim neighbors.

With all this, Quadaffi wanted to retain an image of a neutral and impartial peacemaker, supporting the legitimate government and following its will – just like France. Quadaffi repeatedly mentioned that his "troops were in Chad at the request of the GUNT and its president, and that they would withdraw immediately if the Chadian president demands so."[25] Finally, being in Chad for a long time and assuming responsibility for domestic security, and, as a consequence, control over the country's international policy, was running the risk of collisions with less pro-Libyan Chadian neighbors, among which were Sudan, Egypt and Nigeria.

After Libya had retreated, the IAF (Inter-African Force) of the Organization of African Unity, consisting of 2,000 Nigerian, 2,000 Zairian, and 800 Senegalese soldiers entered Chad. Because of the vague mandate of the peacekeeping force

24 Nolutshungu, S.C. 1996, 155.

25 Nolutshungu, S.C. 1996, 156.

and the hesitations of all three countries to openly engage any force, IAF made no effort to block Habré's military comeback after the Libya exited. The most decisive factor in abstaining from fighting against Habré was the wish of the IAF countries to prevent Libya from spreading its influence in the Northern Africa, in which Habré could play an instrumental role.

After the defeat, it took Habré almost a year to regain control of the North. In response, GUNT again tried to seek support from Libya, but it was refused: Quadaffi was feeling that the military advantage was on FAN's side and that he might lose if openly confronts rapidly advancing Habré. He was also "hurt" by changes of the GUNT's stance towards presence of his troops in Chad and denunciation of the merger deal. Eventually Libya decided to refrain from helping Goukouni militarily. Facing little resistance from the GUNT or the IAF, FAN moved toward the capital and in June 7, 1982 captured N'Djamena and proclaimed Habré head of state.

French and Libyan Interventions

After his defeat, Goukouni had not vanished from the political scene completely. Numbering from 3,000 to 4,000, his own troops were joined by the remnants of FAP, FAT, CDR, the First Liberation Army, the Volcan Army, and the Western Armed Forces. The new force was christened the ANL (Armée Nationale de Libération – National Liberation Army) and had a total strength of 12,000 troops. Habré had also regrouped his forces and the new FANT (Forces Armées Nationales du Tchad – National Armed Forces of Chad) had an estimate of 10,000 force. At first, Goukouni managed to make some progress on the battlefield and in June 1983 after a decisive bombing of FANT's forces by Libya, captured Faya Largeau. Moving further South, ANL occupied Kalait, Oum Chalouba, and, finally, Abéché. Unlike in June 1982, now Libya decided to assist Goukouni: Libya feared that Habré, if gained momentum, might endanger its possession of the Aouzou Strip.

Habré was also seeking help from the outside, however, without much success. Finally, he took command of the FANT forces himself, and first liberated Abéché four days after the city's fall, then Faya Largeau, and finally retook the Northern posts. Habré's counter-attack in the North led to an inevitable collision with the Libyan contingents stationed there. The Libyan force enjoying overwhelming superiority in military power (around 4,000-5,000 troops), tanks, armored personnel carriers, battle aircrafts, self-propelled artillery, and multiple rocket launchers finally expelled FANT from Faya Largeau.

Seeing that Chad might fall victim to the Libyan dominance, which France was very much eager to prevent, the French finally decided to intervene which created a four-player intervention game where each of the belligerents had a corresponding "patron-state". This internationalization of the domestic conflict in Chad, however, did not escalate into an open conflict between France and Libya, since their respective interventions "...had some of the characteristics of a cooperative game. Each kept to its side of the line of demarcation, France unwilling to retake the North for Habré and Libya unwilling to press its military advantage to help the GUNT move toward the capital…"[26] Both countries were afraid of taking the Chadian civil war to the level of an international conflict between them and, therefore, limited themselves to a mere show-of-force, abstaining from any direct military confrontation.

With the aim of preventing Libya from large-scale and long-term occupation of Faya-Largeau and minimizing its role in the Chadian domestic politics, in particular, and in the African continent in general, in August 1983 France initiated the *Operation Manta* (Stingray) with the airlift of 180 military advisers and equipment, followed by 3,500 troops, including its air force, the Foreign Legion, and the airborne personnel. The French troops used the same tactics as before – the secured N'Djamena and fortified their positions near the routes leading to the capital, where the government was based. France also tried to separate the belligerents via establishing a no-fly zone on the 16th parallel to the North, which was supposed to put a stop to Libyan bombings.

By 1983 the country was divided into two parts: BET belonged to ANL, and the rest of Chad was under FANT. Libya was increasing its presence in the region by building new, modern radar stations in Chad and bringing in additional troops. The country was on the verge of collapse, and the conflict threatened to spill-over to an interstate war between France and Libya. Seeing this, in September 1984 these two states decided to deescalate the conflict and pledged to pull their troops from Chad (for France) and from the contested Aouzou Strip (for Libya). The promise, however, was fulfilled only by France, who left the country in November, in accordance with the agreement, while Libya defected and continued to keep its 3,000 troops in the BET.

The outcome of the French intervention was that Libya refrained from further advances southward and from threatening N'Djamena. The *Operation Manta* bore a real credible threat of punishment to ANL and its supporter-Libya. At the same time, Libya did not want to engage in open conflict with France. The establishment of the no-fly zone helped FANT strengthen its positions in the regions immediately adjoining the demarcation line. Finally, although after France had retreated Libya remained in the BET, the *Operation Manta* stalled its further Libyan occupation of the territories beyond the BET. France's presence also led to a rapid increase in numbers of the FANT and boosted morale of its soldiers with opposite developments on the side of ANL, including defection and dissention. At this point, FANT included around 15,000 personnel from the former "Codos rebellion" in the South.[27] Seeing this, Libya decided to increase its presence in Chad, and the combined ANL-Libyan forces totaled to 10,000 soldiers in Tibesti and Fada.

26 Nolutshungu, S.C. 1996, 189.

27 The Codos rebellion was insignificant for the purposes of the book since it had neither serious consequence for future political developments in Chad, nor did it cause any third party interventions.

The strengthening of Libya's position by building a new airbase and radar stations galvanized the French to return in February 1986 with the *Operation Epervier* (Sparrowhawk) with 2,500 personnel including a detachment of top-level Jaguar and Mirage aircrafts. This deployment, however, was not an intervention in a full military sense of it, since the French troops participated only in a few military activities, instead using "swaggering" tactics to dissuade Libyans from attacking N'Djamena and Abéché. The only French force in the BET, where the real military operations were taking place, was a group of 150 engineers engaged in de-mining of the territories.

The build-up of the FANT and the French contingent coincided with a split within ANL. Acyl was receiving separate assistance from Libya, which antagonized other factions. This led to resentment of Goukouni's own forces, especially, FAP, to the Libyan presence in the North and their unwillingness to continue offensive against FANT. This discord escalated into an open military confrontation between FAP and CDR, and the latter, with the Libyan support, forced Goukouni's men, who constituted around 2/3 of the whole ANL reserves, to retreat to the mountains. Under such circumstances Goukouni made a reverse move and sided with his old rival – FANT. Such backstab to Libya was very much favored by Habré, who signed an agreement with FAP, while Goukouni himself was under house arrest in Tripoli.

At first, FAP launched attacks against CDR, but was pushed back by the Libyans to the Tibesti Mountains. In December 1986 Libyan armored columns attacked the FAP settlements in Tibesti with using napalm and poison gas, and forced FAP to retreat. At the same time, with the economic help of France and equipped well for a desert war with light Toyotas pick-ups carrying arms, FANT attacked CDR and Libyan troops in Fada. Libyans, together with the Islamic Legion's heavy armored tanks were not suited for such warfare, where highly maneuvering Toyotas fired antitank missiles and recoilless rifles at them from a close range. The total losses of Libya mounted to 700 dead and 150 war prisoners, and one billion US dollars worth of the military equipment.[28]

This defeat, however, did not stop Quadaffi from another attempt to regain control over BET. However, his resumed offensive in February 1987 with a total of 11,000 troops was not successful either: FANT had not only crushed the two tank squadrons, but also managed to capture the Libyan base in the North, with the Libyan death toll reaching 1,200 and additional 450 soldiers as prisoners. This was a severe blow to Libya further decreasing the already-low morale of its military. Without a pretext of intervention upon request from the government and without any support from its former Chadian allies, Libya found itself deeply bogged down in Chad as an occupant. Libyan troops were isolated in an unfamiliar terrain, and with no effective radar systems and airbase to guide their air strikes in support of their ground personnel that could inflict no harm on mobile FANT units.

28 Azevedo, M. and Nnadozie, E.U. 1998, 59.

Eventually, suffering heavy losses in personnel and military equipment and failing to reach its goal of securing the North for CDR and spreading its influence in the BET, Libya retreated. Following this, FANT successfully attacked the town of Aouzou urging Libyans to leave their base. Libya retaliated by bombing the Northern cities occupied by FANT. In return, Habré asked for French intervention, although without success. France did want to continue hold its presence in Chad, but still did not want to intervene in Aouzou, which was a territory under Libyan dominance. The French Ministry of Defense declared that there would be no French soldier or aircraft intervening on behalf of the Chadian government to liberate Northern Chad from Libyan occupation, and that the 1,000 French troops and aircrafts stationed in N'Djamena would be used exclusively for the purpose of defending the capital.

FANT was left alone, and, as a result, was driven out of Aouzou by the Libyan air strikes followed by ground troops copying Chad's own desert warfare tactics with the usage of light vehicles. Habré responded with a surprise attack on the Libyan airbase, killing 1,000 and capturing 300 soldiers and also a considerable number of Libyan fighter aircrafts and choppers. Later, France tacitly assisted Habré by establishing an air defense system to prevent any further Libyan military actions southward of the 16th parallel and bombing the Libyan radar installation at Qadi-Doum.

Finally, seeing the fruitlessness of further military confrontation, both Habré and Quadaffi decided to suspend fighting. Chadian and Libyan foreign ministers met in August 1988, and the two governments agreed to conduct further talks with the OAU mediation. Chad suspended its attempts to regain the Aouzou Strip, and Libya stopped bombing the Southern regions of the country. The two states subsequently signed an agreement that ended their confrontation, while the Aouzou Strip continued to remain within Libyan hands until 1990.[29]

From 1989 onward, in his nearly seven years in power, Habré pursued a mix of national reconciliation policy with punishment of leaders of factions who openly and actively opposed his regime. In domestic politics, he advocated national integrity and a unitary state. However, faced with internal threats to his regime, he used repression against his political opponents. On the international level, Habré expressed strong preference for French rather than Libyan patronage. France continued to maintain a sizable military and security presence in Chad as well as providing strong economic and financial support.

Ethnic rivalry continued. Collisions between different ethnic groups, especially between the representatives of Hadjerai, Zaghawa and Gorane factions in the

29 The dispute over the Aouzou Strip between Chad and Libya was taken to the International Court of Justice in 1990 for a binding ruling. According to the ICJ decision made on February 3, 1994, the land shall remain within Chad. The Strip was formally transferred from Libya to Chad on May 30, 1994 [Online: the ICJ Judgment]. Available: http://www.icj-cij.org/docket/index.php?sum=424&code=dt&p1=3&p2=3&case=83&k=cd&p3=5 [accessed: May 6, 2009].

central government, led to the defection of Idriss Deby, a Zaghawa and one of Habré's leading generals, to Darfur, Sudan in April 1989. In December 1990, with no opposition from the French stationed in Chad, Deby successfully occupied N'Djamena and ousted Habré to Senegal. Three months later, Deby, supported by his MPS (Mouvement Patriotique du Salut – Patriotic Salvation Movement), became the new president of Chad.

Analysis of Interventions

The modus of the French interventions in Chad was developed as a result of the intricate interplay of its domestic politics, perceptions of its role on international arena and changing nature of international environment by the 1960s. Ever since the independence of its former colony, France had been playing an important role in the domestic Chadian politics by supporting its governments in many military, economic, and administrative aspects.[30] The French presence was always noticeable in the country: their troops had either physically been in Chad for a limited time or were stationed in neighboring states with the purpose of coming to salvation of the governments at any time needed. France was the most important supplier of economic aid through offering development assistance, loans and other grants to uphold the Chadian economy. Although no longer a consumer of Chad's agricultural goods, as was the case during colonial times, French aid still accounted for a substantial part of the country's budget.

At the same time, apart from assisting various Chadian governments, France had its own intervention goals, some of which, in fact, had nothing to do with Chad per se. Important insights into France's continuous support and presence in Chad were given by Noluchungu (1996): "In France, the fate of Chad was always linked to the security of French influence over the rest of his former colonies in tropical Africa. The kind of domino theory seemed to apply: if one were lost…others might be lost (or abandoned); if France were unable to protect one dependent state, its guarantees to others might become less credible…France's global status as well as its African economic interests and prestige would be undermined."[31] Thus, France considered Chad as an inherent component of its security and wanted to keep the situation stable.

From that prospective, starting from 1968 all the subsequent French interventions were well-fitted within the views of France on its roles in the international politics of 1960s known as *Gaulism* (after its prominent president

30 According to some sources, the value of French military assistance to Chadian government from 1983 to 1987 was around $175 million. During the first half of 1987 alone, all aid, including *Operation Epervier*, amounted to nearly $100 million (for more information on France's military and economic role in Chad see http://www.country-data.com/frd/cs/tdtoc.html, [accessed: May 6, 2009]).

31 Nolutshungu, S.C. 1996, 11.

Charles de Gaulle). France had to possess an independent nuclear arsenal – *force de frappe*, emphasizing its *grandeur* in the world political arena and fulfilling its special mission of spreading democracy worldwide. In this way, the reasons of the French interventions were deeply rooted, as Chaigneau noted (1984), in their "need for…global presence and influence, [with] Africa having a major role to play in such a scheme."[32] Successful international operations of France, especially outside of statutory borders of Europe, would affirm its (regional) superpower status and would show to the allies in NATO that France was capable of acting independently on international arena (especially when France let the NATO Integrated Military Command in 1966). Also, restoration of its international role would help France domestically to redeem itself from the stigma of German occupation during the WW II and revive the potency of the country in the eyes of its own citizens.

There was yet another reason for the French involvement in Africa, and specifically in Chad – the desire to limit the influence of pro-Soviet and Muslim Libya on the territory it considered its own backyard. France opposed Libyan advances in the North-Central Africa, and Chad, in particular, because Libya might have brought not only overwhelming "Islamization" of the country, but also "Arabization" of the Chadian population and a slow decrease in the usage of the French language, which would be substituted by Arabic, presaging the demise of the French cultural aura (which, in fact, happened during the first years of Habré's rule). As a result, France stood to lose the traditional linkages between the French and their African ex-colonies. Besides, the Libyan build-up in Aouzou Strip threatened access of France to uranium resources of neighboring Niger, which were vital for France's national interests.

Success of French interventions was largely due to three factors: its support to the political factions, which were in the government of Chad; externalization of interventions through limited operational involvement and institutional approach to interventions. The variable that characterized continuous pattern of the French interventions and that made them largely successful in different time was the direction of French support: France always supported the government, which, in majority of cases, was the strongest of all military factions in Chad. This stance stemmed from a general "paternalistic" attitude that committed France to supporting its Francophone African states. With the specific reference to Chad, French remembered the loyal role the Chadian government played in the WW II under its ex-governor Félix Eboué and were grateful for its support of de Gaulle's Free France at that time. In its interventions in independent Chad France continued to shield its governments from domestic disturbances in the face of sometimes blatantly non-democratic practices.

This path-dependence in providing support to the nominal governments of Chad took sometimes paradoxical forms, when former enemies of the government once in office could count of continuous French backing. For instance, during

32 Chaigneau, P. 1984. *La Politique militaire de la France en Afrique*. Paris, 1984, 18-19.

the first intervention in 1968, France protected Tombalbaye against FROLINAT, and then it supported Malloum, who overthrew Tombalbaye, against FROLINAT. Furthermore, during the *Manta* and *Epervier*, France assisted Habré, whom they did not particularly like due to his past anti-France rhetoric and former hostile acts against the French citizens.

Another reason for supporting the government lied in purely rational calculus of France. Since France preferred to keep security in Francophone Africa and protect its economic and political interests in the state. Governments, by having comparative advantage in military and economic resources and larger territorial coverage were, in most cases, stronger than the opposition factions and were easier to be assisted by limited outside inputs in their actions against various rebellions that rarely represented potent forces. Also, it was much easier to support nominal governments who had the task of preserving security in their respective countries, rather than by contributing to the capacities of the opposition, which posed threats to security and the causes of domestic instability.

Another significant factor of success of the French interventions was that France always remained an external player – the stance born out of general post-colonial vision of France limiting their large-scale interventions and heavy military presence in the African countries. Starting from the policies of de-colonization, France tried to avoid deep immersion into the conflicts in African countries, thus distancing itself from being a significant domestic actor. Externalization from the conflicts was visible in France's attitude towards the sides they had supported during their interventions, as well as in their operational characteristics.

In nearly all its interventions France closely followed the commitment of disassociation from the peculiarities of domestic politics in Chad, the belligerents and their internal rivalry. This externalized approach interventions was reflected by their limited agendas, scopes, geographic coverage, and resources. Starting from the first intervention aimed at salvation of Tombalbaye's regime, as well as in ensuing attempts to save subsequent rulers, France never aimed at replacing the Chadian government in any way. France shunned exercising domestic law enforcement functions and other administrative tasks, which would remind both Chad and France of their colonial past and would mean long-term commitment in allocation of enormous economic and political resources. Neither did France want to install any external authority and put in place its "own" persons.

Furthermore, France never intended to be tied up by the committing itself to uphold the security of the Chadian state in such a way that would require its large-scale presence. Such an operational posture stemmed from France's general stance towards African countries: it was not going to be involved in major external actions in Africa; it did prefer to have stability in the region, however, not through massive military interventions. This viewpoint largely limited the goals of interventions in Chad. France had never intervened with the aim of total annihilation of the various opposition factions which would seriously antagonize the population supporting them against the French. Neither had it undertaken the role of a peace-enforcer or a peacekeeper, under which it would provide external security guarantees for the warring parties. Moreover, France had never actually led or mediated any formal peace talks or negotiations, or had any agreement with FROLINAT with the purpose of ending the conflict, except for the release of the kidnapped French citizens.

Although the French presence in Chad was always felt, the French troops had never been stationed in the country for lengthy periods of time. Their interventions had a repeated, concurrent, but not continuous or prolonged character. France had never maintained a large-scale presence in Chad, except for the actual interventions and extracted its military immediately after their operations were over. During non-combat phases, French personnel were limited to a military training officers and service personnel of the N'Djamena Airport. The French detachments operated on their own – they did not mix with the Chadian army, and always represented a separate entity. Thus, they created a sense of credibly autonomy for the Chadians, who believed they were acting on their own. Such an attitude facilitated high morale within the Chadian ranks that they were supported by a strong patron and, at the same time, had a feeling of self-sufficiency.

Externalization approach to interventions led to their limited operational scope: on a very few occasions did the French directly collide with the opposition factions' military detachments. France had never had any substantial face-to-face combat with the other intervener, Libya, and this posture protected France and Libya equally from an inter-state conflict. This also held France to maintain limited combat losses that presupposed popular domestic support for its military operations. The narrow scope of the operations also limited their geographical coverage: unlike the Libyan troops, which was largely scattered all over the Northern Chadian terrain, the French, when present, always maintained a close pattern of deployment being stationed in N'Djamena and protecting the inbound routes. These tactics allowed them to keep good communication lines, high mobility of troops, dense concentration in the case of combat, and to avoid extensive combat casualties. Unlike the Libyans, the French military had never been forced to operate in an unknown and hostile environment against the wishes of the population – in N'Djamena and close to the capital the local dwellers were usually highly receptive of the French presence.

Finally, a very important aspect of success of the French interventions was their institutionalization both in the eyes of local Chadians as well as the international community. Institutional frameworks for the interventions were achieved by supporting the Chadian government, which had a legitimate institutional authority, and by legalizing their presence in the country in corresponding legal acts. By supporting an actor with, at least, nominal institutional legitimacy – the government with its administrative apparatus, military and law enforcement agencies – France institutionalized its presence in the country. With the reference to much disputed discussions on governments' losing their legitimacy when undertaking illegitimate actions against their people, none of the Chadian governmental leaders had ever engaged in any large-scale domestic atrocities and ethnic cleansing. Although far from being fully democratic, they enjoyed the French support not because of their personal qualities but because of the offices their held. Opposition factions, on the other hand, lacked the institutional legitimacy of the country government – their legitimacy confined in the regions they were located.

From legal viewpoint, the bases for French interventions were different multilateral and bilateral cooperation agreements signed with the African states. For instance, the Defense Agreement between France and the members of the AEF (Afrique Équatoriale Française – French Equatorial Africa): Chad, Central African Republic, and Congo, signed in August 15, 1960.[33] In accordance with its terms, military forces of the AEF states "shall participate, with the French armed forces, under a single command, in the joint defence system." They also gave France the right "to discharge its responsibilities with respect to their joint defence" but granted to "the French armed forces free use of the bases they require." France pleaded to "provide the [states] with the aid needed to constitute their armed forces." This included, but was not limited to "unimpeded movement on the territory, in the air space and in the territorial waters…exercices and manuvres…use[age of] port, sea and river, road, railway and air installations…" The "discharge from responsibilities" clause meant that France would intervene to salvage the Chadian regimes from internal and external threats whenever it considers necessary, thus letting France act upon its sole discretion.

In return, France was obliged not only to provide economic support and military technical assistance to the Chadian army, including training and coaching of the Chadian officers but also to protect Chad against external threats and supply domestic security, law and order (this clause was invoked by Malloum when he asked for the French assistance to put down FROLINAT). The agreement with its legal force would have tied France to long-lasting commitment and provision of permanent aid to the government, which could have been a serious burden. Such a legalized institutional approach to interventions from the viewpoint of Chadian domestic politics was significant in maintaining public support for the French interveners. This way the French were never considered by the general public as interveners but as protectors of security and keepers of stability of the country.

The other intervener in Chad, Libya also carried out its vital national interests in Chad for nearly two decades. Even from the beginning of the 20th century, when it was ruled by the Ottoman Empire, Libya attempted to exercise its influence over Chad. During the colonial period that a decisive event laid the basis for future its interventions with Chad: in 1935, under pressure from the Fascist Germany, France was forced to change its administrative borders in Chad in favor of its colonial next-door neighbor – Mussolini's Italy, which held what is now independent Libya.

---

33 Defence Agreement between the French Republic, the Central African Republic, the Republic Of The Congo And the Republic Of Chad. 1960. United Nations Treaty Collection. [Online]. Available at: http://untreaty.un.org/unts/1_60000/23/33/00045646.pdf [accessed: May 13, 2009].

As a result of these arrangements, the Libya-Chad boundary was relocated about 100 kilometers Southward across the Aouzou Strip. After the independence of Chad, Libya attempted to retain the Strip by stationing their troops in the region. Unlike the usual intervention scenarios, which commonly start at a certain point in time marking specific issues to be followed and end up with fulfillment or failure to achieve their goals, Libyan actions resembled more an occupation and annexation of a foreign territory. With its forces stationed in North and Center of the country Libya was "libyanizing" the local population through introduction of its own national ID cards, its currency, educating young people in Libya, establishing local People's Committees, and flying Libyan flags on governmental buildings. Such an excessive endeavor was the key reason of continuous failure of the Libyan interventions. Unlike France who always viewed itself as an external player to Chad, Libya strived to become an internal actor on the Chadian domestic political scene from the very beginning of its involvement – not merely an intervener with its own agenda, but as an occupant and service-provides on the territories it covered. While the French entered Chad only when needed and asked for, Libyans from the very beginning of their involvement were aiming at long-term prospects of territorial annexation.

Failures of subsequent Libyan intervention can also be explained by Libya's going out of the original area it had previously occupied and expanding its intervention agenda, which turned out to be fatal. While stationed in Aouzou, its troops could easily coordinate their actions, receive continuous supplies of military equipment and ammunition from Libya proper, and economically sustain their presence. They could also install their own administrations (which they, in fact, did), and conduct heavy expansion of the Libyan culture and traditions as well as the Arabic language. Also, limited territorial coverage allowed Libyans to effectively survey the land installations and back-up their infantry actions by aircraft fire.

Once, however, Libya decided to engage southward, it proved difficult to effectively sustain a presence of its troops on larger territories and an unknown terrain. Airlifts of cargo from Libya proper became increasingly difficult. Air surveillance was limited due to the absence of radar installations in the South, and the troops received no support from the air. Libya also had to operate in a territory populated by other ethnic groups, which, apart from decreasing the morale of its soldiers, led to greater popular resistance.

An important factor in internalization of intervention that led to Libya's failures was that it had not limited itself to mere operational presence but undertook the steps directed towards provision of external security and external governance for the Northern territories. As a result of being in the Aouzou Strip for a long time, Libya got deeply immersed in domestic Chadian politics and its subsequent problems. This involvement intensified even as Quadaffi tried to rein in Libya's commitments in Chad: Libya could not remain upon another state's sovereign territory indefinitely. A decision had to be made either to legalize its status in Northern Chad via its complete unification with Libya, or to retreat. Libya, who did not have large support in the international community for its actions in Chad, and which had poor relations with power states on the international arena, such as the US and the USSR, was unable to effectively annex the Chadian territory and receive international blessing for that. Thus, it chose the third, the less beneficial option: to de facto remain in Chad as long as possible, undertaking an increasing number of state functions and responsibilities that it was unable to bear.

Another important factor in continuous defeats of Libyan interventions was that it supported the opposition against legitimate governments. Acting on behalf of the opposition made Libya seen as an unwelcome outsider to the majority of the country's population. Opposition was usually operationally weaker than the government it fought against, and Libya's inputs barely equalized the capacities of the belligerents. A clear case of this was the fight against Habré's FAN once it came to power: the opposition was tactically and operationally inferior to FAN and Libya proved to be unable to effectively enforce its will against the government. Although FAN received no sizable assistance from the French, who mainly played the role of observers and protectors of the European expats, Habré's troops fought a decisive war, which, according to Ottaway (1987), was the result of "the most successful collaboration between a Western army and a Third World army in modern times."[34] After its initial defeat at N'Djamena, FAN forces became operationally more suited to the desert warfare and tactically flexible. The Libyan army, on the other hand, "…favored conventional Soviet-style operations in which infantry are backed up by armor, making them vulnerable to that FAN's hit-and-run tactics".[35] As for its single victory against Habré in 1988, when FAN was driven by Libyans out of previously occupied Aouzou, this was done by mimicking FAN usage of highly maneuverable light vehicles and short-range self-propelled missiles.

Only on one occasion did Libya manage to fulfill its intervention agendas when it supported the opposition. This was the case of late 1980 Libyan intervention, when its troops brought GUNT to power. From an operational point of view, Libyan troops succeeded in helping GUNT to stifle FAN and for almost a year pushed Habré's supporters out of N'Djamena. This happened due to operational superiority of the combined Libyan-GUNT troops who possessed more advanced military equipment and, in general, outnumbered FANT. However, the most important factor here was that GUNT, while being in exile, was still a legitimate government of Chad. As in the French interventions, institutionalization was the crucial determinant of success for the Libyan actions. On the basis of the official agreement with Goukouni, Libya supported GUNT, a legal entity installed as a result of the Lagos II conference. Apart from securing public support in Chad, this allowed Quadaffi represent himself as a peacemaker and not as an annexer, and to distract international attention from his real interests in Chad.

---

34 Ottaway, D. 1987. The US May Send Chad Some Stingers. *The Washington Post*, September 17, A36.

35 *Africa Confidential* 28(8). April 15, 1987, 2.

If Libya had enjoyed popular support in the territories to the North, including their fellow-Arabs and other African Muslims, the appreciation of their presence in Chad was decreasing with their movement southward. The South had always rejected the domination of the North, especially when this supremacy was installed and supported by an outside force. When Libyans were aiding the legitimate government of the country, Tripoli's actions looked also legitimate, helping it to achieve a certain level of popular support entrusted to the GUNT.

The institutionalization of interventions was an indispensible precondition for success both for the internal Chadian politics, and the international arena. The institutionalized intervention increased the confidence of Libyans and the Chadians they supported that they were acting for the right cause and the right government. Quadaffi went even further and claimed that, since Goukouni had asked Libya to intervene, he might also ask it to go away and that he would be bound by that decision. Libya, as a responsible member of the international community, would respect this request and leave. This may also have been a face-saving act since, following the request of Goukouni, Libya did in fact leave.

The legitimacy of GUNT, nurtured and endorsed by four reconciliation conferences, might have been an additional reason for why France did not support Habré in 1980-1981. Although minister of defense, for them Habré was still an opposition rebel, who, now out of GUNT, was acting against the legitimate government, whom France once had supported. A logical question to ask would then be why did France not support GUNT, as a legally placed government, as it did Habré's government? A possible explanation of this behavior could be is that GUNT enjoyed the backing of Libya, with which France had a competitive relationship in the region, at large, and Chad, in particular. It was difficult for the French leadership to arrange popular support at home for their possible cooperation with a country, which, if not an enemy, was certainly not a friendly state, and the influence of which threatened France's interests in Africa. Thus, a rational explanation, taking into account the general line of the French support for legitimate governments in Chad, no matter who was in office, would be that once a new government was in place, France could easily exercise its influence over it.

Conclusions

The conflict in Chad and its concurrent interventions represent various degrees of success in fulfilling the objectives of interveners. The interventions of France and Libya were characterized by considerable path-dependency in their actions: they had always supported the same side, with the first providing aid to the government, which was generally the stronger of the two, and the latter – to the opposition, being usually weaker. In both cases, the interventions were successful when they were backed up by institutional arrangements safeguarded by formal legal agreements. Even when Libya supported GUNT in opposition to Habré's ruling regime, it was still considered by the many, including internationally, as a government in exile, on behalf of which Libya made a commitment to intervene.

The direction of third party support had an important effect on the subsequent developments: the government-sponsoring intervener enjoys a higher degree of legitimacy both locally (in the target country), domestically (in the own country) and internationally. Hence, an intervener is considered by the populations abroad and at home as having a noble task of an upholder of law and order, helping it to achieve its objectives. In contrast, when the intervener aided the opposition, it had the backing of that party and its supporters alone, which by definition was quite limited.

Another decisive factor in the success of interventions was the externalization of intervention, which contributed to a higher degree of success: made it increasingly easy operationally and logistically for an intervener to keep the troops out of the target country and intervene only upon the request of the party it supported. The French presence remained largely external to the situation in Chad, allowing France to retain its limited agendas. In contrast, Libya's decision to extend its presence by going out of the area, both literally and figuratively – extending its territorial coverage and including additional components of intervention, like state-building and external governance – worked against its ability to effectively achieve its intervention goals.

Externalization was also complemented by limited intervention agendas: both France and Libya were effective when they had narrower goals: the former not wanting to engage in long-lasting conflict with the opposition and succeeding in having a say in the Chadian affairs, and the latter effectively keeping its presence in a small area of the Aouzou Strip. Once Libya went beyond its initial scope of intervention, it could hardly sustain multidimensional presence composed of infantry, armored vehicles, artillery and air power, as well as public administrators on a large territory away from their home base. Such a gargantuan endeavor would have required not only high degree of coordination between highly dispersed units, but also a huge economic commitment to maintain their presence. It turned out to be a daunting task for Libya to go southward and to attempt to provide for the local administration of the territories it was covering, mainly due to its limited economic resources, and the diversity of population it encountered to the South.

Chapter 4
Georgia (1992-1994): Intervening for the Sake of Intervention

Map 4.1 Map of Georgia

Source: Reprinted with permission of the UN Cartographic Section.

The Georgian-Abkhazian civil war is a typical post-Cold War secessionist conflict, which was rooted in the history of the ethnic majority-minority interactions and which appeared immediately after the collapse of the Soviet Union. Nationalist forces nurtured and, at the same time, restrained, by the Soviet system for more than 70 years, which had created self-identified quasi nation-state republics, found their revelation into clashes on ethnic grounds unleashing long-lasting identity wars in Abkhazia, South Ossetia, Nagorno-Karabakh, Osh, and Transdniestria. Initially having been started as a communal collision between Georgians, ethnic majority in the former Georgian Soviet Socialist Republic and on the territory of Abkhazian Soviet Autonomous Republic, which was a part of it, and ethnic Abkhazians, being the minority, the conflict later developed into a full-scale war.

The conflict witnessed two interventions: a unilateral intervention by the Russian Federation in early 1990s and a multilateral intervention by the same actor under the aegis of CIS (Commonwealth of Independent States) peacekeeping forces, which were technically multilateral but were composed exclusive of the Russian military. Both interventions were unsuccessful – the first failed to achieve its goals because of their ambiguity and inadequate resources it allocated whereas the latter was completely inefficient in fulfilling its peacekeeping mandate. Abkhazian conflict was preceded by the war in South Ossetia, another region of Georgia populated by ethnic minority – the Ossetians. The result of the both conflicts was de facto secession and a "no-peace-no-war" situation, which lasted for nearly 14, when, in August 2008 the Russian Federation intervened on behalf of the South Ossetians. This quick and successful intervention, which was promptly capitalized by Abkhazia, who pushed the Georgian forces busy with rebuffing the Russian attack away from its borders, brought independence and sovereignty to both breakaway regions by unilateral acknowledgement of Russia.

Conflict Background

To understand the causes and consequences of the unilateral and multilateral intervention interventions, it is necessary to view them from the prism of historical relations between majority and minority ethnic groups in the former Soviet Union. At the heart of ethnic tensions was the primordialist issue rightly noted by Varshney (2003): "Those who came earlier to a land have often argued that they are more entitled to political privileges or to a preeminent place in the national culture than those who came later".[1] The land aspect had a number of accompanying attachments: language, culture, religion, and, last but not the least, political loyalties, all of which constituted the inherent components of identities of these two ethnic groups. The question "Who came to Abkhazian land first – Georgians or Abkhazians?" was the part and parcel of historical domestic rivalry between Georgians and Abkhazians, which was put down during the Soviet Union but which found gaps in its ethnic homogenization policies once the central rule slowly but surely weakened by the beginning of the 1990s.

Geographically Abkhazia, indeed, is pictured as a separate entity. It is located in the North-Western part of Georgia, is detached from the center, borders Russia and is washed by the Black Sea. During the Soviet times, Abkhazians represented a notable minority being largely confined to the territory of the autonomous republic. According to the public census of Georgia undertaken in 1989, out of the total of 105,308 Abkhazians living in Georgia, the majority – 95,853, or 91 per cent – resided in Abkhazian Autonomous Republic, whilst the rest lived in the western parts of the country. Georgians, on the other hand, were a title nation

1 Varshney, A. 2003. Nationalism, Ethnic Conflict, and Rationality. *Perspectives on Politics*, 1(1), 92.

– in the multiethnic republic with 239 nationalities totaling to nearly 5.5 million people, Georgians were 65 per cent.[2]

In the matter of timing of the land arrival, mutually contradictory statements and historical sources were used: both nations claimed to have come to Abkhazia first. In trying to "age" their dwelling, another important aspect of interethnic relations was endangered: identity. Abkhazians were claiming being totally different from Georgians, while the latter insisted on their Georgian origins belonging to the Iberian-Caucasian family of peoples, the principal member of which is Georgians. Contrary to this, Abkhazians claim to be autochthonous in the region with no ties whatsoever to the Georgian nation.

Historically, Abkhazia used to constitute a separate principality within Georgia kingdom divided between Iran and Turkey. The modern history of the region starts with the Great Caucasian Wars between Russia and Turkey (1830-1864), in which Abkhazians supported their kin Muslims in Turkey, while Georgia sided with Christian Russians. Following the Russian victory, Abkhazia fell under the direct Russian rule, which perpetuated in Soviet times.

In 1918 Abkhazia became a part of the Democratic Republic of Georgia with an autonomous status. The situation with the ethnic minorities was far from perfect in the new independent country: ethnic minorities faced discrimination and oppression, which lasted until 1921, when the communist Red Army eliminated the statehood. In March 1921 Abkhazian Bolsheviks declared independence and proclaimed establishment of Abkhazian Soviet Socialist Republic – a union-level republic directly subordinated to Moscow with no formal links to the newly created Georgian SSR. In 1931, however, Abkhazian SSR was included in the Georgian Soviet Socialist Republic with the autonomous status. This was the first time when formal administrative, vertical and hierarchical relations were established between Tbilisi, capital of Georgia, and Sokhumi, capital of Abkhazia.

The whole process of development of Abkhazian nation during the Soviet Union, which is the root of this identity conflict, can be characterized as the struggle between their forced assimilation by Georgians and willful assimilation by Russians, one of the signs of which was imposition of the usage of Cyrillic script. The nature of this disagreement was indeed vital: the nationalist Georgians claimed that Abkhazians were newcomers to the region and had nothing to do with the ancient population of Abkhazia. This argument was over the very existence of Abkhazians nation: while Abkhazians claimed their uniqueness, Georgians asserted that they had no distinct national identity: they believed that "Abkhazian identity is entirely a product of the Soviet corruption of history, and was artificially reinforced to destabilize and weaken the Caucasus."[3]

---

2 The data on ethnic minorities residing in Georgia was taken from the "Demoscop" website. Available at http://demoscope.ru/weekly/ssp/sng_nac_89.php?reg=6 [accessed: May 6, 2009].

3 Goldberg, S. 1994. *Pride of Small Nations: The Caucasus and Post-Soviet Disorder*. London and New Jersey: Zed Books Ltd, 102.

The problem was more than a mere forced ethnic transformation – it had deeper institutional origins rooted in the administrative formation of the Soviet Union and its ethnic policies. In the matter of future conflict the factor of Abkhazian autonomy was of paramount importance. Autonomies, which, according to Cornell (2002), "…impl[y] introduction of ethnoterritoriality – territorial control linked to ethnicity",[4] in post-Soviet Union meant "separation"; that is, the institutionalized feeling of "otherness". The system of Soviet republics and autonomies, as Brubaker (1994) claims, "…actively institutionalized the existence of multiple nations and nationalities as constitutive elements of state and its citizenry…[through] sponsoring, codifying, institutionalizing…[and] inventing nationhood and nationality on sub-state level, while at the same time doing nothing to institutionalize them on the level of the state as a whole".[5] Furthermore, ethnic autonomies within Soviet Republics were, according to Suny (1993), an important condition for future unrest: "[n]ational self-determination to the point of separatism had been enshrined in a constitutional guarantee of a right of secession from the union, a time bomb that lay dormant though the years of Stalinism, only to explode with the Gorbachev reforms."[6] This constitutional guarantee – a formal right of secession of Soviet Republics, envisaged in Article 72 of its Constitution, though without any real mechanism – given to Soviet-level republics meant to their respective autonomies that if former could secede, they could break away, too. While under the Soviet Union, the status of autonomous republic merely denoted administrative separation from their titular nations, after its collapse, a minority's autonomous status implied potential independence.

The Soviet system, though its public administration mechanism, bred the framework for future Abkhaz separation from Georgia. Having the de jure administrative separation status Abkhazia had been governed by its republican authorities in Tbilisi, the capital of Georgia, which, in their turn, had been rules by the central authorities in Moscow. Such a double administrative hierarchy belittled the importance and power of republican organs vis-à-vis their autonomous ones, who increasingly turned for support and advice to the Soviet center. Remembering that once Abkhazia was a Union-level republic, its nationalist forces during the history of cohabitation with Georgians in the Soviet state nurtured self-identification of masses as being Abkhazians and distinct from Georgians, and constantly express wishes for entering the Soviet Union with the same status as Georgia or, at least, having a stronger and a bigger patron – the Russian Soviet Federal Republic.

4 Cornell, S. 2002. Autonomy as a Source of Conflict: Caucasian Conflicts in Theoretical Perspective. *World Politics*, 54(2), 246.

5 Brubaker, R. 1994. Nationhood and National Question in the Soviet Union and Post-Soviet Eurasia: An Institutional Account. *Theory and Society*, 23(1), 52.

6 Suny, R.G. 1993. *The Revenge of the Past: Nationalism Revolution, and the Collapse of the Soviet Union*. Stanford University Press, 128.

Nearly every decade, starting from 1947 and especially in 1988-1992 Abkhazian leaders were submitting petitions to join the Russian Federation, the requests that had been consistently turned down by Moscow.[7] The official position of Russia was neither to satisfy Abkhazians appeals petitions nor to reject them completely. The cause for such attitude of Moscow lied in the hierarchical composition of the Soviet state and, specifically, the Russian Federation: if the Abkhazian claims had been satisfied, similar demands would have been made from 16 autonomous republics, 5 autonomous regions and 10 autonomous districts. This was not inadmissible for the nationalist policies of the USSR with vertical national subordination.

From the point of view of ethnic majority standings, within the Soviet Union, in words of Suny (1989), "Georgia became a protected area of privilege for Georgians. They received the bulk of the rewards of the society, the leading positions in the state and the largest subsidies for cultural projects while Armenians, Abkhaz, Ossetians, Adjarians, Kurds, Jews and others were at a considerable disadvantage in the competition for the budgetary pie."[8] Close to the end of the 1980s the national consciousness of Georgians became more politically salient through asserting the superiority of the Georgian people over the other nationalities living in the Republic. Ethnic chauvinism continued under the administration of Zviad Gamsakhurdia, a former a self-proclaimed leader, dissident and future President of independent Georgia. Chauvinist and pejorative rhetoric of the Gamsakhurdian political party "Round Table – Independent Georgia" equally threatened all ethnicities, whom it called "newcomers" and "guests" on the land where they had lived for centuries. Gradually nationalist statements increased and representatives of other nations started leaving the country in large numbers out of fear of persecution. However, no serious, large-scale and systematic harassment and mistreatment of the representative of any ethnic group had been recorded.

Close to the end of the Soviet Union credible commitment problem developed leading to interethnic security dilemma. Minorities were worried that Georgian nationalism would incite aggressive actions against the minority groups. On their part, the Georgians tended to blame Russia for all their ills and the minorities residing in autonomies for secessionist aspirations. The mere fact of existence of Abkhazian autonomy gave Georgian authorities sufficient grounds to consider these ethnic minorities as threatening their right to self-determination as nations. A classic security dilemma made the Georgians regard "…Abkhazians and Ossetians merely as a tool and instrument of Russian in its attempts to destabilize Georgia and prevent its accidence to independence…[T]he demands or claims from Abkhazians and Ossetians…were seen as artificially created by Russia, with

7 For a full account of the history of Abkhazian ethnic mobilization and separation attempts, see Lezhava, G. (ed.) 1997. Mejdu Gruziei i Rossiei: Istoricheskie Korni I Sovremennie Faktori Abkhazsko-Gruzinskogo Konflikta (XIX-XX gg.) ["Between Georgia and Russia: Historic Roots and Modern Factors of the Abkhazian-Georgian Conflict" (XIX-XX)]. Moskva: UNMO.

8 Suny, R.G. 1989. *The Making of the Georgian Nation*. London: I.B. Tauris, 290.

no domestic roots of their own…"[9] Hence, the zero-sum nature of the forthcoming conflict: while Georgians were concerned with the territorial integrity of their nation-state, Abkhazians were fighting for their very existence as a nation. In sum, according to Zdravomislov (1997), "Imperial components of the Georgian politics towards Abkhazia stimulated Abkhazians nationalism, which gave an impetus to the Georgian nationalism."[10] In response to political mobilization of Georgians that continued after the end of the Soviet rule, Abkhazians formed their own nationalist movement, *Aidgilara*, and began pushing for separation from Georgia and becoming independent subject within the Soviet Union.

The first real step towards escalation to open conflicts with Abkhazians and Ossetians was the introduction by the Georgian authorities of the State Program of the Georgian Language in August 1989, which proclaimed the Georgian language as the only official media of communication in the country leading to negative reactions from Georgia's minorities. The Language Laws were succeeded by the Elections Law of Georgia banning regional parties from participation in the Republican Supreme Soviet. This was a direct signal to Abkhazians and South Ossetians that they would be out of political life of the country and would not be able to lobby their interests. The most important legal document was adoption of the "Act of Restitution of Independence of Georgia" on April 9, 1991, stated indivisibility of the territory of Georgia and fixed its borders. Abkhazia promptly responded with declaration of these acts null and void, and on August 25, 1990, the Supreme Council of Abkhazia adopted the resolution "On Legal Guarantees of Protection of the Independence of Abkhazia" and the "Declaration of State Sovereignty". These declarations were duly revoked the next day by the Supreme Council of Georgia. From that point the security dilemma could only get worse, where each subsequent move of one group to increase its own security provoked a harsher reaction by the other side, increasing the likelihood of a preemptive war.

Russian Intervention

Gradually Abkhazia began strengthening its ties with Russia and their ethnic kin living over the border in the North Caucasus. In November 1991, the Third Session of the Mountain Peoples of the Caucasus in Abkhazia signed the Treaty for a Confederative Union of the Mountain People of the Caucasus. This was a perfect window of opportunity for Abkhazians to lobby for their independence from Georgia, since Georgia was currently preoccupied with internal civil war against Gamsakhurdia.

9 Cornell, S.E. 2001. *Small Nations and Great Powers: A Study of Ethnopolitical Conflict in the Caucasus*. Curzon Press, 163.

10 Zdravomislov, A.G. 1997. *Mejnacionalnie Konflikti v Post-Sovetskom Prostranstve* [Inter-ethnic Conflicts in Post-Soviet Space] Moskva: Aspekt Press, 21.

The first sparkle that opened Pandora's Box of violence between Abkhazians and Georgians occurred with the establishment of the branch of the Georgian State University in Sokhumi where the language of instruction was Georgian. This was considered by Abkhazians as a direct threat to their identity, but Georgian authorities managed to calm the tensions. On August 14, 1992, however, the troops of the State Council of Georgia crossed the administrative border of Abkhazia under the pretext of protection of railroad cargo from looting. Abkhazians labeled this act as Georgian intervention upon their territory and started the war. From the beginning the Georgian forces were gaining momentum: they easily managed to Sokhumi and nearby towns and villages. However, with assistance in a form of mercenaries from various parts of Russia, especially from Northern Caucasus and some 1,500 Cossacks from the southern provinces of Russia, and military support from the Russian military bases in Abkhazian towns of Gudauta and Ochamchira, Abkhazians managed to retake Sokhumi in September 1993. The Russian role in the conflict was framed by providing war-related supplies and ammunition to Abkhazian forces, keeping its borders open and allowing groups of mercenaries, goods and arms to move in and out.

On political front, Russia's Supreme Soviet repeatedly denounced Georgia's resort to violence. It suspending the delivery of Russian arms, equipment and other resources to Georgia: an embargo, which led to a real economic disaster. During the Soviet times, Georgia depended heavily on supplies of raw materials and energy carriers from Russia. With the closure of its border with Abkhazia, where one of the main electric power plants was located, and stoppage of oil and gas imports from Russia, the country entered a severe energy crisis lasting for almost a decade. Such actions of Russia openly supporting secession of Abkhazia created strong anti-Russian sentiments in Georgia.

Apart from participating in the conflict on the side of the Abkhazians, Russia was eager to keep the image of a neutral peace-maker. Russia mediated several agreements, which were aimed at secession of hostilities. Some of these agreements were almost immediately broken, others provided only temporary remedies to the situation, and neither of them resolved the conflict. The first attempt to stop fighting was made right after the beginning of the conflict in Sochi in July 1992 with the Russian mediation. The Sochi agreement provided for the withdrawal of the Georgian troops from Abkhazia, demilitarization of both sides, and the return of the legal (Georgian) pre-war government to Abkhazia. Russia stepped in as an external guarantor of the agreement. The Georgian side observed the agreement and withdrew their heavy weaponry from Sokhumi to the port of Poti in the Western Georgia. Abkhazians weapons, on the other hand, were stored near the front and kept handy in case of resumption of the hostilities. The agreement was soon violated, and the war resumed.

The war led to the deaths of 20,000[11] people from both sides and more than 250,000 Georgian IDPs. Despite Russian denials of involvement in the Abkhazian war, 46 Russian soldiers of various ranks were killed in Georgia in 1992[12] and several fighter aircrafts, bombers and helicopters piloted by the Russian officers were shot down. However, no former military regiment from the regular Russian army had officially participated in the war.

On September 3, 1992 the leaders of the conflicting parties, together with Boris Yeltsin, then President of Russia, signed a cease-fire agreement in Moscow, in which Russia officially supported the territorial integrity of Georgia, the inviolability of their frontiers, and protection of the interests and rights of national minorities living on their territories.[13] Most importantly, Article 5 of the Agreement envisaged facilitation of creation of the conditions for safe return of the refugees, which was later included in the mandated provisions of the CIS intervention. Yeltsin also proposed that Russia would act as a third party to guarantee the peace agreement. There were then a series of fruitless discussions and meetings in Moscow between Shevardnadze and Vladislav Ardzinba, Abkhazian leader, although nothing actually worked when, finally, the parties reached a temporal armistice in 1993 and began a real negotiation process. The Russian Duma (Parliament) adopted an extremely negative approach to Georgia and passed several resolutions condemning the activities of legal authorities in Abkhazia.

To avoid large-scale confrontation with Russia, Eduard Shevardnadze, who replaced Gamsakhurdia, had to bring Georgia into the CIS, a regional intergovernmental organization successor to the Soviet Union, created in December 1991 by Russia, Ukraine and Belarus. Negotiations to end the conflict were conducted also on a bilateral level between Georgia and Russia. On February 3, 1994, the sides signed the "Treaty on Friendship, Cooperation and Peaceful Coexistence between the Russian Federation and the Georgian Republic". On April 15, 1994, Georgia, as a new member of the CIS, signed the "Resolution of the Sovereignty, Territorial Integrity and Inviolability of the Borders of Nations Belonging to the Commonwealth of Independent States", in order to safeguard its own borders.

The conflict eventually moved to the international level when the UN became involved in with a parallel conflict resolution process. The United Nations Observer Mission in Georgia (UNOMIG) was established on August 24, 1993 by Security Council resolution 858 mainly to monitor the situation and report to the UN on the

---

11 UCDP/PRIO Armed Conflict dataset v.4-2008 [Online]. Available at: http://www.pcr.uu.se/research/UCDP/data_and_publications/datasets.htm [accessed: May 6, 2009].

12 Brecher, M. and Wilkenfeld, J. 2000. *A Study of Crisis Data Project*. University of Michigan Press, 2000.

13 Rossiya-Gruziya Itogovii Dokument Moskovskoi Vstrechi 3 Sentyabrya 1992 Goda [Russia-Georgia. Final Document of the Moscow Meeting on 3 September 1992] [Online].Available at: http://lawrussia.ru/texts/legal_185/doc185a417x330.htm [accessed: May 22, 2009].

belligerents' compliance with the peace agreement.[14] The OSCE also participated in the conflict resolution process; its involvement increased since Georgia became a member of the Council of Europe in 1999. Peace-making activities of these organizations were limited to situational monitoring and reporting to the belligerents about violations of peace. None of these actions, however, managed to solve the essential cause of the conflict: the incompatibility of the views of the belligerents on their political statuses.

There is a considerable controversy over the Russian intervention in the conflict. On the one hand, there is no clear-cut evidence of direct participation of the Russian regular troops in the military activities on either side. Neither there is a proof of the role Russia played in instigation of the secessionist aspirations of the Abkhazian minority. Its involvement was clandestine, uncontrolled on the ground, hectic and vague. As the Human Rights Watch report goes, "Russia's presence [in Georgia]…is…fluid, ambiguous, and appears to represent varied interests and commands. It may involve the supply of weapons, logistical, financial or planning support, intelligence sharing, or military intervention by Russian forces. Yet who gives the orders often cannot be determined." At the same time, the same report claims that "The Russian military took a direct role in hostilities on several occasions, and appears to have provided logistical support and supplies to Abkhazians"[15] especially during its air attacks on Sokhumi occupied by that time by Georgians.

It is commonly known that Abkhazians were largely outnumbered by Georgians, which put them in clearly unfavorable position: they were not in position of solely withstand the Georgian majority having overwhelming advantage in numbers of soldiers but for the sizable outside support. The arguments of Mack (1975) and Areguin-Toft (2001) on minorities being weaker and still winning wars against stronger majorities by employing asymmetric military warfare and engaging in guerilla tactics of attrition[16] cannot be valid in this case, since all the warring parties used guerilla tactics due to the specific mountainous and forest terrain. This geographic specificity made large-scale regular military actions from both sides quite complicated and forced the two sides to engage in similar irregular and mostly partisan military actions. Also, by the early times of collapse of the Soviet Union, Georgia had no proper army of its own. Even the National Guard, the name of the Georgian regular military engaged in warfare, suffered from a low

---

14 Mandate of the UNOMIG [Online]. Available at http://www.un.org/Depts/dpko/missions/unomig/mandate.html [accessed: May 6, 2009].

15 Human Rights Watch Arms Project, 1995. *Georgia/Abkhazia: Violations of the Laws of War and Russia's Role in the Conflict*. Human Rights Watch/Helsinki, 7(7), 12 [Online]. Available at: http://www.hrw.org/reports/pdfs/g/georgia/georgia953.pdf [accessed: May 6, 2009].

16 Mack, A. 1975. Why Big Nations Lose Small Wars: The Politics of Asymmetric Conflict. *World Politics*, 27(2), 175-200; and Areguin-Toft, I. 2001. How the Weak Win Wars: A Theory of Asymmetric Conflict. *International Security*, 26(1), 93-128.

level of development and expertise. Poor discipline inside army ranks, irregular movements of troops to the conflict zones and the recruitment of mainly volunteers with no prior military experience all contributed to this position. However, even in this case Georgians still had considerable superiority in their military and human capacities.

Where did Russia participate in the conflict directly was in keeping its borders with Abkhazia open, which allowed the irregulars, volunteers and hired mercenaries from its Northern Caucasian and Southern territories to freely enter Abkhazia and to participate in clashes with the Georgian forces. The fact remains that Confederation of Mountainous Peoples and its military groupings and soldiers, which fought on the side of Abkhaz against the Georgians, were officially citizens of Russia, and were under that country's jurisdiction. In addition to paramilitary personnel, Russia also supplied arms and ammunition to the Abkhazian rebels from its military bases. Finally, it contributed to their secessionist claims economically from its nearby Krasnodar region.

There is, obviously, a predictable divergence between Western and Russian sources about the Russian role. Western scholars directly ascribe loss of Georgia in this conflict to the Russian factor. For instance, Goldberg (1994) notes that "Georgia's unforeseen defeat was almost entirely due to the reinforcement from Russia which fought on the side of the rebels…[The] forces from the former Soviet army base at Sokhumi were aiding Abkhazians…The disintegration of the Red Army had left hundreds of thousands of servicemen without employment and housing; signing on an as a mercenary provided a convenient alternative…"[17] Hertzig (1999) also supports the idea of the Russian hand behind Abkhazian victory: "The Abkhaz…benefited from Russian military support channeled through the Russian bases in Abkhazia at Gudauta and Bombora, though the scale of that support and the level at which it was authorized remain disputed."[18]

For his part, Horowitz (2004) also notes the long-lasting effect of the separatist movement in Abkhazia as a function of the support coming from Moscow: "The Soviet Center encouraged and supported South Ossetian and Abkhaz resistance, as a way of discouraging Georgian separatism. This also provided a green light to local Soviet Commanders sympathetic to the Ossetian and Abkhaz causes."[19] He continues that "[l]ocally based Russian troops provided crucial aid, while hard-liners in the Russian parliament and military threatened to intervene on a large scale. This placated Caucasian mountain peoples within the Russian Federation

17 Goldberg, S. 1994. *Pride of Small Nations: The Caucasus and Post-Soviet Disorder*. London and New Jersey: Zed Books Ltd, 109.

18 Hertzig, E. 1999. *The New Caucasus: Armenia, Azerbaijan and Georgia*. London: Pinter Publishers, 77.

19 Horowitz, S. 2004. Identities Unbound: Escalating Ethnic Conflict in Post-Soviet Azerbaijan, Georgia, Moldova, and Tajikistan, in *Ethnic Conflict and International Politics*, edited by S.E. Lobell and P. Mauceri. Palgrave Macmillan, p. 63.

that were ethnically related to Abkhazians…"[20] A student of the Caucasus, Cornell attributes the defeat of Georgia after its quick early victory to Russia's pro-Abkhaz stance in the conflict. He ascertains that after quick victory Georgian troops "…were pushed back, with the assistance of the Russian units to Abkhazians side, in particular, air force units bombing Georgian positions."[21] For him the fact that Abkhazia possessed "T-72 tanks, Grad rocket launchers, and other heavy equipment…that over 100,000 landmines were pulled out during the war is another factor indicating Russian military support…, as there were simply no such amounts of armory in the region…"[22]

Another side of the role of the Russians in the conflict is presented by Russian scholars. As an example, Pryakhin condemns anti-Russian Georgian attitudes during the conflict and believing that Russia had "stifl[ed] Georgia for centuries, which had finally chosen Abkhazia…as a 'working tool' for bringing back breakaway and free Georgians."[23] He considers Russian interest in the Caucasus region as a sine qua non of its foreign policy, and its involvement justified by the simple fact that the conflict bordered Russia. Important insights to defining the scope of the Russian intervention in Georgia are given by Zdravomislov who notes non-homogeneity of the Russian domestic politics, undergoing drastic transformation from communism to democracy. After the dissolution of the Soviet Union, especially in early years of its statehood, it was increasingly difficult for the center to control its peripheries, which was especially true for the army. The army, which once represented a strong force capable of ruling nearly half of the world, was left not only unattended, but out of control as a result of the collapse of the USSR. Majority of the Russian/ex-Soviet political and military elites blamed Gorbachev and Shevardnadze for breaking up the Soviet system, and sop-Yeltsin for supporting them. The conflicts in Georgia, in words of Zdravomyslov, represented a perfect opportunity for them to avenge "democrat-Shevardnadze, who took an active part in dissolution of the Soviet Union" and to use Abkhazia and South Ossetia for the sake of territorial interests of the "unified and indivisible Mother-Russia within the borders of 1917."[24]

The paradoxical part of the Russian actions in Abkhazia and Georgia was that it supported both sides. Apart from supplying arms and personnel to the Abkhazian rebels, Russia also provided assistance to the Georgian military from their bases located in Georgia proper. As Hertzig argues, as a result of Moscow's complete lack of control over the military forces, "Russia also equipped the Georgian forces.

20 Horowitz, S. 2004.

21 Cornell, S.E. 2001, 171.

22 Cornell, S.E. 2001, 171.

23 Pryaxin, V.F. 2002. *Regionalnie Konflikti na Post-Sovetskm Prostranstve. Abkhazia, Yujnaya Osetia, Nagornii Karabakh, Pridnestrov'e, Tajikistan* [Regional Conflicts on the Post-Soviet Space. Abkahzia, South Ossetia, Mountainous Karabakh, Transdniestia, Tajikistan], Moscow: Publishing House GNOM and D, 134.

24 Zdravomislov, A.G. 1997. 63.

Local Russian units and their commanders, as well as generals in Moscow, made ad hoc decisions based on personal preferences and local loyalties, with scant regard for official policy."[25] An important thing to keep in mind is that Transcaucasia was traditionally a buffer zone between the Soviet Union and NATO, which bordered the region from the side of Turkey. After the collapse of the USSR, the Transcaucasian Military District, with its headquarters in Tbilisi, had left vast amounts of arms – armored units and a variety of artillery and missile systems – in the region.

The main problem was the fact that the troops from the former Transcaucasian Military District lacked a clearly defined legal status, creating danger for the Russian personnel stationed in what had become a conflict zone. It, thus, became increasingly easy for both belligerent sides to obtain weapons. The only sources of weapons for Abkhazians as well as for Georgians were these Russian military bases. Despite the official position of Russia in early 1990s of supporting territorial integrity of Georgia and not jeopardizing the peace near its borders, different Russian politicians and rogue army generals were vitally interested in supplies of arms and escalation of violence notwithstanding the ceasefire agreements their state mediated.

CIS Intervention

The most important peace deal was signed in May 14, 1994 (also known as the "Moscow Agreement") with the Russian mediation. By stressing the urgent need for ceasefire and removal of heavy equipment from the conflict zone, the Agreement created a delimited area of 12 km on either side of the Inguri river (a border between Abkhazia and Georgia proper) for separation of the belligerents. The parties also agreed to dissolve and remove all informal military groupings upon the request of Georgia who complained about mercenaries from Russia.[26]

Further to the agreement in May 1994 Georgians and Abkhazians jointly appealed to the CIS countries to act as intermediaries and third parties in the resolution of the conflict. Acknowledging the territorial integrity of Georgia (which, in this case meant acknowledging that Abkhazia is also a part of Georgia) and support for protection of the rights of the multinational population of Abkhazia, the Heads of CIS States decided "[t]o deploy in Georgian-Abkhaz conflict zone the Collective Force composed of military contingents of interested states – members of the CIS of 2-3 thousand of people, as well as military observers in order to maintain the peace."[27]

---

25 Hertzig, E. 1999, 156.

26 Agreement of Ceasefire and Separation of Forces, May 14, 1994, UNOMIG [Online]. Available at: http://unomig.org/data/file/276/moscow_agreement.pdf [accessed: May 6, 2009].

27 Decision of The Council of The CIS Heads of States on Usage of Collective Forces to Maintain Peace in The Conflict Zone of Georgian-Abkhaz Conflict, Office of the State

The Statute of the CIS Peacekeeping Forces (PKF), which arrived to Abkhazia to become guarantors of peace, defined them as a "coalition grouping",[28] which, in principle, should have include military personnel from more than one of its member-state. Contrary to the idea of multilateralism stemming out of the intergovernmental nature of the Commonwealth of Independent States as an institution, the intervention was formed exclusively by the Russian military, which turned to be the main reason of its subsequent failure to reach its goals.

Initial aims of the CIS intervention were separation of belligerents and provision of a buffer zone between them. Another goal of the peacekeeping operation was to conduct monitoring over the fulfillment of the ceasefire agreements reached by the parties. Larger issues were humanitarian assistance, among which were de-mining actions. More specific operational tasks included disarmament of the illegal paramilitaries from both sides, supervision on the fulfillment of the International Humanitarian Law, demining and demilitarizing the conflict zone and preventing fighting between the sides.

The peacekeeping operation was scheduled to end in May 1995. From the point of view of fulfilling their mandate – keeping de facto peace – the CIS peacekeepers, indeed, managed to reach their goals: they separated the warring parties and, although small clashes were normally happening with relative frequency, they prevented large-scale military activities and resumption of the conflict. Such a "no-peace-no-war" situation was, in fact, acceptable for both parties, who, for a while, rested on their gains and losses. Abkhazians were successful in keeping control over the majority of the land: the only place they could not access was the Upper Kodori, populated by mountainous Georgians and being under jurisdiction of the central government. Abkhazia was seemed to be content decided with a longer-term de facto independence furthering it by a possible legal separation from Georgia. Abkhazians did not fear retaliation on the part of the Russian peacekeepers in case of their defection, knowing that majority of them, having been stationed for years in Abkhazia, would have natural sympathies towards the local people.

The situation was the same for the Georgians: the CIS peacekeepers were a good face-saving tool for the Shevardnadze government, which had actually lost the war in Abkhazia. The country with a population of more than 4 million could not effectively use its majority advantage to secure a territory with a population of some 90,000 people. Therefore, Russian peacekeepers served as an excuse for the government to explain away the loss of their land. Also, any repeated military

---

Minister of Georgia for Reintegration, August 22, 1994 [Online]. Available at: http://smr.gov.ge/en/abkhazia/documents/cis_cpkf [accessed: May 6, 2009].

28 Decision on Adoption of the Statute of Collective Peacekeeping Forces in the Commonwealth of Independent States. Uniform Registry of Legal Acts And Other Documents of the Commonwealth of Independent States. Moscow, January 19, 1996 [Online]. Available at: http://cis.minsk.by/webnpa/text.aspx?RN=N99600003 [accessed: May 6, 2009].

assaults from the part of Georgia would mean increased casualties for both sides and, taking into account the support Abkhazians gained from Russia, prospects for their victory were vague, if not gloomy.

However, that same month the Head of CIS amended the mandate of the peacekeepers and included the most important task – establishment of "the necessary conditions for security and return of displaced persons to their places of residence."[29] This meant that the Georgian majority would return to the places it had been evicted from and that Abkhazians would again find themselves with an uneasy minority status. This was the vital issue for the Georgian government: once the Georgian refugees returned to their prewar homes, the balance of power would shift back to its pre-conflict stage, i.e. almost entirely to the benefit of the Georgian majority. Georgia also tried to legally strengthen the provision of the CIS PKF mandate through concluding a bilateral agreement with Russia in 1994 on facilitation of return of the internally displaced persons in Abkhazia.[30]

The return of refugees would have also allowed the Georgian forces to regain an initial foothold in the conflict zone, since the supportive kin population would provide a sizable influx of human power to the Georgian military. The refugees were eager to defend their interests, rights and properties abandoned during the active warfare. In case of a peaceful conflict resolution outcome– such as, for example, power-sharing arrangements through a referendum on the political status of the region – the increased Georgian population in the region would serve as an indispensable asset for bringing Abkhazia back into the Georgian realm since all the Georgian national would definitely voted for unification of the breakaway region with Georgia.

The failure of the CIS peacekeepers to successfully implement that part of its mandate was due to a number of reasons, the most important one being defection of Abkhazian side from the terms of the agreement as well as the mandated objectives. Many of the houses belonging to Georgians have been occupied by Abkhazians and their return to their owners would mean forceful eviction of the former from the property. Also, Abkhazians knew that the Georgian population would support the unification idea and were against this scenario. Neither was Russia fully committed to conduct the return of the refugees. It was afraid of

29 Decision of The Council of The CIS Heads of States on Usage of Collective Forces to Maintain Peace in The Conflict Zone of Georgian-Abkhaz Conflict, Office of the State Minister of Georgia for Reintegration, August 22, 1994 [Online]. Available at: http://smr.gov.ge/en/abkhazia/documents/cis_cpkf [accessed: May 6, 2009].

30 Soglashenie MejduPravitelstvom Rossiiskoi Federacii i Pravitelstvom Respubliki Gruziya o Regulirovanii Processa Pereseleniyha I Zashite Prav Pereselencev (Zaklucheno v g. Tbilisi (03.02.1994) [Agreement Between the Government of the Russian Federation and the Government of the Republic of Georgia on Regulating the Process of Re-settlement and Protection of the Rights of Displaced Persons (Signed in Tbilisi on 03.02.1994)]. Online. Available at: http://lawrussia.ru/texts/legal_783/doc783a787x781.htm [accessed: June 1, 2009].

possible resumption of hostilities by the Georgia side but reluctantly agreed to amend the PRF mandate to appease Georgia, a new member of the CIS, over which it was to exercise its full, with the aim to procrastinate the matter as long as possible.

The task of assisting in bringing back indigenous Georgian population to Abkhazia remained the core of the peacekeepers' mandate and a lightning rod of its perpetual criticism by the Georgian government. There was an incessant perception within the Georgian establishment that Russia was a strong lobby of Abkhazia politically, economically and militarily. The Georgian parliament was continuously making proposals to the CIS Heads of States to stop legal power of the peacekeepers, not to prolong their activities beyond the mandated deadline, or to replace them completely with other peacekeeping forces or, at least, to include forces from other countries in their contingent.

These Georgian proposals to change the CIS peacekeepers' format were repeatedly rejected by Abkhazia locally and blocked by Russia in the CIS. Abkhazia had quite justifiable fears of losing the initial advantage they gained by inclusion of any other external player into the PKF contingent who may not necessarily have such a benevolent attitude towards them as Russia. For its part, Russia was also concerned with retaining control at its southern borders and not letting any outside power enter its spheres of influence.

The issue of fulfillment of the mandated tasks remained the key controversy with the CIS peacekeepers. Apart from keeping de facto peace, the most important part of their mandate – facilitation of peaceful return to refugees and peace-building efforts – failed to be properly executed. Although there had not been any significant military activities in the region since the deployment of the peacekeepers (barring the unsuccessful assault of Abkhazians forces in 1998 in the Gali region), the PKF continued to serve merely as a conflict separator between the two sides.

The real problem was that the military command of the nominally multinational intervention force undertook the task it was either unable or unwilling to achieve out of the wish to appease the both sides of this zero-sum gain. Since in the minds of Georgia and Abkhazia the only possible outcomes of the conflict were diametrically opposing: unification of Abkhazia for the former and separation from Georgia for the latter, tasking the intervener with enforcing such mutually excluding options upon the belligerents, was initially doomed to failure. The CIS forces failed to reach their main goal and establish favorable political climate for safe relocation of forcefully displaced people, which means failure to successfully fulfill their mandate and objectives.

This volatile state of a self-proclaimed and unrecognized republic in Abkhazia continued until August 2008, when military activities resumed in South Ossetia by military intervention of Russia. Abkhazian forces were in full mobilization along the Inguri River during the Ossetian conflict and feared no retaliation since Georgia was clearly not in position to wage a war on two fronts simultaneously. Seeing the successful advancement of the Russian troops in South Ossetia and knowing that Georgians would be preoccupied with buffering these attacks, Abkhazian military units seized this window of opportunity and launched an offensive on the Georgian troops located in Upper Kodori and soon occupied the whole region. Not long after the secession of hostilities in South Ossetia Russia legally institutionalized the results of its intervention by officially recognizing South Ossetia and Abkhazia as new independent countries and members of the international community of states. In this sense the resumption of military actions in Abkhazia was a by-product and a direct consequence of the war in South Ossetia. Currently Abkhazia is strengthening their political gains by seeking further military assistance from Russia: its navy military base is being built in Abkhazia; its frontier guards are controlling the borders of a new independent state and communication facilities, including railroad network and ports are handed over to Russia.[31]

Analysis of the Interventions

The Abkhazian conflict is still far from being settled for all the parties concerned. Abkhazia will continue its strife for becoming a full-fledged member of the international community or inclusion into the Russian Federation. Georgia will continue to appeal to the world community and use international legal norms of state sovereignty and infallibility of state borders to make the international actors force Russia to renounce its decision to acknowledge Abkhazian sovereignty. For its part, Russia will also use same international frameworks but of different nature – the right of nations for self-determination, the need for humanitarian interventions and its obligation "to protect the rights, freedoms and legal interests of the Russian citizens living in Abkhazia…"[32] – to make the most of the situation and to institutionalize their initial gains.

What were its objectives of Russia during its first "intervention for the same of intervention"? Why was it not capable of fulfilling its tasks? Why did the CIS peacekeeping forces fail? The issue of failure of its first intervention of Russia has a number of components to be diligently scrutinized. The role of Russia in Abkhazian conflict before 2008 was quite equivocal and less publicized. After the dissolution of the Soviet Union Russia remained vitally interested in political developments in the post-Soviet space and tried to retain its primus *inter pares*

31 *Abkhazia Vrememnno Peredast Rossii Jeleznuyu Dorogu i Aeroport* [Abkhazia will temporarily transfer railroads and airport to Russia]. 2008. Gazeta.ru News Agency. May 15 [Online]. Available at: http://www.gazeta.ru/news/business/2009/05/15/n_1362210.shtml [accessed: May 16, 2009].

32 Soobshenie Dlya SMI. O Porucheniyax Presidenta Rossii Pravitelstvy Rossiiskoi Federacii v Otnoshenii Abkhazii I Yujnoi Osetii. 2008. (#501-16-04-2008), Moskva, MID [Information for Mass Media. About Decrees of the President of Russia to the Government of the Russian Federation in relation to Abkhazia and South Ossetia (#501-16-04-2008), Moscow, Ministry of Foreign Affairs] [Online]. Available at: http://www.mid.ru/brp_4.nsf/sps/FD56A80A7198CD7CC325742D003F807C [accessed: May 7, 2009].

role in the CIS to influence politics of the former Soviet Republics. Initially with the under Gamsakhurdian nationalist policies Georgia abstained from having close connections with Russia: the stigma of 1989, when the Soviet (or Russian) troops crushed anti-governmental demonstration in Tbilisi causing the death of 15 teenagers and elderly was still very vivid. At some point in the midst of the war with South Ossetia Gamsakhurdia even declared economic embargo on Russia. With the ascent to power of police general and ex-Soviet foreign minister Shevardnadze, Russia was hoping to make the Georgian leadership more placate and susceptible to its influence.

What Russia could not do was to let Abkhazians be defeated by Georgians, which would place it in a very uneasy, in the best case, position in relation to the nations of the Northern Caucasus whose kin the Abkhazians were. At the early 1990s Russia itself suffered much from secessionist and ethnic conflicts between own ethnic minorities and occupying the North Caucasus and predominantly bordering Georgia (for instance, the wars in Chechnya and the conflict in the North Ossetian). Without direct ethnic ties with Abkhazians (unlike South Ossetians who have their kin in North Ossetia), Russia became, in the words of Jenne (1990), their "surrogate lobby state"[33] – an external patron not by ethnic links but, rather, by political and economic interests. By allowing the North Caucasian volunteers to help their alleged brethren in Georgia, Russia, thus, redirected its own domestic unrest and quenched dissatisfaction thus acquiring in the eyes of its North Caucasian nations the image of a protector of their kin.

In essence, Russian actions were directed at severing Abkhazia from Georgia. By not closing its borders with Abkhazia, by letting mercenaries from its territories, including both paramilitaries and hired regulars from the Russian army fight with the Georgian troops, by supplying arms and ammunitions to Abkhazian rebels, Russia aimed to achieve separation of Abkhazia. At the same time, Russia wanted to keep good relations with Georgia by publicly supporting infallibility of its borders and providing military equipment from its bases.

As a result of such a bifurcate logic behind Russian behavior in relation to Georgians and Abkhazians, Russia failed to satisfy the aspirations of both sides: the quest of Abkhazia for own statehood or entity within Russia, and the desire of Georgia to keep its territory intact. Moreover, it failed to achieve its own goals of interventions because of bipartite support born out of unclear intervention aims.

Historically, Russia had strong ties with the Georgian nation. Many Georgians were prominent political and military leaders of Russia/Soviet Union nearly at all times. Even after the independence, there had always been good connections between the "young" Russian and Georgian military. Russia, according to its leadership, kept strong neutrality in the conflict, but, as dubious as it may sound, Zverev postulates this Janus-faced Russian behavior of early 1990s: "…(although it was in line with a consistent Russian policy of supplying both sides in a

33 Jenne, E.K. 1990. A Bargaining Theory of Minority Demands: Explaining the Dog that Didn't Bite in 1990 Yugoslavia, *International Studies Quarterly*, 48(4), 748.

conflict), at a time when Russian-supplied warplanes were bombing Georgian-held Sukhumi, other Russian units continued to supply the Georgian Army."[34] Abkhazians and Georgians alike had large caches of arms and ammunition for long-lasting confrontation even before the start of the conflict, and only place they could get these arms were the Soviet/Russian military bases located in Georgia and Abkhazia.

Together with military support, Abkhazians and Georgians received completely different and diametrically opposed commitments from Russia. The official position of Russia has been to support the territorial integrity of Georgia. While acknowledging participation of some non-state actors and irregulars from the territory of the Russian Northern Caucasus in the conflict, according to Pryaxin, "...the official position of Russia did not allow for any deviations from the principal line of respect for sovereignty and territorial integrity of the friendly Georgian state."[35] At the same time, Abkhazians were constantly receiving indications of the Russia's will to protect its Abkhazians and its fellow-citizens. Even if Russia wanted to establish its presence in the conflict zone, have a say in the domestic affairs of the country, and keeping its role as (at least) a regional power, it did it with no specific agenda and no actual steps towards decisive end of the conflict. Russia failed both to submit Georgia to its will and to institutionalize Abkhazia's independence because of the lack of pure political will.

The main problem of imposition of the conflict resolution options on the belligerents was absence of clear policy goals and identity crisis within Russia. The country was undergoing immense transformation after the collapse of the Soviet Union, which resulted in a struggle between the new democratic forces and the old totalitarian elements. The conflict coincided with the time when reactionist forces occupied the Russian White House and the future of the democracy in the country was seriously jeopardized. Under such circumstances, controlling separate military regiments, the heads of which could quite successfully launch their own mini-wars, was quite difficult. Russia, which had a difficult time of keeping control over its political establishment, failed to act decisively and preferred no-war-no-peace to an actual solution of the conflict. All of these led to absence of clear self-interests, hence foggy self-benefits, and an oxymoronic wish to satisfy all parties, which put Russia in quite an awkward position, very correctly pointed out by Zverev in the following description: "Throughout 1992 and 1993, Russia had no single policy with regard to the Georgian-Abkhaz conflict. It was not clear which would best suit Russian interests – to see Georgia strong and united or weak and dismembered."[36]

---

34 Zverev, A. 1996. Ethnic Conflicts in the Caucasus 1988-1994, in *Contested Borders in The Caucasus*, edited by B. Coppieters. Brussels: Vubpress [Online]. Available at: http://poli.vub.ac.be/publi/ContBorders/eng/ [accessed: May 7, 2009].

35 Pryaxin, V.F. 2002, 138.

36 Zverev, A. 1996.

Indecisiveness and unclear intervention strategies led to low level of engagement of Russia in the conflict. This was, in a sense, an intervention for the sake of intervention: Russia had not used its regular military regiments, or deployed large numbers of troops and military equipment, or widely engaged diverse types of military (land, air, and navy). No large-scale regular military force was used to bring victory to Abkhazia institutionalizing its independence. Low intervention commitment to itself and absence of clear political will led to lukewarm actions engaged fewest resources possible. The intervention tools were limited to economic support in the form of transfer of weapons, ammunition, allowing the flow of goods across its border, irregular military support in the forms of Russian soldiers fighting on Abkhazians side and free movement of mercenaries from its southern regions to Abkhazia.

With its presence in and support to Abkhazia, Russia contributed to a longer confrontation. Increase of military powers of the minority group, from a moral perspective, protects it from punitive actions of the majority. However, from the longer-term viewpoint, it extends the conflict by bringing in additional forces of a third party and imposing such a situation where neither of the sides is able to reach a decisive victory. In Abkhazia, successful support to the minority meant establishing a new geopolitical environment for the target country, where the minority would receive either concessions from the central government, or secede from it and create its own state or join another state. On the other hand, successful support to the majority government would likely mean a more moderate solution of incorporating the minority into the existing state, out of the general protectionist policies of the Soviet Union/Russia aiming at supporting the rights of smaller ethnic groups.

Another important point in the negative role of the minority support is difficulty of institutionalization of the conflict outcomes. In case a third party aides the majority government, not only the conflict may last considerably shorter, but also the third-party presence and its results can be easier institutionalized through agreements and treaties. Whenever a third party directs its support to the target government, this usually done, as Regan also claimed earlier, in a open fashion, and third-party troops are legalized and institutionalized on the territory of the target country, usually on the basis of bilateral agreements (as it was the case of the French interventions in Chad). In Abkhazia, this was absent and the most important political treaty after the end of the Soviet Union that Georgia concluded with the Russian presence was the CIS membership agreement.

With all these uncertain political moves Russia was considered by Georgia as an aggressor and occupier, which put additional pressure of Russia to pursue its objectives in the region. Even though Russia gave indiscriminately its citizenship to Abkhazian population, these actions clearly directed towards institutional dominance, were unsuccessful for almost fifteen years. Eventually, foreign policy vagueness of early 1990s in Russia took the form of a neutral peacekeeping, which molded the faint "just-to-be-there" interests of Russia with fear for chain reaction at home and bitterness of its elites into endless, weary and unsuccessful peacekeeping benefiting no one. However, neither multilateral intervention orchestrated and performed solely by Russia managed to achieve its objectives.

With the CIS intervention, Russia tried to institutionalize its presence in Abkhazian conflict. Being unilateral in form, the PKF had to impose the options of the sole player upon the belligerents, leading the side that benefited less from imposed arrangements view mistrust the interveners. The CIS as an organization, and corresponding operations of its peacekeeping forces were heavily influenced by Russia. This was evident in the decision of the Heads of CIS states, who abstained from sending their troops, thus acknowledging the Russian domain in the matter of resolution of the Abkhazian conflict. For instance, Kazakhstan, Kyrgyzstan and Tajikistan promised to send only observers, while Belarus and Armenia signed the agreement with the proviso that they will consider their participation in the course of future negotiations with the conflicting parties. Apart from purely organizational problems, none of the CIS state operationally shared the composition burden of the peacekeeping force, leaving Russia the only decision-maker and actor without any real international monitoring over its operations.

This fact, together with previous Russian participation on the side of Abkhazians, meant that the Georgian side failed to see this organization as an effective mediator. At first, it may seem that the CIS participation in conflict resolution would be quite fruitful for all parties, and that Russia, as the main actor on the ex-Soviet political stage, would be acceptable to both of the belligerents as a mediator able to keep peace, and, in future, to restore a political settlement acceptable for all. For Abkhazians, "official" Russian involvement would gave the blessing to their previous actions, since they received official support from the Russian Federation in the form of its governmental military forces stationed there, instead of some unidentifiable non-state paramilitaries. For Georgians, too, presence of Russia in CIS was acceptable at first, as it was officially supporting Georgia's territorial integrity, which meant the end of further losses and a possibility for retaining their land.

As the time went by, Georgia became strengthened in its belief that there were two Russias involved in the CIS. The one officially supported territorial integrity of the country in accordance with the international legal standards, peaceful settlement of the conflict, including facilitation of return of the refugees as envisaged in the mandate of multilateral intervention. The other accused Georgia of violations of peace process, sent its regional and federal delegations to officially meet Abkhazian representatives, at all international meetings lobbied for Abkhazian interests and only in few occasions fulfilled the CIS mandate, although completely ineffectively.

This was due to dubious position of Russia towards the conflict settlement, which substantially influenced operations of the CIS peacekeepers, who were receiving sometimes directly contradictory orders from Moscow that were in violation of their mandates and impeded their actions on the ground. A clear example of such inconsistencies of the Russian approaches to peacekeeping, in general, and the specific activities of its peacekeepers, would be an incident in

September 1994, when the Russian deputy defense minister Kondratev, visiting the dislocations of the troops in Abkhazia, ordered peacekeepers to direct fulfill the part of the mandate on return of the refugees by "forceful rebuffing anybody who tries to hinder this."[37] The protesting Abkhazian militia in the Gali district was surrounded and ordered to disarm. The peacekeepers also closed the access routes to Gali to prevent main Abkhazian troops from entering the district. This decision was immediately overruled by Russian defense minister Pavel Grachev, who flew from Moscow on the order of Yeltsin to stop these actions of peacekeepers.

Among the indications of Russia's bias toward Abkhaz were indiscriminate issuing of Russian citizenships to the population of Abkhazia and in all occasions "implying" the need for protection its citizens on the territories of other states by all means; constantly blaming Georgia in all skirmishes in the conflict regions; and trying to use the fact of Kosovo independence as an international legal precedent for solution of other secessionist conflicts (here – Abkhazia and South Ossetia). Such duality of approaches and one-sided actions greatly undermined trust of Georgia to the neutrality both of the CIS peacekeeping mission. On a number of occasions, Georgians have accused the PKF of failing to fulfill its mandate, since the return of the approximately 250,000 Georgians displaced from Abkhazia has not been achieved. They see Russia, particularly, its military, continuing the general line of supporting Abkhazian cause, and therefore as unfit to act as an impartial peacekeeper. The Georgian side also complained that, with passage of time, status quo strengthened Abkhazian territorial gains and made the refugees psychologically accustomed to permanent exile.

This reasoning gets to the heart of the problem with the CIS forces and its mandate – reliance on a single actor in allegedly multinational operations. Russian sole presence in the PKF meant lack of control from the side of the CIS – the organization mandating the mission – over the activities of its peacekeepers on the ground. In an impartial multilateral intervention, bias (if any) towards conflicting sides is shared by the member-states of a coalition, thus being internationalized and institutionalized within organizational frameworks. This makes it easier for the intervener to force belligerents to accept the offered options. With the CIS PKF, bias was only de-jure institutionalized. In reality it remained largely unilateral, antagonizing Georgia against Russia, and CIS, as a whole and creating gloomy future for the organization per se.

From operational perspective, the military capacities of Russia, as a regional superpower within the CIS scale, surpassed those of any other CIS state, alone or even collectively, which made it easier for this state to impose any solution onto the belligerent parties. Instead of acting impartially and fulfilling the terms of its

37 Sokolov, A.V. 1997. *Mirotvorcheskaya Aktivnost I Mirotvorcheskie Sili Rossii v SNG* [Peacekeeping and Peacekeeping forces of Russia in CIS], in *Restructuring the Global Military Sector, Volume 1: New Wars*, edited by M. Kaldor and B. Vashee. London and Washington: Pinter [Online]. Available at: http://www.memo.ru/hr/hotpoints/peace/chapter1.htm [accessed: May 7, 2009].

mandate, the PKF took clearly one-sided stance towards the conflicting parties, which reflected negatively on its ability to perform its functions. Failure to fulfill the paragraph of the mandate on return of the refugees put the PKF in an absolute and unsolvable quandary. The fact that Russia was the only real participant in these peacekeeping forces, and repeatedly blocked other countries' participation in it (be it the UN peacekeepers or, for instance, Ukraine, a CIS member, which is famous for its ties with Georgia and the West) sent a clear message to Georgians: first, that Russia was not committed to preserving Georgian state borders, and second, that CIS peacekeepers were there simply as window dressing for Russian interests.

As a result, the PKF failed to effectively assure the Georgians of its neutrality and impartiality, because for the Georgians the peacekeeping forces were formed exclusively by the military of the country that was blamed for their loss in the war. The problem with unilateral composition of multilateral force was further aggravated by the nature of the intervener present. Russia, being accused by Georgia in participation in the conflict on Abkhazian side, was also accused of biasness in its multilateral operations. At the same time, it was indeed a former unilateral actor vitally interested in a specific outcome that would suit its own best interests. Presence of a former unilateral player in multilateral coalition, even composed of many member-states, jeopardized its impartiality and efficiency of performing of its tasks. In Abkhazia the situation was even more difficult since the multilateral intervention was composed by one state who previously participated in military actions against the target government agreeing on deployment of this multilateral force. This greatly undermined the image of multilateralism. For Georgians it became increasingly clear that the options, solutions and actions offered by the peacekeepers were framed in accordance with previous intervention agenda of Russia.

The CIS peacekeepers had not only failed to fulfill their mandate, but also had no success in articulating the mandate per se. The PKF, acting as a "buffer zone" between the Georgian and Abkhazian troops, failed to fulfill the main aim of their presence: peace-building with assistance to return of the refugees and facilitation of peaceful reconstruction processes. The issue here was not that this particular task was difficult, but that there was not enough will and commitment on the part of Russia, as the one and only figure of the multinational intervention to fulfill it. Instead of engaging in fulfilling the intervention mandate, Russia used CIS peacekeepers as a tool of its influence on the situation in Georgia proper.

Conclusions

The two interventions conducted during the course of the conflict were in fact one continuous intervention by a single third party, where the first was clandestine, unofficial and irregular, and the second open, public, more or less official, multinational in form but unilateral in practice. Neither of these interventions managed to reach their goals: the first one was indecisive, clumsy, irresolute and largely a function of the messy transition of a powerful state, which wanted to have a say in the politics of its neighbor. The second intervention – seemingly ambitions – failed to build the needed trust of all sides because of its inability to perform its mandated tasks. As a CIS peacekeeper, Russia fell short of assuring Georgia of its neutrality and impartiality, facilitation of the return of the refugees and overall, assisting in unification of Abkhazia – as it was the wish of Georgia supported by official Russian statements on territorial integrity of the former.

The cause of these two failures was vague intervention agendas, the "fake" nature of the multinational force preformed by one actor, which had participated in previous external actions and consideration of the problem from the prism of domestic politics, which created considerable credible commitment problem. As a result, Russia had entrapped itself in the cobweb of building unfulfilled commitment to Abkhazians for more than a decade. Its subsequent acknowledgement of independence of Abkhazia in 2008 cannot be accounted for success of its actions in early 1990s: the main point is differences in time and Russian foreign and domestic policy, which became more robust and focused on its vital national interest, which developed into actions domestically aimed at consolidation of "vertical of power" and on international level directed towards restoring superpower status and competing with the leading international actors in pursuing its policy goals.

Chapter 5

Somalia (1991-1994): When Force Fails

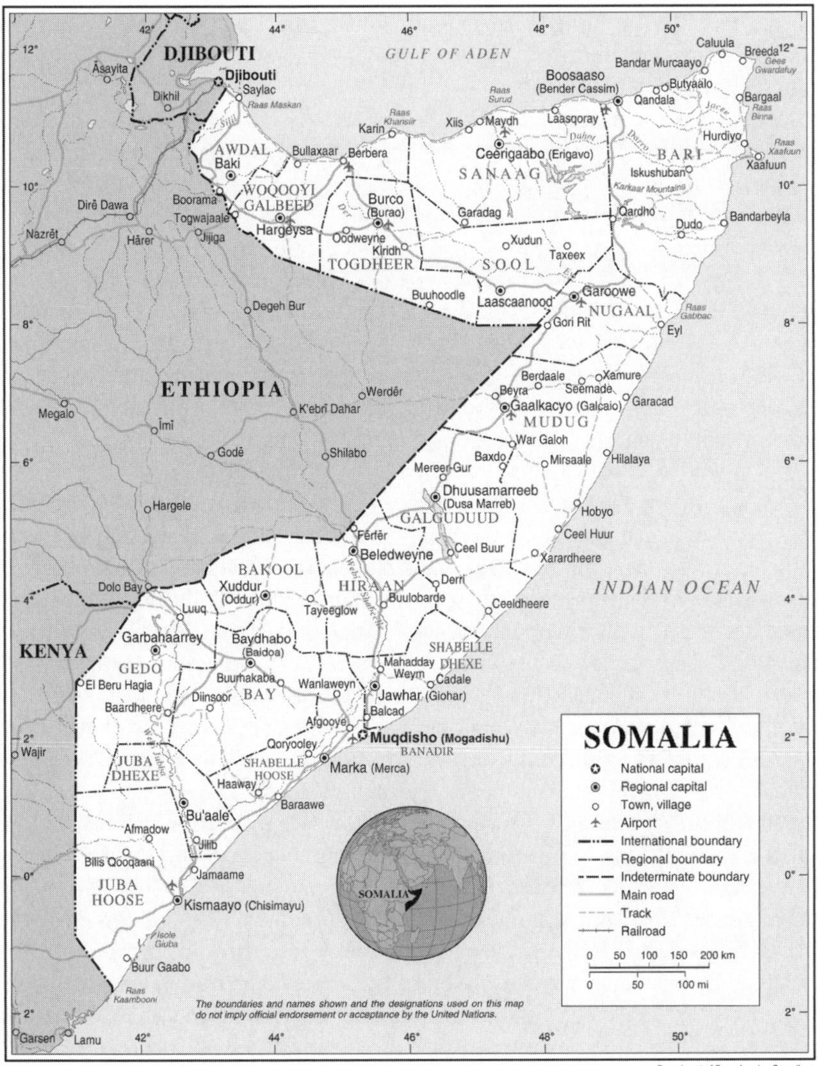

Map No. 3690 Rev. 7 UNITED NATIONS
January 2007

Department of Peacekeeping Operations
Cartographic Section

Map 5.1 Map of Somalia

Source: Reprinted with permission of the UN Cartographic Section.

The conflict in Somalia was born out of a mixture of tensions of oxymoronic identity dualities deeply rooted in the history of the country: common ethnicity versus powerful clan-based cleavages; self-determination of identity groups versus their strong urge for integrity of statehood; history of colonial and post-colonial multiple interests versus present international indifference. The resulting conflict was framed by a power-struggle between mutually antagonistic clan-led groups with own loyalties driven by a common wish for a unified country. Starting from the early 1990s, Somalia remains a "failed state" with the lowest levels of social, economic and political indicators in the world and remains one of its most dangerous and volatile places.

Somalia was one of the first tests of post-Cold War institutional multilateralism – joint interventions of states under the aegis of intergovernmental organization in domestic affairs of a conflict-torn country. The conflict erupted during the rapidly changing international world order where the major players, including intergovernmental organization, were at a considerable limbo about the future fate of the ex-bipolar world. In Somalia post-Cold War intervention, perhaps, for the first time was not tainted with ideological rivalry between communist and capitalist blocks and, as it seemed, would have been, thus, more efficient. Unlike majority of the Cold War interventions where the belligerent groups were aided on the basis of their ideological affiliations with the third parties, early 1990s interventions were devoid of such ideological implications.

The Somalian case was also representative of one of the few instances of intervention where the third-parties were clearly neutral without any apparent or hidden own agendas and self-interests. Two interventions in the country were conducted by the same multilateral organization – United Nations. While the first mission, UNOSOM I, was successful from the point of view of fulfilling its mandate-defined agendas (monitoring over the implementation of the ceasefire agreement provisions and supporting reconciliation efforts between numerous warring clans), the second one, UNOSOM II, failed to reach its goals (peace-enforcement, post-conflict reconstruction and state-building). To understand the causes of successes and failures of interventions it is necessary to immerge deep into domestic Somalian inter-clan environment, interaction between sub-clans, popular support these clans enjoyed and the structure of the Somalian nation, which were in the heart of the conflict and which largely stipulated corresponding outcomes for the interveners.

Evaluation of successes and failures of interventions in Somalia becomes a relatively straightforward task due to a number of reasons. First and foremost, the goals and agendas of UN peacekeeping missions are easily identifiable in their corresponding mandates, which were open, transparent and responded to any field contingencies by subsequent mandate amendments. And, second, the fact that the nature and identity of the intervener were the identical in both cases, UN, allows to have control over a whole number of factors pertinent to the character of the third party (for instance, their method of internal decision making, the power of interveners vis-à-vis the target state, geopolitical considerations, relationships between the interveners and the belligerents, and many more).

Conflict Background

Population of Somalia represents an ethnically homogenous group: all Somalis, being Muslims, consider themselves to be descendants of the mythical Samaal, after whom the country was named. With the arrival of two (also mythical) warlords Sheikh Daarood and Sheikh Isahaaq, the two principal clans named after these leaders were created. The feeling of belonging to one ethnos is very strong among the Somalis, who, in the words of Laitin and Samatar (1987), have "...a sense of common national identity...", possess common territory, "...common language universally spoken and understood...a way of life, that is predominantly pastoral, a shared poetic corpus; a common political culture; a profound Islamic heritage; and a deeply held belief that nearly all Somalis descend from the same source..."[1] The notion of division, difference, and specific and conflicting identities is virtually absent in Somalis' mentality.

The paradox with the Somalian society with all, at first glance, ethnic unity and homogeneity, is its high fragmentation and division along clan and sub-clan identities, which lie in the heart of all the past and present conflicts. A typical Somali citizen "...gives political allegiance first to his/her immediate family, then to his immediate lineage, then to the clan of his lineage, then to a clan-family that embraces several clans, including his own, and ultimately to the nation that itself consists of a confederacy of clan-families."[2] These clan-based cleavages serve as a crucial factor in understanding the origins and nature of power struggle in the country.

Located at the commercial and cultural crossroads between the West and the East along the Gulf of Aden and the Indian Ocean, facing the Arabian Peninsula, Somalia attracted outside actors for its strategic location, and not natural resources or any other land-based wealth. Unlike majority of other African countries, which had generally one colonial occupier, Somalian colonial history was characterized by abundance of foreign powers controlling different parts of the country: the British North-Central part; French East and Southeast territories (modern Djibouti); Italian Southern Somaliland; Kenyan NFD (Northern Frontier District); and Ethiopian Ogaadeen region. Traditionally, Ogaadeen was the most sensitive geographic area for the Somali nationalism: with its predominantly Somalian population, it has long been a central issue of confrontation between Ethiopia and Somalia. For the short period, it was "united" with Somalia proper under the Italian administration, but after the WW II was returned to Ethiopia upon request of the latter.

The path to independence in Somalia started, as in many ex-colonial nations, with an increased sense of national consciousness and, in such a divided country, a collective quest for unification of all Somali people, which lead to creation of political parties almost exclusively based on clan membership. Such "political

1 Laitin, D.D. and Samatar, S.S. 1987. *Somalia: Nation in Search of a State.* Boulder, Colorado: Westview Press, 21.

2 Laitin, D.D. and Samatar, S.S. 1987. 30-31.

clanization" was also one of the determinants of future polarization of clan-based rivalries. The first and the only non-clan-based political movement to appear with the permission of the Italian colonial administration was the Somali Youth Club, created by young educated Somalis in 1943 and later transformed into the Somali Youth League (SYL) with the aim of unifying all Somali territories and opposing clan-based rule. In contrast to SYL, another major southern party, the HDM (Hisbia Digil Mirifle), represented two clans of Digil and Mirifle and enjoyed financial support from the Italians to balance SYL. Other parties were also clan-associated: the SNL (Somali National League, the Isaaq clan-family), USP (United Somali Party, the Dir and Daarood clan-families), and the NUF (National United Front).

Immediately after its independence on July 1, 1960, problems of combining the former colonial entities in one state appeared. The Italian and British Somalian lands, according to Contini (1969), had "...different judicial systems; different currencies, different organizations and conditions for service for the army, the police and civil servants...The governmental institutions, both at the central and local levels, were differently organized and had different powers; the systems and rates of taxation and customs were different, and so were the educational systems."[3] The southern territories were much better developed under the Italian administration than the British North, which led to possession of key administrative posts in nearly all the governmental branches by better-educated representatives of the southern clans and marginalization of the northern clans in the new state.

The inter-clan rivalry continued after the independence of Somalia. In the 1967 presidential elections, former Prime Minister Abdirasdiid Shermaarke (from the Daarood clan) was elected president of the country with strong support of the SYL. Other factions, divided along clan lines, began accusing government of political fraud, nepotism, protectionism, and corruption. Tensions grew, and in October 1969 Shermaarke was assassinated. The military seized power and major-general Siyaad Barre became the Head of the SRC (Supreme Revolutionary Council). Initially, Barre took a democratic stance in his governance – abolishing clan-based parties and aiming at ending tribalism and clan-based political decision-making. However, himself not being free from his clan baggage, Barre, as a typical Somalian, paid particular tribute to his own clan (Mareehaan), his mother's clan (Ogaadeen), and his son-in-law's clan (Dulbahante), popularly known as "MOD".

Unable to settle domestic problems internally, Barre tried to move the popular attention away from inter-clan rivalry to a common international matter that would amalgamate the Somalian society – the war. Unsuccessful confrontation with Ethiopia in 1977-1978 for unification of Ogaadeen, in which Somalia lost due to the fickle support of the Soviet Union and Cuba, was a crucial factor in understanding subsequent fall of Barre's regime and the resulting civil war. Domestic situation deteriorated soon after the loss in the war, further undermining the faith of Somalis in a unified country. The defeat in Ogaadeen rendered unrecoverable blow to Barre:

3 Contini, P. 1969. *The Somali Republic: An Experiment in Legal Integration*. London: Frank Cass, 11.

in the eyes of common Somalis, it was not the country that had lost, but Barre's MOD had, which was blamed by majority of other clans for poor performance in Ogaadeen. Probably the most dissatisfied with the war was the Ogaadeen clan itself, which more than others had serious grievances against Barre for the defeat and for "selling out" country's interests in negotiating a subsequent peace treaty.

Unsuccessful military campaign in Ogaadeen led to creation of political and, unsurprisingly, clan-based opposition to Barre's regime. After the failed coup d'etat organized by the Majeerteen officers in 1978, the anti-governmental SSDF (Somali Salvation Democratic Front) was set up. The SNM (Somali National Movement) was formed by the Isaaqs in London in 1981 with the same agenda – to overthrow Barre. The Hawiye clan formed its own political movement – USC (United Somali Congress), which closely cooperated with the SNM in the North. The South was controlled by the SMP (Somali Patriotic Movement). Other lesser political organizations included the SDM (Somali Democratic Movement, Rahanwayn clan) and the SDA (Somali Democratic Alliance, Gadabursi clan). The common enemy temporarily united the opposition clans in the interest of changing the regime and decreased their inter-clan confrontation, which was, paradoxically, the aim of Barre at first place when starting the war. Demonstrations and pubic unrest sponsored by these movements soon spread all over Somalia, forcing Barre to flee the country in January 1991.

Chronic failure to consolidate the society by any ruler through effective power-sharing mechanisms among clans became clear soon after creation of the provisional government. The fault in this case was not even along clan-family lines, but rather within single clans. The warlords were pursuing the policy of all against all with unclear political agendas and vague political representation. The resulting domestic anarchy was not only on the central, but also regional, levels, where clan loyalties were clashing, as well.

It was the inability to reach consent even on sub-clan level and to mollify potentially belligerent groups that caused the country to collapse. In May 1991 the ruling SNM proclaimed the independent Republic of Somaliland, which until now remains as recognized internationally. Another self-administered part of the country is Puntland, located in the north-east part of Somalia, which does not aspire for independent statehood, but wants regional self-administration. Finally, the SPM (Somali Patriotic Movement) created its own de facto state under the name of Jubaland in the southwest.

It did not take long after the fall of Barre that the military clashes between clans and sub-clans started. USC tried to form the central government, which was against the interests of the other clan-families. Although the new government tried to incorporate within its ranks representatives from the main clan-families (president Ali Mahdi Mahammad was a Hawiye and Prime Minister Umar Arteh Ghalib – an Isaaq), other clan-families and their corresponding sub-clans considered themselves to be marginalized in this power-struggle. Some of them, such as the SSDF and the SMP, temporarily aligned themselves against USC.

The conflict started in September 1991. The worst fight occurred between the members of the same clan-family, Hawiye, which was instrumental to the overthrow of Barre's regime. Former General Mahammad Faarah Aideed (a Habar Gidir sub-clan) declared his opposition to the rule of President Ali Mahdi Mahammad (an Abgal sub-clan) and created his own faction within USC. In November 1990 Aidid, on behalf of his group, signed an agreement with the SNM and the SPM to unify military operations against Barre. However, the real issue behind the inter-clan confrontation was the fact that the leaders of Abgaal sub-clan were considered by others as outsiders in the fight against Barre or, as Metz (1992) calls them, "upstarts trying to usurp control of the opposition movement,"[4] and now being "undeservedly" in power.

The situation reached a deadlock when Aideed formed his own provisional government opposed to that of Mohammad's in the southern part of the capital of Mogadishu. This move defined the future battlefield, a single city, and divided it into two parts. Troops loyal to Mahammad controlled the north of Mogadishu, while the south remained in the hands of Aideed. Neither of them was able to decisively win the war or even to effectively control the territory it held. By the end of March 1992, according to some estimates, 250,000 people had been killed. Additionally, 500,000 became refugees in Ethiopia, 300,000 in Kenya, 65,000 in Yemen, 15,000 in Djibouti, and about 100,000 in Europe.[5] Additionally, around 300,000 people died and 1.5-2 million people became internally displaced as a result of the famine in 1992.[6]

UN Intervention (UNOSOM I)

Right from the onset of the conflict the situation in Somalia drew international attention as a local humanitarian catastrophe and a regional hot spot. Although humanitarian relief workers had long been active in the country, efficiency of their work, which was limited mainly to distribution of food supplies and medicines, was much undermined by different armed groups who controlled distribution channels and extorted money or in-kind contributions from the humanitarian agencies willing to pay the paramilitaries but still provide help.

From the very beginning of the conflict the fate of the people suffering from unrest in Somalia has entered the domestic political discourse of major

---

4 Somalia: A Country Study, Federal Research Division, Library of Congress, 1992, edited by H.C. Metz [Online]. Available at: http://www.country-data.com/frd/cs/sotoc.html [accessed: May 7, 2009].

5 Somalia: A Country Study, Federal Research Division, Library of Congress, 1992.

6 van Beurden, J. 2000. Somalia: From Permanent Conflict to More Peacefulness? Searching the Peace in Africa, European Center for Conflict Prevention. European Center for Conflict Prevention [Online]. Available at: www.conflict-prevention.net [accessed: May 7, 2009].

international players. The time was especially noticeable: the international system was undergoing rapid transformation from bipolarity into something else; Russia was undergoing rapid and painful transformation after the dissolution of USSR; a new figure, Boutros Boutros Ghali, was to lead UN, which was overwhelmed with preserving the international system after its sudden and unexpected mutation. Important changes were also underway in US: the term of the Bush administration was coming to an end and a future US President – Clinton – was to enter the office. Gilkes (1993) describes how the issue of Somalia became a cornerstone of domestic politics in US: "Candidate Bill Clinton seized on the issue as evidence of President Bush's failures in foreign policy…The decision [to intervene] came too late to influence US election results, but it suggested that Bush believed that US can and should intervene at will."[7] Such "domestication" of the international conflict put additional pressure on UN Security Council which was used as a tool of the first test of US actions outside its borders.

From the beginning of the conflict, UN was closely monitoring the situation on the ground. When the death toll reached the point where it could no longer be ignored by the international community, UN Security Council with its Resolution 733 appointed Mohammed Sahnoun as resident coordinator to oversee humanitarian activities and negotiate a ceasefire with the belligerents. The resolution also established a "general and complete embargo" on weaponry and military equipment to all the conflicting sides.[8] Subsequent deployment of UN peacekeeping mission was done mainly under pressure from US administration, which was eager to take a more active role in the world politics after the end of the Cold War. Sahnoun's task was to organize the peace process under extremely difficult settings in Somalia with no central authority and constantly changing political and military conditions. Special attention was to be paid to the role of elders, who represented historically developed way of conflict resolution in the Somalian society. At the same time, Sahnoun was negotiating an agreement with quasi-independent Somaliland and bringing together the belligerents in Mogadishu to reach reconciliation with Ethiopia in order to avoid further complications in the Ogaadeen region.

In less than six months, Sahnoun managed to establish good working relations with the both sides of the conflict and the local population, especially with the elders. Sahnoun was a proponent of an incremental approach to conflict resolution and advocated for an increased involvement of the local communities in bringing the belligerents to negotiation table. It was due to his action that the first agreement was reached between Aideed and Ali Mahdi, which was signed on March 3, 1992. The "Agreement on the Implementation of a Ceasefire" also included the acceptance of a United Nations security component for convoys of humanitarian

7 Gilkes, P. 1993. From Peace-Keeping to Peace Enforcement: The Somalia Precedent. *Middle East Reporter, Despots and Democrats Political Change in Arabia*, 185, 22.

8 The UN Security Council Resolution #733. 1992, New York. [Online]. Available at: http://www.un.org/documents/sc/res/1992/scres92.htm [accessed: May 7, 2009].

assistance and the initial "deployment of 20 military observers on each side of Mogadishu to monitor the ceasefire."[9]

The real problem in successful enactment of this and further agreements was deeply rooted in antagonism on a personal level between Aideed and Ali Mahdi, who viewed any possible developments within the context of their own rivalry. For instance, for Aideed, according to Drysdale (1997), "Mahdi's agreement to the deployment of UN military observers…and…UN support for Mahdi's unilateral appeal for the deployment of foreign troops in Mogadishu…[meant] formal UN backing for Mahdi as interim president, real or imagined, [and] was enough to ensure that Aideed's further cooperation with UN would require exceptional diplomatic skills."[10] The reason was that Aideed considered himself alone responsible for the victory over Siyaad Barre, and any real or imagined cooperation of any of the remaining groups with UN meant diminishing his role as a liberator of Somalia, which he was not going to yield either to Ali Mahdi or UN.

Initially, the agreement was largely respected. However, the causes for confrontation essentially remained unchallenged: absence of a uniform government and lack of enforceability of any outcome upon any belligerent parties. Neither Aideed nor Ali Mahdi was ready for political compromise and none was able to impose his will over his opponent. As a result, Mogadishu remained divided into several parts controlled by warlords from different sub-clans subordinate to the two rival figures. Food, as before the ceasefire agreement, was largely used as a weapon by the paramilitaries from different camps who frequently looted the aid supplies and interfered in the operations of international relief agencies on the grounds that they were providing assistance to their enemies.

On the side of UN, the peacemaking process was also impeded by the internal organizational management mismatch. Sahnoun's incremental approach toward building trust among the key stakeholders of the Somali nation and careful actions adapted to the local environment were not favored in UN headquarters. The Security Council, under pressure from US administration and several other member-states, who wanted to score a success in Somalia and who argued for immediate and forceful intervention with the purpose of alleviation of human suffering, led UN into another stage: active involvement in peace-building. UN, in the words of O'Neil and Rees, "…sought neither to assume fully the reins of power nor to propose what form any new Somali authority should take."[11] Further

9 Somalia – UNOSOM I. Background [Online]. Available at: http://www.un.org/Depts/dpko/dpko/co_mission/unosom1backgr2.html [accessed: May 18, 2009].

10 Drysdale, J. 1997. Foreign Military Intervention in Somalia: The Root Cause of the Shift from UN Peacekeeping to Peacemaking and Its Consequences, in *Learning from Somalia: The Lessons of Armed Humanitarian Intervention*, edited by W. Clarke and J. Herbst. Westview Press, 120.

11 O'Neill, J.T. and Rees, N. 2005. *United National Peacekeeping in the Post-Cold War Era*. New York: Routledge, 124.

worsening of the humanitarian situation in Somalia and UN bureaucracy led to the dismissal of Sahnoun and authorization of the military intervention.

Established in April 1992 by Resolution 751, UNOSOM I was initially composed of 50 ceasefire monitors mandated with provision of "protection and security for United Nations personnel, equipment and supplies at the seaports and airports in Mogadishu and escort[ing] deliveries of humanitarian supplies from there to distribution centres in the city and its immediate environs".[12] Subsequently after considerable delays and difficulties, an agreement was reached with Ali Mahdi and Aideed to deploy 500 United Nations security personnel in the capital as part of UNOSOM I. Pakistan had agreed to contribute a large unit for this purpose. The first group of military observers arrived in Mogadishu on September 14. In following resolution 775 Boutros Ghali recommended the deployment of four additional United Nations security units with 750 personnel to protect the "humanitarian convoys and distribution centers throughout Somalia".[13] The total UNOSOM I manpower in Somalia at its peak amounted to 4,219 personnel, including 500 observers authorized for Mogadishu and 719 for logistical support.[14]

However, UN resources were still too limited to cover the whole country and to respond to the needs of the local population affected by the crisis. Following UN actions, US National Security Council authorized its own humanitarian intervention the same month. Together with UN monitors, 400 American soldiers were deployed to Kenya during the Operation Provide Relief, airlifting aid to remote areas in Somalia and to protect the personnel of humanitarian organizations. The problem of humanitarian aid remained: in a country with no central authority to facilitate aid distribution by providing primary security, humanitarian assistance suffered from constant looting, pillaging of supplies and extortion of money by different and sometimes unidentifiable armed groups.

In view of mass casualties and displacement, a non-functioning central government, and frequent albeit low-scale attacks on UN personnel, Boutros Ghali decided to reframe UN strategy in Somalia. The Resolution 794 allowed use of force, which allowed for "all necessary means to establish as soon as possible a secure environment for humanitarian relief operations in Somalia". UN was determined "to restore peace, stability and law and order with a view to facilitating the process of a political settlement under the auspices of United Nations."[15] With this purpose the Resolution called on member-states to provide military forces or cash or in-kind contributions to United Task Force (UNITAF) established under US field command.

---

12 The UN Security Council Resolution #751. 1992, New York. [Online]. Available at: http://www.un.org/documents/sc/res/1992/scres92.htm [accessed: May 7, 2009].

13 The UN Security Council Resolution #775. 1992, New York. [Online]. Available at: http://www.un.org/documents/sc/res/1992/scres92.htm [accessed: May 7, 2009].

14 Information of the UN Department of Peacekeeping Operations [Online]. Available at: http://www.un.org/Depts/dpko/dpko/co_mission/unosom1backgr2.html [accessed: May 7, 2009].

15 The UN Security Council Resolution #794. 1992, New York. [Online]. Available at: http://www.un.org/documents/sc/res/1992/scres92.htm [accessed: May 7, 2009].

UNITAF, with the agenda creation of a secure environment for humanitarian relief operations, was, in fact, an interim body in transition to UNOSOM II with broader goals and objectives. 37,000-manned UNITAF included 28,000 American soldiers and the remaining personnel from 23 countries. Commenting on its mission, US Special Envoy Robert Oakley, while sending a message of minimal involvement of UN in the matter of imposing peace, "We are not an occupying power. We have no power to arrest. There is nothing in the Security Council resolution about war crimes"[16] specifically stressed the neutrality and supposed operational low-intensity of UNITAF. The main reason behind US involvement in Somalia, however, was not that altruistic as it seemed at first sight.

There were no particular and apparent vital national US political or economic interests involved in Somalia. Neither was Somalia a member of any alliance or union that was particularly receptive to US interests in Africa, which could be used by US to spread its influence over the region in accordance with the ideological reasoning common for the Cold War times. Albeit this, at first glance, low-benefit intervention, there were still clear institutional advantages for US to be involved in the conflict. Apart from increasing its prestige on international arena as an altruistic peacemaker, US were trying to stress test the ground for possible larger operations outside its borders unimpeded by the clashing interests of the former Soviet Union. The end-result of operation in Somalia would, thus, indicate whether US could undertake the responsibility to play the major role on the international arena.

With the wish to remain a peacemaker, US still wanted to avoid large-scale military operations that would inevitably lead to human losses. According to a US diplomat, President Bush wanted to keep US mission within a limited scope and specific objectives that could be "met in the near term and as soon as they are, the coalition force will depart, transferring its function to UN force."[17] Meanwhile, all political and humanitarian aspects of conflict resolution in Somalia were to remain within UNOSOM I. This separation of responsibilities also had a geographical component: while UNOSOM I remained mainly in Mogadishu, UNITAF's task was to secure major population centers, including the capital, to ensure proper and efficient delivery of humanitarian assistance. From practical side of intervention, UNITAF was engaged in food distribution in the centers in each of the major areas and aiming at stopping the looting with the aim of elimination of food extortion as a main strategy of the belligerents in stymieing the work of the humanitarian agencies.

Retaining multilateralism in form, UNOSOM I remained largely unilateral in essence: US were in full charge of commanding issues of the combined UN intervention force. This fact from the very beginning jeopardized UN neutrality and put the organization is a very awkward position in relation to the belligerents who could not distinguish between who was doing what and considered UN as

16 Perlez, J. 1992. Witnesses Report a Somali Massacre before U.S. Arrival. *The New York Times*, December 29, A1.

17 Bolton, J. 1994. Wrong Turn in Somalia, *Foreign Affairs*, 73(1), 40.

another party in the domestic confrontation. Also, with all their acceptance of UN intervention, both Aideed and Ali Mahdi largely remained suspicious of UN actions and considered presence of foreign troops on their territories as a necessary evil, which would inevitably have led to confrontation with UN once it acted against or in favor of a certain warring faction.

The initial antagonism of UN started in the eyes of Aideed with negative personification: according to O'Neill and Rees (2005), he viewed Boutros Ghali "as having a hidden agenda, that of seeking to make Somalia a UN trusteeship and of wishing to restore Barre"[18] which made him consider UN actions as admittedly hostile. Although this was far-fetched, Aideed accused UN of continuing to support Ali Mahdi both politically and militarily. Unlike UN, United States enjoyed greater acceptance by Aideed because of its humanitarian agenda and because, as Drisdale (1997) noted, Aideed believed that US with no prior colonial ties to Somalia "would not change the political balance of power to his detriment"[19] and would not challenge his standings. This amiable relationship was also based on the ties with the intervener during the Barre's regime, when Aideed and his top opposition leadership had good working relations with the Americans (for instance, his treasurer and advisor was a liaison for US oil company Conoco and a close acquaintance of UN Ambassador Oakley).

The multilateral operation meanwhile continued. Within the framework of UNITAF and in accordance with Resolution 794, US in December 1992 launched Operation Restore Hope with the aim of assisting and protecting the humanitarian activities of UN and other international relief agencies. This goal was divided into two stages – disarmament of the population by UNITAF military personnel and further steps directed towards political reconciliation creating the first level local government – municipalities – and restoring communal services. At the same time, considerable efforts were made in the direction of official conflict management by UN, Ghali himself and US officials.

In general, although limited in operational capabilities and scope of action, UNOSOM I was an effective multinational intervention. From the very beginning, impartiality and low-operational involvement of UN mission guarded the organization against clashes with the belligerents: its mandate was confined to monitoring of the ceasefire agreement, provision of humanitarian assistance, delivery of food and medical supplies, and mediation through reconciliation conferences, and not peace-enforcement.

Until UNITAF stayed out of domestic power rivalry, kept low engagement in active military actions against the warring factions and abstained from actions going beyond peacekeeping and monitoring as state-building, it was perceived as neutral and not supporting any side. In the first UN mission, UNOSOM I, presence and activities of UNITAF had a positive impact on the security situation in Somalia and on the improvement of effective delivery of humanitarian assistance.

18 O'Neill, J.T. and Rees, N. 2005, 114.

19 Drysdale, J. 1997, 129.

As a result of UN presence, the warring groups were effectively separated from each other, and there were no large-scale and substantive military clashes between them. Also, Sahnoun's peace-making efforts set up favorable conditions for further reconciliation by facilitating cooperation among elders and local communities. Different societal actors were becoming increasingly involved in the negotiation process, including wide array of civil society and traditionally developed social structures of the Somali communities. These popular groups were considered by Sahnoun as a cornerstone of the relief operations and an incremental mechanism for further conflict resolution, which was at the beginning of UN mission's operation a promising sign of improvement of the political situation.

Even when this approach had been rejected by UN and the emphasis was made on negotiations with key belligerent leaders, the presence and leadership of US in the multinational coalition, which was not going to use active force against the warring sides, was a sign of effective cooperation and a good start for an eventual solution. Mediation efforts of the international community, started by Sahnoun, continued by UN and, particularly, US high representatives. Altogether, there were 17 nation-wide and 20 local-level reconciliation conferences held in Somalia with the aim of bringing together people from as many conflicting parties as possible. The most representative and, probably, the most important national reconciliation conferences were held in Addis Ababa on January 3, 1993 and March 15, 1993, at which a peace agreement was signed by Aideed and Ali Mahdi. The first peace package included a general agreement on cease-fire and disarmament, which was shared by 14 Somali military factions. Traditional leaders of Somali society – the elders, civil society, businessmen and intellectuals – were left behind the conflict resolution process. This was done primarily upon the request of Aideed who, probably still wishing to capitalize on Barre's overthrow, insisted on inclusion of only those groups, which supported him during the change of the government in early 1990s. Pro-Aideed list of agreement signatories meant that he would eventually achieve control of the negotiation process, and it seemed to many Somalis as if UN was putting warlords in the political center of the country.

The second Addis Ababa conference tried to amend the faults of the first one by including a more comprehensive list of participants. It was at that conference that key divergence in views appeared between the main factions in relation to the administrative issues of their future state. While Aideed advocated for a federalist state giving significant powers to regional clan-based warlords like him, Ali Mahdi, as a statutory government figure, was a proponent of a strong central government. Eventually, the agreement, calling for complete disarmament, established the TNC (Transitional National Council) for a period of two years with the task of creation of central and regional administrative units. SNM from the Republic of Somaliland refrained from signing the Agreement and remained an independent observer.

For UN, which was encouraging rapid solution to the conflict through political means, these conferences were a clear sign of slow but steady improvement of the political and security situation, and of a general will of the conflicting parties to cooperate with each other and UN, at large. That is why UN decided that situation was ripe for transformation of its operations from peace-keeping to peace-building and post-conflict reconstruction. Following UN Security Council Recommendation, it was decided to expand the mandates of UNOSOM I and UNITAF by broad tasks of political reconciliation and country rebuilding.

UN Intervention (UNOSOM II)

The day before signing of the agreement, Resolution 814 was adopted, which extended the mandate of UN operations in Somalia, and, what was more important, included enforcement measures in accordance with the Chapter VII of UN Charter. The civil war in Somalia, which was now viewed by UN Security Council as a clear threat to peace and security in the region, mandated UN mission to undertake large-scale disarmament with the ultimate goal of national reconciliation. In particular, the resolution authorized UN mission to "to assist the people of Somalia to promote and advance political reconciliation through broad participation by all sectors of Somali society, and the re-establishment of national and regional institutions and civil administrations in the entire country."[20] Thus, the peace-keeping of UNOSOM I and UNITAF was enlarged, expanded and enriched by peace-building actions of UNOSOM II.

The mandate of UNOSOM II was indeed overly ambitious: in a war-torn country with a proliferation of different clan-groups engaged in constant conflict, UN personnel was tasked with the continuation of UNITAF's mandate of restoring peace, law and order and general stability in a country where relative peace was still very much confined to its capital. In addition to this, UNOSOM II was to assist in economic, social and political development of the Somali society, to foster revival of the national security institutions and to facilitate reconstruction of administrative functions of the state. In sum, the goal of UNOSOM II was not only peace-enforcement, but, more importantly, provision of external security guarantees to the warring parties and the population, reconciliation of all the belligerent factions, and (re)creation of a fully functional country.

Jonathan T. Howe was appointed to lead UNOSOM II as the head of the civilian component and Lieutenant-General Çevik Bir of Turkey as the military commander of UNOSOM II. The military ranks of UNOSOM II included 28,000 personnel with approximately 3,000 civilian administrative officers. UNOSOM II's personnel was to be involved in nearly all post-conflict reconstruction activities, including repatriation and resettlement of refugees and IDPs, training of civilian officers and local police, removing anti-personnel mines, reconstitution of general public services and economic rehabilitation of the country.

It was the scope and essence of its tasks in the particular Somalian multi-actor conflict environment that soon became fatal to UNOSOM II. The problem with

20 The UN Security Council Resolution #814. 1993, New York [Online]. Available at: http://www.un.org/Docs/scres/1993/scres93.htm [accessed: May 7, 2009].

the new multi-dimensional mandate was that UN wanted to carry out post-conflict reconstruction during an active war phase, with numerous domestic players with their own agendas and no clear winner and loser. Encouraged by the initial accomplishments of UNOSOM I and the slow but promising peace-building, UN accelerated the pace of its actions. The real quandary was that even if a fragile peace remained, the conflict was far from being de facto settled. Somalia had no effectively operating government, neither in the center nor in the periphery, to act as the counterpart of UN state-building efforts or even to be its main interlocutor. There was no organized civil service, nor any effective army and police force that would obey the orders of a central government.

Somalia was divided by military groups with own agendas and aims and possessing enough human resources and military equipment not only not to fight with each other, but also oppose any UN actions that would jeopardize their interests. The warlords were unwilling to consider peaceful existence that would yield them far less profits if compared with the war-related gains. Not only was the local population under constant attacks of various warring militants, but also UN personnel itself and that of international humanitarian agencies suffered from numerous "loose cannon" groups that could not be even properly identified. The real problem was unavailability of a single credible force that UN could rely in its peace-enforcement and reconstruction efforts. In the words of Menkhaus (1997), "...in the absence of either a Somali state authority or clearly recognizable social and political leadership, reconciliation efforts were chronically weakened by disputes over legitimate and effective authority. Who had the right to represent whom in Somali peace talks?"[21] This was an unsolvable quandary for any neutral external actor.

Another set of problems pertinent to political and military fragmentation of the Somali society represented uncontrollable and accumulating difficulties for UN from the point of view of information-sharing: the communication pipeline between UN and these groups was difficult to control. Moreover, UN soon became hostage to their parochial interests, as the representatives of various factions used their ties to the international body to pursue their own agendas. In a country with so many political figures and participants, who were using UN for their own benefit, "...peacebuilding soon degenerated into a cynical cottage industry dominated by entrepreneurial Somali politicians. Factional leaders were quick to appreciate, and exploit the fact that UNOSOM [II] needed Somali national reconciliation far more than they did."[22] Political fragmentation of the local environment substantially complicated and slowed down UN peace-building attempts. Due to the multiplicity of actors, efforts of the international community involved in the intervention had to be performed with a sense of awareness of the domestic situation, with

21 Menkhaus, K. 1997. International Peacebuilding and the Dynamics of Local and National Reconciliation in Somalia, in *Learning from Somalia: The Lessons of Armed Humanitarian Intervention*, edited by W. Clarke and J. Herbst. Westview Press, 57.

22 Menkhaus, K. 1997, 46.

increased sensitivity to the main players and, which was the most important, with the decisive and wholehearted will to impose externally offered peace option.

This was quite difficult to achieve in practice. Important insights to the problem inherent to inter-clan rivalry are given by Menkhaus (1997), who claimed that UN's efforts to revive the governmental structures and agencies artificially imposed on the Somalis previously by Barre, "...worked at cross purposes with its reconciliation efforts, often fueling conflict instead of reducing it...Different clans were often able to coexist in relative peace in a single location. However, if asked to form a local government structure with a fixed number of seats, they often fell into heated disputes, sometimes ending in casualties, and dramatically worsening local security."[23] The Somalian society had liberated itself from Barre's oppressive administrative structures and a return to them, even in a democratic form, as proposed by UN, was unacceptable to the warlords, their supporters from the general public, and even to those who were not engaged in warfare but continued to accuse UN for extending the conflict by re-imposition of public administration offices. As the World Bank report goes, "via locally-selected district councils [which] directly threatened the interests of a number of militia leaders and their clans, who controlled valuable riverain and urban estate through conquest, and who viewed UNOSOM's program as a move to disenfranchise them. A confrontation was inevitable."[24]

The first serious challenge blow to UN prestige and authority happened when, due to incorrect and faulty communication between UN Headquarters and several factions of Somali militia, on June 5, 1993 24 Pakistani peacekeepers were ambushed and killed. The peacekeepers were doing their routine reconnaissance duties at the SNA arms depot near the radio station controlled by Aideed's forces and had not expected such a severe retaliation. The blame quickly fell upon Aideed, who soon became the target number one of US and UN alike. UN promptly issued Resolution 837 urging the arrest and trial of all those responsible for the brutal assault upon UN troops.[25] With the new task UNOSOM II launched large-scale operation to find and capture Aideed. US had own Operation Gothic Serpent with the same task.

On July 12, 1993 in response to the incident with the Pakistani peace-keepers, UNOSOM II destroyed the building, which was reportedly occupied by Aideed's clan, killing about 50 Somali clan leaders but failing to capture Aideed. This move further enraged the Somali public, who viewed the Americans as a rogue force acting with its own agenda. However, the turning point of the intervention was the "Battle for Mogadishu" when on October 4, 1993 the attack was launched on

---

23 Menkhaus, K. 1997, 59.

24 *Conflict in Somalia: Drivers and Dynamics*. 2005. The World Bank, 11-12 [Online]. Available at: http://siteresources.worldbank.org/INTSOMALIA/Resources/conflictinsomalia.pdf [accessed: May 7, 2009].

25 The UN Security Council Resolution #814. 1993, New York [Online]. Available at: http://www.un.org/Docs/scres/1993/scres93.htm [accessed: May 7, 2009].

the Olympic Hotel, an alleged hide-out for Aideed. During the attack more than three hundred Somalis were killed and about eight hundred wounded.[26] US also suffered casualties: 18 soldiers were killed and 79 more injured in combat. Scenes of mutilation of US soldiers were transmitted all over the world.

Opposition to UNOSOM II and, especially, inability of its military component to effectively impose its peace option onto the belligerents seriously jeopardized any further activities of the interveners. The death of US soldiers had very harsh reverberation at home, causing negative public opinion to press the administration to withdraw from Somalia. In two days after the notorious event known as the "Black Hawk Down" incident, President Clinton ordered a halt to all US actions against Aideed except those in self-defense. Ambassador Robert B. Oakley was appointed a special envoy to Somalia to arrange a peace settlement and subsequent pull-out of US troops by March 1994. Tragic events of October 1993 played as a critical role in subsequent military developments in Somalia: for Aideed, it was clear that such defiance, even if brought him relative brief gains, would further antagonize the Americans, and he decided to temporarily cease military actions and seek respite. On October 9 his USC declared a unilateral cessation of fight against UNOSOM II. On March 24, 1994 Aideed and Mahdi signed an UN-brokered peace agreement, which later met the same pitiable fate as all its predecessors.

After the departure of US forces, the remaining UN contingent kept quite a low profile until it, too, was eventually removed. In 1995, within a year after US had left UNOSOM II, UN intervention mission, which already continued a nominal presence in the country, ceased to exist, with one of the highest rate of UN mission fatalities – 155 battle deaths.[27]

Analysis of the Interventions

The exorbitant tasks undertaken by the international community in Somalia from the very beginning connoted daunting difficulties. In the country torn by different rebel groups fighting among themselves for possession of fractions of the state, with humanitarian suffering increasing every day, and vague prospects of actual lasting peace the interveners had their objective to restore the state structures and to put all political forces under a unified form of governance. At first sight, the strategy employed by UN, was quite simple: to come, negotiate

26 Atkinson, R. 1994. The Raid That Went Wrong: How an Elite U.S. Force Failed in Somalia. *The Washington Post*, January 30, A1. Another estimate of casualties was given by Bowden – more than 700 killed and more than 1,000 injured. See: Bowden, M. 1999. *Black Hawk Down: A Story of Modern War*. Atlantic Monthly Press. Berkeley, California, US.

27 Fatalities by Mission and Appointment Time. 2009. The UN Department of Peacekeeping Operations. [Online]. Available at: http://www.un.org/Depts/dpko/fatalities/StatsByMissionAppointmentType per cent203.pdf [accessed: May 7, 2009].

with the belligerents, establish peace (at least, temporarily), and assist the leaders of military groups in rebuilding their country.

The conundrum of this approach was the solution it offered and was trying to enforce: a centralized state in a chronically decentralized society. As Lederach and Storks (1993) assert, "Centralization in governance had been a root cause of Somalia's breakdown…The rebellion that developed in Somali society was a revolt against this centralization."[28] With all the paradoxes of Somalia – general political wish for unity of Somalian population for maintenance of the territorial integrity of their country – the counterproductive forces that made all Somalis politically different was the fundamental problem with UN mission: the option it was trying to impose – a unitary state. Issa-Salwe (1994) claimed that "The Somalis had never been subjected to institutionalized government except under that of the authority of elders, and felt uneasy with the interruption of their traditional way of life…"[29] This implied failure for any form of governance different from Somalia's traditional structures – elders, intra- and inter-clan unofficial governance.

At the same time, there was nothing inherently wrong with this option: Somalia needed to have normal executive, legislative and judiciary structures common to the rest of the states institutionally governed by UN. That is why the forms of governance other than those pertinent to the international system – informal public administration mechanisms historically developed and approved by time in the Somalian society – were simply not considered as an option by the third parties.

A comparative assessment of the two interventions undertaken by a single actor is valuable from the point of view of keeping constant the variables inherent to the nature of the intervener. Although organized under the auspices of the same organization, the two UN interventions were quite distinct in their nature, character, operational objectives, and modus operandi.

During the first UN intervention, UNOSOM I, although entailed deployment of observers, was still largely externalized. It had a low operational mandate and a narrow profile and was confined to monitoring and peace-keeping activities. The aim of the mission was the "…imposition of neutral and lightly armed interposition forces following a cessation of armed hostilities and with the permission of the state on whose territory these forces are deployed, in order to discourage a renewal of military conflict and promote an environment under which the underlying dispute can be resolved."[30] The mandate of UNOSOM I, as initially defined by the Security Council, was to monitor the cease-fire in Mogadishu, to provide protection and security for own and other agencies' humanitarian personnel in fulfillment of their duties and to escort and protect humanitarian supplies in distribution centers.

28 Lederach, J.P. and Stork, J. 1993. The Intervention in Somalia: What Should Have Happened: An Interview with John Paul Lederach. *Middle East Report, Radical Movements: Migrants, Workers and Refugees*, 181, 39.

29 Issa-Salwe, A.M. 1994. *The Collapse of the Somali State*. Monograph. Published by the Author in association with HAAN Associated. London, 30.

30 Diehl, P.F. 1993. *International Peacekeeping*. Johns Hopkins University Press, 13.

This kept UNOSOM I out of direct contact with the belligerent factions and their internal rivalry.

Another key determinant of success of UNOSOM I involvement was its limited geographic coverage: UN forces were restricted in their operations almost exclusively to the capital of Mogadishu. This aspect was, of course, negative from the viewpoint of enforcing and preserving peace beyond the capital and in Somalia proper and gaining control over the territory. This is especially true when considering extremely negative reaction of self-proclaimed territories of the Republic of Somaliland, Puntland, Djibouti and Jubaland to enlargement of UN presence, which would consider such actions as encroachment to their own statehood. However, neither the resources not the tasks of UNOSOM I permitted it to go beyond what was defined in its mandate at that stage. Neither peace-enforcement not state-building was included in the mandate of UNOSOM I.

With all these actions, UNOSOM I was not involved in the political arrangements on the national and regional levels. Refraining from substitution for the duties of the local governmental services, its monitors were busy with gathering of information on fulfillment of the peace deals and provision of aid to the population. No wide-scale administrative assistance aimed at restoration of statehood had been envisaged. In essence, although UN was de-jure present in Somalia, it still remained largely absent from the internal political scene.

It was due to the confinement in operational objectives that UNOSOM I enjoyed wide acceptance of the warring parties. The mission was not tasked with power enforcement of peace on the belligerents, and even its disarmament efforts were limited to the territory it had covered and had more of an ad-hoc nature. With its limited numbers, it could not pose any significant threat to the positions and interests of the belligerents who, although accusing UN of supporting each others' rivals, in reality, were not afraid of UN sanctions. With its limited resources at hand, UNOSOM I could not effectively impose peace or punish the defectors. The very features that signaled its lack of bias made the first UN mission a credible and trustworthy mediator, which also meant that it could not effectively enforce any peacekeeping agreement that was reached.

Externalized intervention granted to UNOSOM I the aura of neutrality which allowed it fulfill its aims without significant hindrance on the part of the conflicting parties. Its objectives of peace-keeping and monitoring were not supposed to impose any sort of external solution to the conflict to the belligerents, to restore law and order, or to act, in Walter's terms, as an "external guarantor" of peace agreements. It was this modesty of aims that facilitated Sahnoun's successful conflict mediation in the case of the first intervention. Sahnoun, favoring a bottom-up approach without large-scale military involvement, was successful in establishing dialogue and good working relations with the local chieftains, elders and community leaders, women's associations, tradesmen, professionals and intellectuals.[31] During the negotiation process, he favored nobody in particular and aimed at inclusion of

31 Lederach, J.P. and Stork, J. 1993, 39.

all the parties – both military and societal actors. This incremental and cautious process of building peace through talks, negotiations and reconciliation efforts had scored substantial success under the first UN intervention. The initial success did not mean that the conflict was over; neither were Aideed and Ali Mahdi ready to hand over their weapons and return to normal civilian life. It merely meant that both of the key belligerents had accepted UN presence as a neutral intermediary, or were at least not hostile to it.

Externalization of UNOSOM I has been considered a drawback of the mission by some scholars, one of which claimed that "The overall flaw of UNOSOM I was UN's failure to address the fundamental problem, namely collapse of state authority. UN had behaved towards the factions as it would with sovereign governments."[32] However, the strategy of exclusion of the warlords in the negotiations processes, if employed, would have led to marginalization of the actual conflict sides. Forming a sovereign government at the outset would also have forced UN to negotiate with an amorphous and nominal entity and societal actors who had no actual power on the ground. Ignoring the key players in the mediation process would have been a mistake leading in the best case scenario to meaningless peace agreements.

The other significant factor that contributed to success of the mission was its timing. UNOSOM I was deployed after the actual cessation of hostilities. Although there still were large caches of arms within the hands of belligerents, and sporadic fire was also present, no large or particularly bloody clashes took place after the signing of the Addis Ababa agreements. These agreements signed by Aideed and Ali Mahdi were the starting point for deployment of UNOSOM I. Although the agreements provided for no actual peace-building mechanism, they offered a clear window of opportunity for further UN prudent steps: not to intervene with the purpose of stopping fire, but to act as a neutral and impartial force, which would separate belligerents and contribute to the peace-building process. Absence of active warfare provided a secure environment for UN operations and the low casualties encouraged the member-states to remain in the coalition, which contributed to the successful fulfillment of its mandate. The figures of casualties of the corresponding UN missions significantly support this argument: by the time of transition from UNOSOM I to UNOSOM II the casualties of the former amounted only to six field-related deaths.[33]

Movement from UNOSOM I to UNOSOM II meant internalization of UN intervention and extension of its mandate with the state-building and post-conflict settlement activities, which invoked active conflict developments in the country. State-reconstruction, in general, requires wide involvement of the public, which would serve as a cornerstone of the society to be rebuilt. The focus of peace-building is usually on all the layers of the society, which should enjoy wide representation in a new government, participate in power-sharing in all administrative and legal

32 O'Neill, J.T. and Rees, N. 2005, 112.

33 Somalia – UNOSOM I. Facts and Figures. [Online]. Available at: http://www.un.org/Depts/dpko/dpko/co_mission/unosom1facts.html [accessed: May 7, 2009].

aspects, as well as in reconstruction of their identities.[34] This was the initial area which UN would target by involvement in facilitating negotiations between traditional social components of the Somalian society. When these developments were forcefully accelerated in the direction of state reconstruction while the conflict was far from being over, UNOSOM II failed.

The volatile political environment of Somalia forced UN to use its military power, especially after the deaths of its Pakistani peacekeepers. UN had two options: either to leave to avoid additional casualties or to curb hostilities. With the second option chosen, UN actually entered the conflict scene for the first time. The key reason why UNOSOM II failed was indecisive imposition of the peace option onto the warring factions: although considerable forces had been involved, internal organizational problems and overdependence on a single (although theoretically mighty) member – US – jeopardized overall its mandate.

When UNOSOM II tried to forcefully capture Aideed, this put it in a seriously biased position since, in ethnic war supporting and/or acting against one faction automatically means acting against and/or supporting its rivals. According to Gilkes, UNOSOM II's "...action against Aideed becomes support for the Darod clan, the main Hawiye rival for control of Mogadishu."[35] Without doubt, with the launching of large-scale manhunt for Aideed, UN became a major player in the internal Somali game: "Actions taken against a clan's militia leader were seen by Somalis not as justice done to an errant individual, but as a hostile action against the entire clan."[36] The African Rights Report also claims by openly engaging with Aideed, UN for the local Somalis became somewhat inseparable from the rest of the belligerents: it became, in a way, a third force: "Somalis regard[ed] UNOSOM as another faction and Admiral Howe as another warlord."[37] UN, had thus become not an intervener aiming to facilitate cessation of the conflict, but literally a third party participant in the conflict.

Under such conditions of active conflict, even the matters specific to internal UN mismanagement that had nothing to do with the belligerents per se took on a veneer of sinister intent in the eyes of Somalis. For instance, the failure of UN to properly investigate the crash of the Russian plane with UN's World Food Program in July 1992, which was reportedly delivering arms to Ali Mahdi against UN SC Resolution 733 and to impose additional sanctions against a key side of the conflict antagonized Aideed and indicated to many Somalis that UN tacitly backed Ali Mahdi.[38]

---

34 These and other solutions to conflicts in ethnically divided societies are discussed by Lijphart, A. 2004. Constitutional Design for Divided Societies, *Journal of Democracy*, 15(2), 96-109.

35 Gilkes, P. 1993, 23.

36 Gilkes, P. 1993, 56.

37 *Somalia. Human Rights Abuses by the UN Forces*. 1993. African Rights Report. London, 33-34.

38 O'Neill, J.T. and Rees, N. 2005, 111.

Although the forceful option was correctly chosen by UN it was ineffectively imposed. UN should have been aware that Aideed, like Ali Mahdi, enjoyed large support from their fellow-clansmen and that the offensive against them would have been vigorously retaliated. Withstanding popular outrage and resistance would have required substantial resources and, more importantly, will and self-commitment of UN as already a biased intervener. By targeting Aideed UN successfully jeopardized its neutrality and impartiality but unsuccessfully enforced its bias.

An excellent illustration of inefficient violation of UN principle of impartiality and its overall peace-building failure is given by Menkhaus. According to him, "For peace enforcement, UN had to be impartial – that is, it had to enforce certain rules of the game on all parties concerned…As long as the peace-enforcement operation imposes the same penalties on everyone for security infractions, it maintains its impartiality. But having once embarked on enforcement measures against a serious violation (Aideed's attack on UNOSOM forces in June 1993), UN cannot simultaneously play the role of a neutral mediator in national reconciliation."[39] One of these roles should have been abandoned and the other wholeheartedly imposed. By going till the very end and decisively crushing Aideed, UN would have announced Ali Mahdi as a sole winner of the conflict and the future head of the Somalian state. This was, however, out of the general philosophical quagmire of the organization: a pacific body not interfering within political lives of its members. If Ali Mahdi had to become the winner, he would have done by himself, without UN backing.

As a result, UNOSOM II failed to use its insurmountable will to effectively impose peaceful solution at the expense of neutrality and impartiality for the sake of keeping sustainable peace. Any act directed at altering the battlefield calculus was not neutral by definition, and the only way UN could score a success in such a conundrum was to vigorously enforce a peaceful solution, which it failed to do. Its actions aimed at imposing any options equally to every belligerent party, and, in this case, specifically on Aideed, turned out to be not "heavy-handed" enough. As a result, UNOSOM II involuntarily accepted the third option – it became a conflict participant in its own right.

The other significant factor, which made UNOSOM II fail, was peculiar to its composition. Although UN mission was indeed multilateral by its structure and the number of participating member-states, in essence it still remained unilateral, where the main contributor, both economically and militarily, was US. Such over-reliance on a sole (strong) coalition member made UNOSOM II vulnerable structurally: it had to follow the single-state guidance both strategically and resource-wise.

From the very beginning, the issue of intervention in Somalia became part and parcel of US domestic politics. US had its own rationale for intervention – strengthening its role in changing global political settings after the end of the

39 Menkhaus, K. 1997, 59.

Cold War, and its own vision of success and failure of operations. Inclusion of the conflict into US domestic party rivalry had a mirror-reflection not only on its operation in Somalia, but also on further effectiveness of the whole intervention. US involvement in Somalia was heavily politicized domestically from the very beginning. Its modus was strongly affected by changes in US administration (from Republicans to Democrats), which involved stressing negative points of the former and over-emphasizing gains of the future presidential administrations.

From his side, President Bush was feeling an urge to resurrect his image on the foreign front after the fiasco of the first Gulf War for the benefit of his presidential campaign. After having lost the presidential elections to Bill Clinton, Bush, according to Chopra et al. (1995), was "no longer constrained by domestic considerations" and wanted to do "a last good thing."[40] The same situation held for new President Clinton, who criticized Bush for the failures of his foreign policy and wanted to do things differently, i.e. better. Such a commitment was clearly described by Madeline Albright, then US permanent representative in UN, who declared that "With this resolution [814], we will embark on an unprecedented enterprise aimed at nothing less than the restoration of an entire country."[41] This was an overly ambitious start of the new administration, which wanted to score early visible victories in foreign policy and to distance itself from the failures of the Bush administration, especially in Somalia.

Having self-interests in and being guided by own rationales in intervention, in principle, should not jeopardize impartiality of a third-party coalition and affect its success, unless it strictly follows its mandate and is transparent in the actions of all its members. Indeed, it is hard to imagine a member of intervening alliance who pursues no self-benefits whatsoever and acts from purely altruistic reasoning. Even if no tangible gains are apparent, states would still try to fulfill their own interests through multilateral coalition, which may not point-blank clearly visible: prestige on international arena, strengthening domestic constituencies, testing and promoting home-made weapons for future trade and many more.

The problem with UNOSOM II was not so much of US pursuing its own intervention line in making strategic and field decisions and having the remaining member-states to follow – UN mission over-dependent on operational capabilities and strength of US. When US had eventually departed the scene, UNOSOM II became incapable of fulfilling its mandated intervention objectives on its own. Its actions aimed at enforcement of peace and state-building turned to be baseless without substantial military and economic resources previously secured by US to be used for the belligerents comply with the will of an external power. From the point of view of resource allocation, even when US were present, UNOSOM II suffered from insufficiency of material-technical base to project its will in an active conflict environment. Except for US troops, the majority of the remaining

40 Chopra, J., Eknes, A. and Nordboe, T. 1995. *Fighting for Hope in Somalia*. Oslo: Norsk Utenrikspolitisk Institutt, 38.

41 Bolton, J. 1994, 62.

peacekeepers were underequipped. Even though this was a multilateral coalition, according to O'Neill and Rees (2005), "UNOSOM II was composed of contingents from states all too many of which either had not the equipment required or were unwilling to provide it."[42] Different military contributions of the member-states made it difficult to for the coalition to operate in combat conditions – for instance, the heaviest armored vehicles with the Pakistanis were M42 A2 tanks, model 1957, which were totally obsolete and unreliable, especially in the harsh climatic conditions of Somalia. With US troops performing much of UNOSOM II tasks this structural disparity was neglected and gained significance when US government had withdrawn its troops.

US left Somalia suffering not from excessive and unacceptable rate of human casualties but a blow to its international prestige and domestic political rivalry unleashed by party opposition and CNN-strung-up common citizens criticizing Clinton for the death of US soldiers. UNOSOM II was unable to carry out the same peace-enforcement with the resources it was left with. This led to overall reconsideration of the intervention mandate, its strategic objectives in the field, and, as a result, to final total withdrawal marking its failure in Somalia.

Conclusions

The causes of success of UNOSOM I and failure of UNOSOM II can be divided into two sets of factor – inherent to the conflict environment and subjective for the intervener. Such a dual view of causal factors is best described in the Report of the International Commission on Intervention and State Sovereignty: "Somalia is a clear example where the initial response [UNOSOM I] to insecurity and famine was not also accompanied by sufficient support to achieve long-term solutions. The follow-on UN operation [UNOSOM II] included ambitious security and political tasks but without commensurate means to realize them."[43] On the conflict level, the major quandary of UN was the solution it was going to offer to the conflict participants, which had to be imposed on all the belligerents. Out of its vision and philosophy UN had developed an outcome that was outside of the conventional structures of Somali governance. The idea of a centralized country with its own governance rules was foreign to the mentality of a typical Somali, who almost exclusively paid allegiance to his sub-clan and clans.

Another important negative aspect of UN involvement in Somalia was its rush to build a unitary state in a country still engaged in active conflict. As long as UN involvement remained externalized to the conflict environment and the intervener

---

42 O'Neill, J.T. and Rees, N. 2005, 132.

43 The Responsibility To Protect. Report of the International Commission on Intervention and State Sovereignty. 2001. The International Development Research Centre, 60 [Online]. Available at: http://www.iciss.ca/pdf/Commission-Report.pdf [accessed: June 1, 2009].

abstained from direct military clashes inevitably resulting in limitation of political and military options available to the Somalia military factions, it enjoyed security for its personnel and was largely successful in monitoring the activities of the warring parties. However, once UN decided to impose peace, on the one hand, and simultaneously build a state, political instability, domestic anarchy, the absence of legitimate authority, a multiplicity of actors, domestic power arrangements and the peculiarities of a clan-based society, the inability to enforce decision of any sort made it difficult, and, finally, impossible to fulfill its objectives as embedded in its mandate.

Subjectively, multinational intervention in form became a unilateral in essence in UNOSOM II. While there were other nations present in the intervention coalition, the real power factor of the interveners was US, which was responsible for the bulk of operations and on which operational success of the overall mission was largely based. US, as a lead actor, appeared vulnerable to outside attacks on its personnel and to domestic political and popular pressure. Too many promises and too higher stakes were put for US success, and its failure in a single operation caused retreat of its forces leaving UN to face local contingencies which the member-states "alone", without US backing, were incapable to cope with.

Chapter 6
Rwanda (1990-1996): Success during Genocide

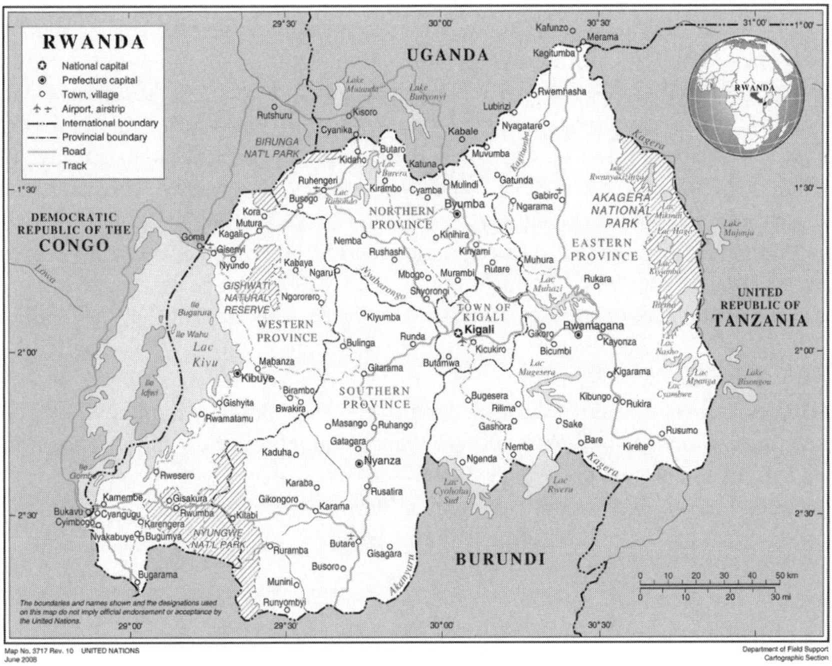

Map 6.1 Map of Rwanda

Source: Reprinted with permission of the UN Cartographic Section.

The conflict in Rwanda was the third large-scale ethnic cleansing of the 20th century, the two previous ones being the mass murders of Armenians in Turkey in 1915 and the Holocaust. The Rwandan civil war took lives of approximately 50,000 Hutus and from half a million to 850,000 Tutsis and led to two million refugees and internally displaced persons.[1] The causes of bloody ethnic confrontation

1 These figures have been taken from various sources, including Prunier, G. 1995. *The Rwanda Crisis: History of a Genocide, 1959-1994*. London: Hurst and Co.; Human Rights Watch. 1999. *Live None to Tell the Story: Genocide in Rwanda* [Online]. Available at: http://www.hrw.org/legacy/reports/1999/rwanda/ [accessed: May 7, 2009]; Sellstom, T.

go back to the colonial times, which were characterized by consistent artificial "ethnicization" of the Rwandan society by the colonial powers occupying the country. However, its outburst and course were largely influenced by outside factors, such as changing geopolitical environment in the region and international arena; historical linkages between the country with its former Francophone patrons; and the fatal impotence of the international community, which turned a blind eye to the appalling massacres of civilians and failed to effectively intervene.

One possible explanation of such a lukewarm attitude to human sufferings in Rwanda can be found in its timing: the conflict succeeded another identity war in Africa – Somalia – where the international community was unable to stop bloodshed. Failure of institutional multilateralism with all its exorbitant force in Somalia predestined its extremely prudent and cautious actions in Rwanda that led to increasing casualties among civilian population. Perhaps the only powerful state still willing to interfere in the domestic fight between the two groups out of its own national interests in Rwanda was France, who wanted to reinstate its influence in the Great Lake District.

Altogether there were four foreign interventions in Rwanda conducted by two parties (France and UN) who intervening twice within the six-year period in the midst of Hutu-Tutsi intergroup rivalry. Notwithstanding the fact that the conflict had not been stopped as a result of the interventions, actions of UNAMIR (the UT Mission in Rwanda) and France shall not be considered as a failure. Peace-enforcement was outside of the scope of goals and agendas of the third parties who nevertheless managed to reach success their initial intervention aims. To identify the reasons for success of the interveners' actions, it is necessary to view not only characteristics of operational environment during each intervention, but also the local context in which the conflict was embedded.

Conflict Background

During colonial times Rwanda represented a case of a minority rule, where the country's wealth together with a considerable number of the country's administrative posts belonged to minority Tutsis (14 per cent of the population) with the overwhelming majority Hutus (85 per cent) and insignificant number of Twa (1 per cent) being politically, economically and culturally marginalized.[2] An explanation for the tragic role of the domestic social settings on the fate of the entire population can be found in the colonial history of Rwanda.

---

and Wohlgemuth, L. 1997. *The International Response to Conflict and Genocide: Lessons from Rwanda Experience. Study 1, Historical Perspective: Some Explanatory Factors*. Uppsala, Sweden: The Nordic Africa Institute, 1.

2 Klinghoffer, A.J. 1998. *The International Dimensions of Genocide in Rwanda*. New York: New York University Press, 9.

Antagonism between Hutus and Tutsis, based on "shamelessly twisted ethnic argument for the sake of class privileges"[3] was nothing more than a man-made creature of the European colonial powers, which wanted to implant their own views on nation-state model in Rwanda. First Germans and later Belgians, who ruled the country in different times, needed a domestic group to rely on in colonial administration and to serve as their counterparts in local affairs. The Belgians, who "inherited" Rwanda from Germans, had chosen Tutsis, who, in their view, more resembled the Europeans in accordance with the "Hamitic Hypothesis".[4] By this theory, according to Sanders (1969), Tutsis were considered as a superior "Caucasoid" race, the lost tribe of Ham,[5] who had migrated to the rest of Africa from Ethiopia and brought civilization to the whole continent.

When Belgians drew the ethnic map of Rwanda, they had used rough procedures of ethnic specification based on household wealth, phenotype (height and body build) and genotype (diverse characteristics of lactose digestion) physical parameters.[6] Such an artificial Barthian "poly-ethnic stratification",[7] in case of Rwanda differentiated people into groups of Tutsis and Hutus in accordance with their European looks and the number of cows each family had: those with ten or more cows and resembling European more were Tutsis together with all their descendants in the male line and those with less number of cattle and with African looks were correspondingly named Hutus.[8] This brought along quite a unique ethno-cultural setting where the whole population of Rwanda represented a "political community deprived of any other characteristics"[9] and Somalis could quite easily move from one ethnic group to the other due to frequent intermarriages and, sometimes, unofficial arrangements. In reality, while all the Somali spoke "the same language…[living] on same hills, and…more or less the same culture",

3 Pottier, J. 2002. *Re-Imaging Rwanda: Conflict, Survival and Disinformation in the Late Twentieth Century*. London: Cambridge University Press, 9.

4 This racist theory was later on employed by the Hutus with the purpose of alienation of Tutsis and depicting them as "foreigners". The most notorious expression of the Hamitic hypothesis was in the famous speech by Léon Mugesera on November 22, 1992 who said the Tutsis "belong in Ethiopia and we are going to find them a shortcut to get them there by throwing them into the Nyabarongo River [a source of the Nile.]" (quoted in Melvern, L. 2000. *A People Betrayed. The Role of the West in Rwanda's Genocide*. London: Zed Books, 47).

5 Sanders, E.R. 1969. The Hamitic Hypothesis: Its Origin and Functions in Time Perspective. *Journal of African History*, 10(4), 521-522.

6 Franche, D. 1996. There's Only One Ethnic Group in Rwanda: Rwandan. *Le Monde Diplomatique/Guardian Weekly*, November 24, 14 and Hiernaux, J. 1974. *The People of Africa*. New York: Charles Scribner's Sons, 60.

7 Barth, F. 1969. *Ethnic Groups and Boundaries: the Social Organization of Culture Difference*. Bergen/Oslo: Universitetsforlaget, 9-38.

8 Shoumatoff, A. 1992. Rwanda's Aristocratic Guerrillas. *New York Times Magazine*, December 13, 44.

9 Franche, D. 1996, 14.

there was still a "purity of social identification…: everyone…identifie[d] as either Hutu or Tutsi [with] no hybrids, none is *Hutsi*".[10]

Nevertheless, the civil war in Rwanda was an identity conflict due to the distinct pattern of violence directed towards a specific group of its residents on the basis of their corresponding social identities. This difference between Tutsis and Hutus become deeply incorporated in the Rwandan society. After the end of the colonial period, Rwanda was governed by the minority Tutsis, who were in a more privileged position than Hutus, had generally higher levels of education, enjoyed greater accesses to urban jobs, and had better economic standings and predominance in the government services. De-colonization process in Africa had a number of particular consequences for Rwanda, taking into account its unique domestic social settings and its relationship with the former colonial powers.

Similar to Chad and Somalia, identity-based political parties began emerging in Rwanda even before its independence of the country and recruited largely from their own constituencies. It was this inter-group political rivalry that led to the first conflict between Hutus and Tutsis at the end of 1959, after false rumors were broadcast to the effect that one of the leaders of the Parmehutu party (Party for the Emancipation of the Hutu People) had been killed by Tutsi extremists from UNAR (National Rwandese Union).[11] As a result, the so-called "Social Revolution" took place, which was inspired and orchestrated by a Guy Logiest, a Belgian colonel. The revolution, resulting in 20,000 Tutsi killed and a total of 150,000 escaped to nearby Uganda, Burundi, Congo, and Tanzania,[12] led to installation of the new government under Grégoire Kayibanda with the decisive support of the majority Parmehutu (78 per cent). Ethnic clashes and pogroms of Tutsis had been launched nearly every year since with frequent counter-attacks from Tutsi refugees living in neighboring countries.

After Rwanda became independence on 1 July 1962, a one-party rule based on Hutu nationalism was installed in addition to a hierarchical administrative system, where the president, in the words of Prunier (1995), applied the "…same style of leadership [as former King], …[with] his deliberate remoteness, authoritarianism and secretiveness…".[13] The one-person rule, also characteristic for majority of post-imperial states, continued by General Juvénal Habyarimana, who removed Kayibanda from the office in a bloodless coup of 1973, and created his own party – the MRND (Mouvement Républicain National pour le Développement).

10 Mamdani, M. 2001. *When Victims Become Killers: Colonialism, Nativism, and the Genocide in Rwanda*. Princeton University Press, 53.

11 *The Rwanda Crisis: History of a Genocide, 1959-1994*. London: Hurst and Co., 48.

12 For detailed accounts of the "Social Revolution" see Mamdani, M. 2001, 103-132; African Rights Report. 1994. *Rwanda: Who is Killing, Who is Dying, What is to be Done*. London, p. 7l; Melady, T.P. 1974. *Burundi: The Tragic Years*. Maryknoll, N.Y.: Orbis, 47; and Segal, A. 1964. Rwanda: The Underlying Causes, *Africa Report*, 9(4), 6.

13 Prunier, G. 1995. *The Rwanda Crisis: History of a Genocide, 1959-1994*. London: Hurst and Co., 48.

Suppression of Tutsi continued with the new government: they were banned from nearly all spheres of public life, including education, government offices, army and church, however, without much physical damage. Popular disappointment with the ruling regime grew not only among Rwanda's Tutsis and moderate Hutus: the biggest dissatisfied group was the community of Tutsi refugees from 1959 and their children in the neighboring countries, mainly in Uganda. The Rwandan Tutsis were instrumental in Yoweri Museveni's seizing the presidency in Uganda in 1986. The Ugandan state was very receptive to their presence, and many Tutsis from Rwanda were rewarded with important posts in Museveni's administration. These Tutsi refugees founded RPF (Rwandan Patriotic Front) in 1979, which became the key contender of Habyarimana's rule.

French Intervention

On October 1, 1990 a group of 4,000 RPF rebels invaded Rwanda from their stronghold in Uganda. Political reasons for the rebellion were the failure of Habyarimana's government to conduct democratic reforms and wide-scale popular discrimination against Tutsis. While Ugandan president Museveni was well aware of the rebellion and the movements of armed personnel across the borders of his country, as well as the rapid build-up of Tutsi forces from Congo, he bluntly denied all allegations of Rwandan authorities of supporting the rebels, officially declared closure of state borders with Rwanda and promised to put in prison anyone who crossed border to go back to Uganda. However, neither of these steps was implemented, and Tutsis in large numbers continued to flow in from the North.

With the purpose of stopping RPF offensive Habyarimana sought French support. The question of why Habyarimana invited the French still remains open. Perhaps, out of two considerations: despite his comparative military advantage of the national army named FAR (Forces Armées Rwandaises – Rwandan Armed Forces), he wanted to be on the safe side and scare the advancing rebels of having the backing of such a mighty power as France. Apart from that, Habyarimana was afraid that the advancing Tutsis might be joined by their in-country supporters, which would increase the capacities of the opposition. Another reason might be geopolitical considerations of possible involvement of Burundi and Uganda into the conflict, which would have internationalized the conflict, which Habyarimana clearly did not want. By inviting the French forces to intervene, Habyarimana sent a comprehensible message to his neighbors to abstain from any further involvement in the conflict and from supporting Tutsi rebels.

France, having its own states in the future political developments in Rwanda, immediately responded by dispatching its military. A number of reasons account for the willingness of France to intervene on behalf of the Rwandan government. First, although not having Rwanda as its colony, French own colonial heritage of controlling a large portion of the African continent presupposed future ties between French and former Francophone African states. As Prunier (1995) puts it, France has always considered Africa "le pré carré" (our own backyard) and viewed itself in African affairs as "a large hen followed by a docile brood of little black chicks"[14] that needed to be taken care of. France had always been committed to supporting countries with which it had common historical, economic, political, cultural and colonial past. This attitude was galvanized by the *lingua franca* of the continent – the French language – which played a decisive role in keeping France and its former colonies together under the common "threat" – the Anglo-Saxon linguistic and political influence.

Realpolitik was, perhaps, the second important factor in the matter of provision of assistance to Rwanda. Both Klinghoffer (1998) and Prunier (1995) point to the role played by the historical universal struggle of the French against Anglo-Saxon influence, starting from the 100-years war with the Britain, Napoleon's times, occupation of Canada by the "les Ricains",[15] aftermath of the WW II, de Gaulle's *grandeur*, and, last but not the least, the spread of the influence of the "les Angliches": the Fashoda syndrome[16] has been the primary driving force for the specific French attention to Africa.[17] Thus, English-speaking Uganda, with its large Tutsi population, and, particularly, its President Museveni, was considered the forefront of "Anglo-Saxonization" of the continent which was for a long time under the Francophone dominance. On top of that the fact that many Tutsi RPF leaders, including future President Paul Kagame, had received military training in Britain and US was another sign of advancing Anglo-Saxonization.

Another explanation of the commitment of the French to assist the government of Rwanda in the crisis can be found in historical heritage of the French nation following the French Revolutions of the 18th century and their similarities with Rwanda's own "Social Revolution" of 1959. Parallels were drawn between the suppressed *classe ouvrière* in both countries and the revolts of the French Jacobins and Hutus against *aristocrate despotisme* of Royalists and Tutsis, respectively.[18] In words of Prunier (1995), "…in Rwanda the French army was in the position of those revolutionary soldiers of 1792 who fought Prussians and 'émigrés' [here: the refugee Tutsis in Uganda, i.e. RPF] alike".[19] The French moral obligation was, thus, exported abroad: France felt it appropriate to help the Hutu government of Habyarimana based on their own legacy of popular liberation.

14 Prunier, G. 1995, 103.

15 Here: the "Yankees".

16 In 1898 the clash between the forces of Captain Marchand of France and the army of Lord Kitchener of Britain near a small Sudanese village of Fashoda nearly led to another European war (see: Bates, B. 1984. *Encounter in the Nile: The Fashoda Incident on 1898*. London: Oxford University Press).

17 Prunier, G. 1995, 102-112 and Klinghoffer, A.J. 1998, 14.

18 Lemarchand, R. 1970. *Rwanda and Burundi*. New York: Preager.

19 Prunier, G. 1995, 112.

The French intervention had also a strong personal aspect to it. The very day of RPF attack, Habyarimana called President of France François Mitterrand and received promises of support, which materialized less than three days after the first attack of RPF. Mitterrand's son, Jean-Christophe, who was supervising African affairs at the government office in the Presidential Palace, was a close friend of Habyarimana. According to Kakwenzire and Kamukama (1999), Mitterrand-junior owned a plantation in Rwanda and was personally involved in the arms trade with the Hutu government.[20] Such personal links between the governments of the two countries were instrumental in both the rapid deployment of French forces to Rwanda, and the commitment to protect mutual interests of the two leaders. Habyarimana knew that the French would support his regime in the spirit of common Francophone Africa.

In three days after the first attack of RPF, 150 French soldiers were dispatched from the Central African Republic. This number was quite insignificant but the French troops were still a token of support of France to Rwandan government. Belgium and Congo also helped in the intervention, but quickly withdrew due to domestic political pressure on the former and complete inefficiency of the latter. With the purpose of drawing increased support from the French, and alluring them into direct combat with the rebels, Habyarimana further dramatized the situation by organizing a fake attack by Tutsis on Kigali, the capital of Rwanda, which brought him due credits and support from the French ambassador. The French however, kept quite a low profile in the country – their intervention was geographically limited to the capital where they "took care of the airport guards and logistics…looked after the government helicopters and when necessary flew them, organized artillery positioning and ammunition supply, and ensured radio communications,"[21] which was not enough to decisively nip the rebellion in the bud. Soon the French military contingent was increased to 600 soldiers, who played an instrumental role in buffering RPF attack but had not completely destroyed its belligerent potential.

The immediate result of this French intervention was that by November 1990 RPF operation had been stalled and it was forced to retreat to the mountainous parts of Uganda, and Habyarimana's regime was saved. Total suppression of the Tutsi population of the country, even more so, their complete eradication, as well as the creation of racist paramilitary groups as a result of this victory, has never been the objective of France, which attached the sense of morality to their intervention. On the contrary, after RPF was back to its initial positions in Uganda the French advisors pressed on Habyarimana to create favorable political conditions for domestic stabilization through power-sharing and administrative reforms and to allow all citizens' participation in the political life of Rwanda.

---

20 Kakwenzire, J. and Kamukama, D. 2000. The Development and Consolidation of Extremist Forces in Rwanda 1990-1994, in *The Path of a Genocide: The Rwanda Crisis from Uganda to* Zaire, edited by A. Howard and S. Astri. Transactions Publishing, 83.

21 Prunier, G. 1995, 110-111.

As a result political and diplomatic talks with Habyarimana following the French military actions and further pressure from the international community, Rwanda introduced reforms that were meant to be democratic in essence and to provide a remedy to ethnic tensions in the country. In the middle of 1991 Habyarimana adopted a new Constitution, which envisaged multi-party political system, created the office of Prime Minister, limited the term of presidency to a maximum of two consecutive terms of five years, and separated the legislative, judicial and executive governmental branches. International support quickly followed. The World Bank issued a loan of 80 million USD to "help solve chronic economic problems and calm heated political conditions brought on by RPF invasion". For its part, France provided 13.6 million USD to Rwanda in the form of a grant for purchasing its essential imports.[22]

These reforms, however, remained largely superficial and quite ineffective due to continuous suppression of the Tutsi minority. Right from the very beginning of RPF invasion, Habyarimana tried to represent it as an inside effort to bring the Tutsi ethnic group back into power. This further galvanized the Hutu population around the government after RPF's defeat leading to large-scale discrimination of Tutsis and liberal-minded Hutus. Arrests of Tutsi businessmen, teachers, and priests on the grounds of alleged cooperation with RPF were occurring everywhere. To increase the efficiency of suppression of the opposition, Habyarimana established well-trained and armed "death squads" – the so called *Interahamwe* ("Those Who Attack Together") and *Impuzamugambi* ("Those With a Single Purpose"), which were indoctrinated with racial hatred against Tutsis.[23] These were the groups that conducted most of the killings that were to follow.

UN Intervention (UNAMIR I)

The process of negotiations between the Rwanda government and RPF lasted nearly nine months from January to August 1993 and ended with the Arusha Agreement signed by the belligerents on August 4, 1993. The agreement package included four main aspects, agreed upon at various times: cease-fire (July 1992); power-sharing arrangement (October 1992 and January 1993); return of refugees (June 1993) and reform and integration of the armed forces (August 1993). The agreement that was meant to stop confrontation between Tutsis and Hutus became, in fact, the starting point for renewed tensions in Rwanda, and the main legal basis for further interventions. A number of African states concerned with the security situation in the region tried to get directly involved in this process –

22 Rwanda Chronology, University of Southern California, School of International Relations [Online]. Available at: http://www.usc.edu/dept/LAS/ir/cews/database/Rwanda/rwanda.doc [accessed: May 7, 2009].

23 Robbins R.H. (1999, 2002). *Global Problems and the Culture of Capitalism*. Allyn and Bacon, 271-272.

Nigeria, Senegal, Mali and Tanzania formed the Neutral Military Observer Group (NMOG) – which appeared completely ineffective and unsuccessful due to limited operational capacities, financial resources and personnel.

Domestically, due to unstable political situation in Rwanda and the split between moderate Hutus supporting further continuation of the negotiation process, on the one hand, and extremist racist militants, on the other, implementation of the Arusha Agreement was repeatedly blocked at home by Hutus who wanted to have a larger part in the new Transitional Government, including all its relevant spheres, especially the military. There were also the French lobbies of Habyarimana, who, in the words of the French Minister of Cooperation Marcel Debarge, advocated the creation of "a common front"[24] with Habyarimana against Tutsis.

For the purpose of fostering the process of preparation of the agreement and its implementation, in February 1993 Rwanda and Uganda applied to UN to deploy military observers along their 150-kilometre common border in order to prevent the military use of the area, especially the transit of military supplies. With the aim of fulfilling the terms of the Arusha Agreement, on June 22, 1993 UN Resolution 846 established an Observer Mission in Uganda-Rwanda (UNOMUR) with its headquarters in Kabale, a city in western Uganda, which, at its first stage included 81 military observers from Bangladesh, Botswana, Brazil, Hungary, Netherlands, Senegal, Slovak Republic and Zimbabwe.[25]

One month later the mission was renamed UNAMIR (UN Assistance Mission in Rwanda, later to be known as UNAMIR I) and was issued a mandate of "contributing to the establishment and maintenance of a climate conducive to the secure installation and subsequent operation of the transitional Government".[26] The main duties of UNAMIR I were ensuring security of Kigali, monitoring the fulfillment of the provision of the Arusha Agreement through notifying UN of non-compliance with the agreement, and facilitating the repatriation of refugees and IDPs. The Mission also coordinated humanitarian assistance with other UN agencies. UNAMIR I force included 2,539 military personnel from Bangladesh, Ghana, and Belgium, including former observers from UNOMUR and NMOG.

Two months after deployment of UNAMIR I UN Secretary General Boutros Ghali stressed its success when he called the Mission "a factor of stability in the area and that it was playing a useful role as a confidence-building mechanism".[27] With all this progress, UNAMIR I lacked the capacity to forcefully impose an effective

---

24 Prunier, G. 1995, 178.

25 The UN Security Council Resolution #846. 1993, New York [Online]. Available at: http://www.un.org/Docs/scres/1993/scres93.htm [accessed: May 7, 2009].

26 The UN Security Council Resolution #872. 1992, New York. [Online]. Available at: http://www.un.org/Docs/scres/1993/scres93.htm [accessed: May 7, 2009].

27 UNAMIR official website [Online]. Available at: http://www.un.org/Depts/dpko/dpko/co_mission/unamirFT.htm [accessed: May 7, 2009].

cease-fire option upon the belligerents,[28] which went beyond its mandate, which included mere monitoring and reporting on the implementation of the agreement – a far modest task. From the moral perspective, limitations of military capacity of UNAMIR I, in the words of Prunier (1995), meant that they "were completely useless because their mandate prevented them from interfering."[29] Although visible to people, UN impotent presence added to their despair. UNAMIR I was simply not meant for peace-enforcement with its operational objectives essentially limited to "the implementation of the Arusha agreements, including the installation of a Transitional Government".[30] Such a mandate excluded any direct clashes with the belligerents or creation of buffer zones between them to prevent from further atrocities. Nevertheless, with a limited scope of action, UMANIR I still was quite successful – not by ability to stop war but by fulfillment its operational manual. The participants of the Arusha process, indeed, revealed high level of collaboration: notwithstanding their sometimes conflicting positions, such as composition of military forces, both the government and RPF representatives "showed good will and cooperation with each other and with United Nations,"[31] as the UMAMIR itself reports.

After the initial high-spirited start of Arusha, tragic domestic contingencies worsened implementation of the results of the negotiations, endangered the implementation of the agreements and instigated the conflict. The first was the existence of a strong anti-Arusha and anti-Tutsi local lobby and in Rwanda: the ruling Hutu government was quite fragmented, with moderates supporting the peace settlement, and the "hawks" eager to exterminate the Hutus. Such gaps in elite preferences were reflected in the negotiation process itself, as well as in implementation of the terms of the agreement. The major reason why the Transitional Government and Transitional National Assembly had not been installed was differences in opinions within the existing government factions regarding its composition: how many places would be given to Tutsis was yet unclear.

The remaining two unrelated events had very grave consequences for the resumption of the conflict in Rwanda. The first was the murder of Melchior Ndadaye, the first Hutu President of Burundi, on October 1993 by extremist Tutsis and opposition Hutus. The resulting domestic conflict in Burundi ended up with the combined deaths of 50,000 people and the exodus of approximately 300,000 Hutus to Rwanda[32] and around 150,000 internally displaced Tutsis. Such acts of

28 Kuperman, A.J. 2001. *The Limits of Humanitarian Intervention. Genocide in Rwanda*. Washington, D.C.: The Brookings Institution Press, 40.

29 Prunier, G. 1995, 261.

30 Klinghoffer, A.J. 1998, 47.

31 UNAMIR official website [Online]. Available at: http://www.un.org/Depts/dpko/dpko/co_mission/unamirFT.htm [accessed: May 7, 2009].

32 Commission Internationale d'Etiquête sur les Violations des Droit de l'Homme au Burundi depuis le 21 Octobre 1993. 1994. *Rapport final*, Brussels.

violence and their aftermath greatly exacerbated internal anti-Tutsi sentiment and fueled hatred against them.

The other unfortunate turn was assassination of Habyarimana on April 6, 1994, when he was returning from a meeting with President Museveni. Together with him on the French Falcon plane was Cyprien Ntaryamira, a Hutu and the newly elected president of Burundi. While a number of theories have been spun as to who exactly was behind this act,[33] most probably this was done by Hutu warmongers opposing the progress of Arusha and fearing Habyarimana was a defector from the Hutu cause. The death of Habyarimana led to what is known as the Rwandan Genocide. Immediately the groups of violent *Interahamwe* launched wide-scale ethnic cleansing of Tutsi population and moderate Hutus not supporting violent nationalist stance of the masses. Among them was Prime Minister of the country Agathe Uwilingiyimana, who was assassinated together with 10 Belgium blue helmets. This event forced the Belgian government to reconsider its role in the multinational intervention and, ultimately, to withdraw from UNAMIR I under strong domestic pressure.

Following the Belgian retreat and fearful that its forces might become the target of interethnic violence, UN Security Council, instead of increasing its presence in the country and bringing in additional forces to enforce peace, decided to further reduce UNAMIR I forces by up to 270 troops.[34] This move showed absence of the will of the international community to save the lives of people and sent a conniving signal to the *Interahamwe* that they are at liberty to eradicate Tutsis. The remaining observers were given the task to act as intermediaries "between the parties in an attempt to secure their agreement to a ceasefire; assist in the resumption of humanitarian relief operations to the extent feasible; and monitor developments in Rwanda".[35] No additional military inputs were envisaged from the major international players to increase UN force, hence the mandate could not be amended to prevent further killings of the civilian population. The biggest possible contributors, both financially and militarily, had their own problems: Russia was too preoccupied with its ongoing war in Chechnya, and US, according to Klinghoffer (1998), was "reluctant to put peacekeepers in jeopardy in a military conflict with no ceasefire",[36] especially after its painful experience in Somalia.

Given the indications coming from UN monitoring on frequent clashes in Kigali, controlled by government forces and RPF from Uganda, as well as on alleged preparations for further massacres of civilians, Ghali still managed to

---

33 Prunier brings up a number of considerations of who is to be blamed for killing Habyarimana: the PRF, the French, the Hutu extremists, the hired hands (see Prunier, G. 1995, 213-229).

34 The UN Security Council Resolution #912. 1994, New York. [Online]. Available at: http://www.un.org/Docs/scres/1994/scres94.htm [accessed: May 7, 2009].

35 UNAMIR official website [Online]. Available at: http://www.un.org/Depts/dpko/dpko/co_mission/unamirFT.htm [accessed: May 7, 2009].

36 Klinghoffer, A.J. 1998, 51.

pass UN Resolution 918 on May 17, 1994, which included two crucial points: it enlarged the limited UN force by up to 5,500 military observers and, most importantly, included protection of civilians in its mandate.[37] The peace-making component mandate was again absent from the new mandate, although UN troops were given the right to open fire in self-defense. The key task of UN intervention remained implementation of the Arusha provisions.

Deployment of additional UN troops coincided with major advances of RPF, which by mid-April 1994 approached Kigali. At this time, there was a quite evident change within the ranks of RPF: although the "Uganda nucleus" holding key posts within the rebellion still remained, RPF was now recruiting much less selectively from the new arrivals that were fleeing from Hutu Power persecutions. Secondly, RPF now also included Tutsis who had fled from neighboring Burundi out of fears of persecution after the failed coup organized there by Tutsi paratroopers in October 1993. These Tutsis, too, nursed bitter sentiments against the Burundi Hutu in particular, and all Hutus in general, including those in Rwanda. RPF now included not only those who viewed the war as a political and non-ethnic evil, but also large numbers of "new" Tutsis outraged with Hutus and wanting to take revenge against those who had brutalized their kin.

Enlargement of RPF had overall negative consequences for the population of the territories they occupied. Obviously, the Hutu population, although not necessarily participating in mass murders of Tutsis themselves, did their "liberation" by RPF. There was a vital need to separate the two groups: advancing Tutsis, on the one hand, and the remaining Hutu Power politicians, their Interahamwe operatives together with the ordinary Hutus, which might have fallen victim to the gaining momentum RPF.

French Intervention

The poorly functional Transition Government was completely useless in keeping the *Interahamwe* from mass killings of Tutsis, even if they had wanted to. The situation was indeed tense: RPF was capturing region after region. Seeing the rapid advances of RPF, UN needed to prevent another ethnic cleansing, this time the one against Hutus. For this it needed to quickly deploy forces on the ground, taking into account the lengthy decision-making process in the Security Council. France was the one member-country that willingly agreed to serve as a protector and peacekeeper to clear its tarnished image from the 1990 intervention. A "buffer zone" was needed quickly and effectively to save the lives of the people. As a country with traditional interests in the region and having already intervened once in Rwanda, France volunteered to set "safe haven" for the retreating FAR soldiers and the Hutu Power people.

---

37 The UN Security Council Resolution #918. 1994, New York. [Online]. Available at: http://www.un.org/Docs/scres/1994/scres94.htm [accessed: May 7, 2009].

After its initial involvement in Rwanda in October-November 1990, France did not actively participate in conflict resolution processes in Rwanda. On the one hand, France was vitally interested in maintaining its presence in the country, at least, on the cultural level, to re-establishing its patronage over Francophone Africa. When RPF made its advances, France wanted to interfere to redeem itself from the image of Hutu supporters and, at the same time, to preserve Hutus from possible atrocities on the part of RPF. An image of peacemaker demanded from France no participation in direct clashes with the rebels who, as it seemed, would become future leaders of the country. Therefore, France was not aiming at launching large-scale military intervention within Rwanda that would antagonize Tutsis. Also, possible clashes would mean some battle casualties for the French military and carried the risk that France might lose their significance in the region and suffer from the damage to its superpower image both inside France and in Rwanda.

These considerations put French government in a real quagmire: it feared negative consequences of possible collision with RPF but had no wish to restore the Hutu Power from moral considerations. In addition to peacemaking function, according to Klinghoffer (1998), France was interested in a short-term humanitarian intervention to counter the negative international and domestic publicity after its earlier fiasco with Habyarimana.[38] Under such circumstances all France left with was to make a cautious face-saving show of force, which would transfer the entire responsibility in case of failure to other actors, in this case, UN. Prime Minister Balladur even depicted the forthcoming intervention as "a moral act aimed at stopping genocide", and claimed that there were "no French strategic interests… involved".[39] Essentially, France wanted to protect itself from accusations that it was not stepping up to the plate to protect its former colonial possessions from sectarian bloodshed. Nevertheless, perhaps, the main reason for French involvement was a sort of a moral obligation – may be not to overall humanity per se and Tutsis victims of genocide, but, at least, to the Hutu establishment whom France had supported previously during Habyarimana times.

In June President Mitterrand officially requested the intervention mandate from UN Security Council, which was soon granted by UN Resolution 929 under Chapter 7 of UN Charter. According to the mandate, the French mission had to be humanitarian in nature; France would guarantee security and protection of refugees and civilians at risk, and, more specifically, would abstain from direct peace-making entailing military clashes with the belligerents.[40] The French were allowed to remain in Rwanda for a maximum of two months until the final deployment of UNAMIR II. In assigning these tasks and limiting them in time, UN also had its own fears that their mandated intervention, especially if remained longer, could

38 Klinghoffer, A.J. 1998, 82.

39 Klinghoffer, A.J. 1998, 84.

40 The UN Security Council Resolution #929. 1994, New York. [Online]. Available at: http://www.un.org/Docs/scres/1994/scres94.htm [accessed: May 7, 2009].

be suffer casualties and, in the worst case, be even defeated as a result of possible military actions – this would damage its own prestige as a global organization.

By its scale of deployment, French Operation Turquoise was cumbersome: for a total of 2,550 soldiers from French and some African countries (Senegal, Mauritania, Egypt, Guinea-Bissau, Chad, and Niger) there were about 100 armored vehicles, a battery of marine mortars, 10 helicopters, and 12 fighter-bomber aircrafts. This was a real show of force both to Hutu, who warmly welcomed the armada, and RPF soldiers, who were on the ascendant. Seeing these menacing forces creating a buffer between them and Hutus, and fearing that they would also suffer losses, RPF decided to rest on their gains and not to challenge the French. By punishing the genocide perpetrators RPF was eager to establish a positive domestic and international image for itself not as a "Tutsi avenger", but as a true "democratizer" of Rwanda and a human rights protector. This allowed the "Operation Turquoise" to flow practically bloodless and to prevent any casualties. As a result, Operation Turquoise succeeded in prevention of further advances of RPF, who was not ready to get involved in open warfare with the insuperable French force. French intervention created "safe heavens" for the ex-government soldiers and civilians who had fled in the face of RPF advances and even assisted them to leave the country.[41] All this did not go without notice by RPF, who, thought, could do nothing but accept the French presence. Notwithstanding the French presence the rebel troops had not ceased their advances: as a result in less than in two weeks RPF seized Kigali finally ending what became later widely known as the Rwandan Genocide.

UN Intervention (UNAMIR II)

After having successfully separated the antagonists, the French troops were replaced by the contingent of evolved UNAMIR II. The key tasks of the renewed UN mission were "to ensure stability and security in the north-western and south-western regions of Rwanda; to stabilize and monitor the situation in all regions of Rwanda to encourage the return of the displaced population; to provide security and support for humanitarian assistance operations inside Rwanda; and to promote, through mediation and good offices, national reconciliation in Rwanda".[42] UNAMIR II was also mandated with monitoring the activities of local police and gendarmerie and those of the civil authorities with regard to human

41 A number of scholars have indicated a positive attitude on the part of the French military not to *Interahamwe* and government forces per se, but the Hutu civilians and all the French-speaking population in general. See: Omar, R. and de Waal, A. 1995. *Rwanda: Death, Despair and Defiance*. London: African Rights, 1145-1146 and Destexhe, A. 1995. *Rwanda and Genocide in the Twentieth Century*. New York: New York University Press, 54.

42 UNAMIR official website [Online]. Available at: http://www.un.org/Depts/dpko/dpko/co_mission/unamirFT.htm [accessed: May 7, 2009].

rights violations and protecting the workers of the International Tribunal set up in Arusha by UN Resolution 955 on in November 1994. Its special training unit, CIVPOL, was involved in training the Rwandan policemen. Another important side of UNAMIR II was the program of state-building; within this framework, it began operating a radio station in three languages calling for national reconciliation.

In addition to Rwanda per se, UNAMIR II was also active in the neighboring countries, mainly in Congo, where the refugees from both sides were. Its peacekeepers protected the refugee camps and prevented re-influx of Hutu rebels from these camps and other areas. To make this effort more effective and to safeguard Rwanda from Hutu attacks from outside, UN acted in a very a peculiar fashion: it suspended the arms embargo against Rwanda but retained it for other countries, thus, reducing "the likelihood that the refugees would return home as part of a military operation."[43]

One of the examples of successful work by UNAMIR II was the case of the Kibeho refugee camp in the Gikongoro region. Seven out of eight camps had been closed down by the Rwandese Government out of fears that they would harbor former *Interahamwe* elements, thereby posing a security threat to the new government. At Kibeho there were about 80,000 IDPs who escaped the camp and spent five days in the hills without food, adequate space and proper sanitation. Under such conditions, UNAMIR II immediately ensured transportation of IDPs, organized casualty collection posts and provided emergency medical assistance. It also evacuated sick and injured people to nearby medical facilities in the city of Butare. Another example of successful humanitarian assistance within the frameworks of UNAMIR II was UN World Food Program, which distributed food to a total of 420,000 beneficiaries. Other assistance activities included rehabilitation of hospitals and health centers by UNHCR, health training programs undertaken by World Health Organization and United Nations Population Fund, water supply projects undertaken by UNICEF, and assistance by UNICEF to some 2,000 unaccompanied minors.[44]

With the purpose of national reconciliation, UN established the HRFOR (Human Rights Field Operation in Rwanda), which was composed of 113 staff in 11 field offices involved in confidence-building measures. HRFOR carried out investigations of genocide and other grave human rights violations; it created comprehensive human rights field offices with the aim of monitoring the current human rights situation; it started promotional human rights activities, such as rebuilding of the Rwandese administration of justice to human rights education. Another important mission of HRFOR was protection of human rights during the implementation of the process of repatriation and resettlement of former refugees and IDPs, which was an uneasy task. HRFOR also monitored the situation of state prisons and assisted in restructuring the justice system at national and local levels.

---

43 Klinghoffer, A.J. 1998, 69.

44 UNAMIR official website [Online]. Available at: http://www.un.org/Depts/dpko/dpko/co_mission/unamirFT.htm [accessed: May 7, 2009].

After six months of its deployment, the capacities of UNAMIR II reached its peak with 5,740 peacekeepers and military observers. At this point, UN began to gradually decrease its presence in Rwanda, but keeping engaged in such activities as "helping in the distribution of humanitarian assistance; facilitating the return and reintegration of refugees; providing assistance and expertise in engineering, logistics, medical care and de-mining…"[45] This downsizing and subsequent retreat of UNAMIR II happened due to two reasons, the first being the overall political stabilization of Rwanda after the conflict was ended. For his part, RPF quickly started building a coalition government. Although the majority of the executive government posts have been allocated to Hutus as a gesture of ethnic reunion and overall forgiveness, the real power remained with RPF. Gradually, Rwanda started resembling a normally functioning state, and, together with the move to suspend its arms embargo, UN decided that the country should rely on its own military capabilities.

Another reason for UN withdrawal was its chronic internal organizational financial problems and appearance of local conflicts elsewhere in the world, which required immediate UN reaction. On its part, the new government of Rwanda was itself willing to be relieved of UN presence. Its leadership, which had opposed the initial downsizing of UNAMIR I forces in April 1994, accused the international community in conniving at increased hostilities against Tutsis by Hutus. Now that the conflict was over the Rwandan government had no need for UN, which, as they bitterly claimed, did nothing to stop mass killings. New Rwandan establishment also protested against the "unfair" distribution of humanitarian aid by UN to Hutu refugees, whom they considered to be genocide perpetrators, instead of using it for country development.

Most of all, the government's ire toward UN was due to its authorization of the French intervention, which, in the eyes of RPF, had protected Hutu criminals and shadowed their escape from the country's new government. The Hutu-sheltering actions of the French had not passed without notice by RPF. RPF military leader and Kagame, when referring to UN in general, and French peacekeepers, in particular, mused that "[t]hey have been basking in the sunshine, burning fuel, doing nothing and receiving the credit for creating this peace environment. We do not accept that. We're happy they're gone".[46]

UN presence in Rwanda ended on April 19, 1996. Upon withdrawal of UN troops, the new government agreed to establish UN Office in Rwanda for coordination of humanitarian assistance, monitoring of human rights abuses and further peace-building actions.

45 UNAMIR official website [Online]. Available at: http://www.un.org/Depts/dpko/dpko/co_mission/unamirFT.htm [accessed: May 7, 2009].

46 Interview with Paul Kagame in *The Newsweek*, International edition, 1996. April 1, CXXVII/12:54.

Analysis of the Interventions

Altogether, four interventions had been conducted in Rwanda starting with early 1990s. France and later UN intervened twice with the single purpose of putting an end to the conflict but with different rationales. The first intervention of France, as a single state, had the aims of stopping RPF assault and saving the Habyarimana regime. Later Operation Turquoise was mandated by and conducted on the behalf of international community, although not unanimously supported by the Security Council. Its goals were prevention of the further humanitarian catastrophe that would possibly follow rapid advances of RPF and suspected indiscriminative revenge of Tutsis over the fleeing Hutus.

The direct outcomes of the two French interventions, in general terms, corresponded with its initial goals. When intervening in 1990, the French never planned to completely destroy the opposition, which in less than five years (as goes with the peace-centric approach to interventions) resumed its attacks on the Hutu government. A clear evidence of this fact is that RPF's small-scale assaults on Rwanda's territory had not cease even after it had been forced to retreat to Uganda. No massive and large-scale military actions with the purpose of complete, despiteful and decisive destruction of RPF was ever envisaged or planned. The French presence remained largely externalized to the conflict with limited goals. The French troops had never actually participated in one-on-one combat with RPF, but provided other important support to the Rwandan army: trained high-level FAR cadre, provided for the physical protection of President Habyarimana, and supplied technical equipment and know-how to the FAR. Military capabilities of the French troops can be an additional evidence of this: during their first intervention in 1990, the limited presence of first 150 and later 600 French troops was quite low as to reach victory in open military clashes with RPF. The maximum number of French soldiers was still only 15 per cent as big as the 4,000-strong RPF.

Also, for complete destruction of RPF the French would have needed to go across the border with Uganda, where the main RPF bases where. This would already be an interstate war with involvement of the third state, which would have made the French efforts more complicated, long-lasting, costly, and, probably, less likely to succeed. Such a scenario was in the mind of the French intervention: they did not want to be deeply involved with the domestic Rwandan problematique and to undertake the role of an external guarantor of peace. In addition to pure military efforts, such internalization of the intervention would have required substantial economic support coming from France to keep the ongoing intervention. Also, longer presence of the French troops in Rwanda and their foreseeable military actions outside its borders would increase international publicity of their intervention, which would put the French soldiers in the spotlight of media attention. Last, but not the least, prolonged intervention would inevitably have a negatively effect on domestic veto-players in France and public opinion putting additional pressure on successful fulfillment of its goals.

With limited operational inputs, France significantly contributed to the rapid victory of the government forces over the Tutsi rebels, who were credibly threatened by the presence of highly-trained and equipped French personnel. The credibility of French support was further strengthened by the fact that France was clearly a major power, at least, by the African standards. In comparison with the belligerents, it possessed the most up-to-date military know-how; its troops were much better trained and equipped; and it had strategic warfare logic that was absent in the ranks of newly formed Tutsi armature opposition. It was also able to quickly marshal resources and deploy its military personnel.

Abstaining from direct clashes with the opposition also had its share in the success of the Operation Turquoise. An open military fight would have had an overall negative impact on a third party presence both from the viewpoint of domestic veto groups that would question human and economic costs of their country's actions, and the international community, which would also raise issues as to the necessity of direct confrontation. Although the advancing army condemned the French backing of *Interahamwe*, claiming that the killings of Tutsis continued on the French-controlled territory, they never did so openly and defiantly. Even though RPF had long held grievances against France coming from their early defeat in 1990 by the FAR and French combined forces and subsequent French lobbying on behalf of Habyarimana government and Hutu Power, RPF never directly challenged the French presence. RPF also wanted to create the image of a force, which had more of a political, rather than ethnic agenda. Several of its key figures were Hutus (for example, the first after war president Pasteur Bizimungu); a part of rebel troops were also moderate Hutus, who had fled from persecutions in Rwanda. RPF aspired to tell the international community that it had a balanced and fair approach to the solution of the conflict, which did not mean extermination of all Hutus, but, rather, the removal of those who were directly involved in genocide actions.

Another cause of the success of the first French intervention, as a sole actor, was its timing: intervention took place from the very beginning of warfare. The rapid deployment of the French troops to the conflict scene resulted in stopping the advance of the opposition that was poorly organized, had hectic and uncontrolled movements, and, therefore, was quite ineffective. RPF advances had not possessed all the necessary military means to effectively crush the FAR, and the assistance of the French to the FAR from the very beginning of the conflict had an important effect on the course of further clashes.

The fact of early intervention into the target country also contributed to success of the French intervention. As a matter of military tactics, when an advancing group captures certain territory, it tries to use it as an economic stronghold to sustain further attacks. The group will try to use available resources of the land under its control – food, cattle, fuel, etc. – to keep subsequent military activities. The group will also try to recruit additional people, usually having kinship connections or simply sympathizing with them, to join their ranks from the territory it newly controls. In the case of the French intervention, RPF was not given the chance to capture any sizable territory, thus weakening its fighting capacities. To further this timing argument, early entry into the scene helped to prevent large casualties on both sides had the war reached a protracted phase.

The final factor facilitating successes of the first unilateral actions of France was direction of its support, which was offered to the stronger of the two conflict players. Aiding the government, which, at that time was in a much stronger position than the opposing forces of RPF, largely predetermined victorious first French intervention. Hutus represented the majority of the Rwandan population, and the government was mainly composed of Hutus and enjoyed considerable military advantage over RPF. Also, FAR alone possessed sufficient means to subdue RPF, and the presence of French officers among its ranks not only raised their military morale, but also gave a subliminal message that, in case of a possible defeat by RPF, the French, taking into account their strength and their will to uphold the country's prestige in the international arena, would not hesitate to engage militarily against the rebels.

Military and technological advantage was also a variable in success of Operation Turquoise, which had a visible operational and military advantage against RPF. If not the French and, subsequently, UNAMIR, the situation would have been far more serious: taking into consideration the changes within RPF ranks, negative memories of people-genocide victims and fleeing from Burundi. Thus, for example, the French troops secured about 1.2 million people, who, according to Prunier (1995), "would start moving again at any time if they feared that their temporary situation was about to change".[47]

From the time-scale viewpoint, like the first unilateral intervention, success of Operation Turquoise was also partly due to the early intervention timing. France intervened when RPF was just gaining strength, capturing city after city. There was a direct threat of another mass killing taking place, now by Tutsis, and, in this case, it would have been much harder to stop the conflict. Intervening early, the French saved the lives of many thousands of people and sent a clear message to Tutsis to abstain from direct clashes.

From the viewpoint of direction of its support, Operation Turquoise was essentially a neutral mission authorized by the international community. A large degree of success of the second French intervention was due to the fact that it was now a UN-mandated mission, i.e. an intervention enriched with some moral and ethical aspects. This allowed for perception of neutrality in action even though PRF was sure that the French in these settings were not neutral. Nevertheless, RPF perceived Operation Turquoise as a part of UN, and considered that if the French had acted hostile, i.e. engaged in large-scale military operations openly taking sides and backing Hutus, there would have been a quick end to that by other members of the Security Council. Taking into account the already widespread negative international publicity and wide usage of the term "genocide", in case of

47 Prunier, G. 1995, 299.

French battling PRF, UN mandate would have been greatly jeopardized and the French would have been considered hostile interveners.

The process of institutionalization of the intervention under the aegis of UN also showed to Tutsis that if fight erupts with the French soldiers, this would be against the common standing of a larger international community, which gave its blessing to the intervention. UN well-aware of the bitter feelings Tutsis had harbored against the French military. Therefore, with the purpose of prevention of further bloodshed UN gave the French its mandate for operation and brought in other member-states, thus institutionalizing the neutrality of the whole process for the Tutsis, at least, on the surface.

The remaining two interventions were conducted by UN and had diverse goals. Their successes, like those of any other actions committed jointly by states within international organizational frameworks, are judged in accordance with its corresponding mandates. The first multilateral intervention, UNAMIR I, was a pure observer mission with no mandate to directly interfere in the active warfare either by helping either side of the conflict or acting as a buffer force to separated them. The second, UNAMIR II, had more peace-building, national reconciliation and state-reconstruction aims. It is a fact that UN had not stopped the genocide: for this, it had neither the required resources nor the wholehearted will of the member-states. Just as with any monitoring mission that is blamed for inability to stop conflicts, being not mandated with peace-enforcement efforts, UN should not be accused of failing to enforce peace.

The most important factor in the success of UN interventions, also present in the second unilateral intervention of France, was its neutrality. UN was not interested in punishing or rewarding any side of the conflict but was only involved in peacekeeping operations and provision of humanitarian assistance. The neutral nature of the intervention facilitated its acceptance by Hutus and RPF alike who could not accuse UN for siding with their rivals. In this sense, UN neutrality in its institutional arrangements also facilitated the success of the French Operation Turquoise. While not quite welcoming the French presence in their country, RPF had to accept it as a necessary evil and as a part of the overall UN operation. They, of course, thought that the French were helping the Hutu Power to escape. However, since the French intervention was mandated by UN – a neutral and impartial international organization – Tutsis had to trust that France would not go beyond their mandated actions and fight against them as it had done during their first intervention back in 1990.

Another variable that promoted the success of UN actions was externalization of its presence by employing a minimalist approach in its operations. Initially, UNAMIR I was limited to monitoring the fulfillment of the Arusha Agreement. Subsequently, the UN mission was ordered not to intervene directly in warfare and its peacekeepers were yet allowed to open fire if attacked. Obviously, with its limited financial and human resources, it could not stop the conflict in Rwanda or even intervene effectively with the purpose of separating the troops. A clear indication of the fact that the goal of UNAMIR I was not putting the end to hostilities, according to Gourevitch, is a cable sent by its head Romeo Dallaire on April 21, 1994, which read that with "just with five thousand well-equipped soldiers and a free hand to fight Hutu Power he could bring the genocide to a rapid end. No military analyst…has ever questioned his judgment, and a great many have confirmed it".[48] Yet the same day the personnel of UNAMIR I faced nearly a 90 per cent cut; instead of 5,000, Dallaire was left with only 270 troops. This all meant that UN was pursuing an externalized modus operandi in its action: it was present in Rwanda, but its presence from the point of view of interfering into actual conflict was not visible.

Such behavior of UN, how amoral or unethical may seem at first glance, clearly indicates that even though UN, its Secretary General its Security Council as a representative body of decision-making states, were indeed concerned with ending killings in Rwanda, they had not defined the actions directed at stopping genocide within their legal framework. Second, UN had actually acted within its limited mandate of mere monitoring of the situation. Had the Security Council approved extension of the scope of UNAMIR I mandate, ordering it to directly act against the Hutu Power and end killings of Tutsis, and had it failed in this endeavor, then UN intervention would have been considered as failed.

This did not happen, and UN contingent was cut even further, its scope limited and clear instructions had been given to Dallaire to refrain from involvement in warfare. Putting aside moral judgments, UNAMIR I cannot be accused of failing to bring peace simply because this was not its goal. Such reasoning was also confirmed by Dallaire himself, who, when speaking on the Canadian television, admitted with bitterness, "The real question is: What does the international community really want UN to do? …UN simply wasn't given the tools…We did not want to take on the Rwandan armed forces and the *Interahamwe*."[49]

To be fair, a moral aspect of UN involvement in Rwanda was within the focus of international community, mass-media, policy-makers and NGOs. To paraphrase Dallaire's question, why had UN not intervened effectively to prevent killing on both sides? The main bases for wide-scale military intervention of UN is, in principle, its Charter and numerous conventions concerning keeping peace and protection of human lives and dignity, in this particular case, the Genocide Convention of 1948, which clearly describes the human rights abuses that qualify as genocide and defines the conditions under which use of force to enforce peace is required. If the Rwandan situation were acknowledged as genocide as it constituted a violation of the relevant convention, then UN should have acted with the single purpose of fulfillment of the main task it is supposed to serve, i.e. putting an end to it. This would have meant not merely paying a lip-service to concerned states and their populations by bringing the word genocide into popular discourse, but

48 Gourevitch, P. 2000. *We Wish To Inform You That Tomorrow We Will Be Killed With Our Families*. Picador: Macmillan Publishers Ltd., 153.

49 Gourevitch, P. 2000, 170.

also having an open agenda and mandate with clearly stated tasks of ending mass murders, backed up by the decisive usage of force against the perpetrators.

The factors preventing large-scale peace-enforcement mandate was economy and political will of intervention. Key financial contributor to of the UN presence in Rwanda was the US. The timing of the conflict in Rwanda corresponded with the failed UN/US intervention in Somalia. As a result of unsuccessful operation there, US was extremely hesitant to agree to a genocide wording of the events in Rwanda, which would require due inputs. In this connection, Gourevitch (2000) gave a clear account of the US role: "[T]here are obligations which arise in connection with the use of the term…[I]f it was a genocide, the Convention of 1948 required the contracting parties to act. Washington did not want to act. So Washington pretended that it wasn't a genocide".[50] Fresh from the defeat in Somalia, US was not yet ready for another humanitarian intervention, which, taken high level of violence, would place the US soldiers on the fire line. The situation was the same with the international community in general, which preferred not to call this a genocide and hence not to intervene to stop the killing.

All went wrong in Rwanda for the victims and UN: the global intergovernmental organization, which was supposed to uphold the fundamental pillars of peace and security, refrained from using this term for as long as possible in order not to invoke the mechanisms of the Charter and the Convention, thus saving military, economic and human resources of member-states that wishes to stay aside of the murderous situation. Thus, neither the will nor the resources were present for UN to act in accordance with the Convention in order to halt the bloodshed in Rwanda.

Finally, specific timing of intervention also contributed to success of the UN operations, although different from the timing of unilateral actions. Unlike the first French intervention and the Operation Turquoise, which succeeded largely due to intervention in the early times of conflict, UN accomplished its invention objectives primarily because intervening late in the conflict. This difference can be explained in a number of ways. The legal frameworks of secession of hostilities, i.e. the Arusha Agreement, have marked the low level of fighting, saving the UN personnel from direct participation in military activities against any of the conflicting parties. UNAMIR I was not supposed to get engaged in enforcing peace, just providing what Carment and Harvey (2001) called, "…the stamp of institutional legitimacy"[51] to the agreement.

The UN troops were not directly involved in military activities, and but could concentrate on peace-building, rather than on peace-enforcement, which is fraught with serious consequences for the UN, as an institution, in case of the deaths of its peacekeepers. Intervening after the actual end of hostilities had saved UN from additional casualties and kept the decision-making spirit unanimous

50 Gourevitch, P. 2000, 153.

51 Carment, D. and Harvey, F. 2001. *Using Force to Prevent Ethnic Violence: An Evaluation of Theory and Evidence*, Westport, Connecticut, London: Preager Studies on Ethnic and National Identities in Politics, Praeger 129.

within the Security Council. A tragic example of killings of the Belgian troops and subsequent withdrawal of Belgium from the coalition shows how vulnerable the multilateral intervention might be due to attacks on its member's soldiers. An important point to make is that UN, as any international organization, remains very much concerned with its prestige in the international arena. With regards to its operations in Rwanda, and, specifically, concerning its military capacities, UN prestige means two things: fulfillment of its mandated goals and doing this with the minimum human casualties. In other words, in order to be successful, UN had to be realistic, if not minimalistic, in establishing accomplishable and feasible goals of its missions. As for UNAMIR II, its peace-building operations started already when the conflict was over and no large-scale military actions had been conducted elsewhere in the country.

Conclusions

The conflict in Rwanda represents a perfect example of inconsistency of the existing scholarship in relation to defining the success of interventions: for example, the French intervention in 1990 was included among "unsuccessful" third party actions in Regan's dataset, while COW 3 database does not even include outside interventions in the Rwandan conflict. The end of conflict and absence of hostilities, i.e. de facto peace, used as a proxy for successful third party interventions, is, in fact, not applicable in the Rwandan case.

In considering successes and failures of interventions in Rwanda an important methodological part of the comparative analysis should be mentioned: the independence of individual observations. Although France and UN intervened twice, the success of the first two interventions had no relevant influence on the course of the second ones. If anything, the earlier intervention in support of one party should have undermined the success of the subsequent intervention in the environment where the rival faction was a clear winner. For instance, as the French had supported Hutu Power during the first intervention they should have faced more difficulty when intervening later on. This meant that RPF government of the second intervention was not well-disposed to the French presence in the country. Their actions, however, did not appear to have negatively affected the effectiveness of the second intervention; in both the first and the second cases, the French succeeded in reaching their intervention agendas. Same goes for UNAMIR I and II: accusations by Tutsis of UN's turning a blind eye on the Hutu atrocities in the beginning of the conflict should have jeopardized subsequent peace-building mission as lacking credibility and trust.

The factor that equally contributed to successes of the interventions was externalization of their operations. Neither of the third parties was deeply involved in the conflict, nor was it committed to do so. Multilateral interventions also succeeded because of neutrality of their actions: both UNAMIR and the French Operation Turquoise, notwithstanding the considerable belligerent potential of the latter, preferred not to engage in open combat with the warring parties. Although the first French intervention was clearly biased and supported the ruling government (which was an additional factor for its success), their second operation was conducted under the aegis of the international organization, which minimized any existing or potential bias and helped the French achieve bloodless separation of the belligerents. The individual commitment of the French as a regional superpower to the Rwandese as a nation and the Hutus as an ethnic group was, first, neutralized by the international organization of which it was a part, and, second, limited by UN mandated framework.

The factor different in the success of unilateral and multilateral interventions was their timing: while the former two succeeded in intervening early in the conflict, the latter intervened after the end of active hostilities. Apart from avoiding battle-related casualties which would have been more vulnerable for an organization rather than a sole state, the role of the timing can be by actor-relevant peculiarities. For a unilateral intervener it is usually easier to mobilize resources in a short time-frame than for an organization, which has to clear internal bureaucracy and to have commitment from its member-states. In case of the Operation Turquoise, UN gave its mandate to France to act rapidly and to prevent further hostilities, which it itself was not in position to do so efficiently.

Although neither of the outside actors had ended the conflict per se, they still succeeded in fulfilling their tasks, which, in words of Gourevitch (2000), would mean that their “first commitment was not to protect people, but to protect their mandates”.[52] Nevertheless, neither of them shall be viewed as a failure. In sum, the case of Rwanda suggests that, to be successful, unilateral interventions should be conducted by (regional) superpower for immediate and powerful deployment but to include small-scale rapid-deployment operations at the beginning of a conflict with the aim of assisting the government of a target country. For the multilateral interventions to be successful, they need to have a mandate limited to neutral non-combat missions, which should be strictly adhered to.

52 Gourevitch, P. 2000, 289.

Chapter 7
A Successful Intervention: When, Where and How

Sets of challenges and opportunities third parties face during their interventions contributing to or preventing implementation of their stated goals and objectives can be viewed at three separate but much interconnected levels: systemic (international level), internal sub-systemic (domestic settings in the target countries) and external sub-systemic (domestic settings in the interveners' countries). On the first level, developments in the conflict-affected countries are closely scrutinized by the international community of states or individual countries having their vital interests and stakes in possible conflict scenarios. Depending on circumstances, foreign countries may wish to intervene jointly or to authorize intervention of one or more state on behalf of a wider representative body they are members to. For their part, actions of interveners are also closely monitored by other states that are concerned with the courses of the events in target countries. This puts additional pressure on the interveners in the form of discussions of the conflict and intervention-related matters between different "state-stakeholders", or joint reaction of the international community to particular activities of third parties.

On the second level domestic political landscape of target countries comes into play. Administrative, political and ethnic dividing lines may further complicate or enhance actions of interveners depending on the directions of their support. Willingness of warring factions to cooperate with outside actors or, on the contrary, their repulsive reaction to any outside interference in their domestic affairs may take interventions to directions different from those otherwise planned. Diverse levels of hostilities, different timelines of conflicts, the specific power arrangements on the ground, or even geography – all that influences the odds of success of third parties. Presence of valuable resources presents strong incentives for the belligerents to start and continue conflicts, as well as for the outside actors to intervene. History of interethnic relations is also a powerful factor in explaining emergence of conflicts, their courses of actions, causes of interventions, and probabilities of their successes or failures.

Third, who the third parties are, what composition they have, what forms the interveners take, what relationships they have with belligerent groups in target countries, what capacities they possess and what tools they use, what standings they have on international arena – all these matter in the ability of third-parties to successfully reach targeted objectives. Their domestic political climate plays has a significant influence over successful fulfillment of intervention goals. Power games with opposition parties, other interest groups and veto players influencing wider public opinion may seriously undermine actions of their governments abroad. Domestic politics of interveners substantially influences membership of their state in coalitions and represents the forces that state authorities cannot neglect while furnishing their country's interventions. Fearing negative publicity and domestic reaction to their foreign operations, state governments may chose more clandestine and less transparent actions that would further affect their end-results.

Conclusions from the case studies presented in the book that focus on the issue of effectiveness of third parties' actions are divided in two parts. Firstly, combined results for success and failure factors are defined separately for unilateral and multilateral interventions. The findings are further grouped in relation to the variables that help single actors reach their goals, and the variables that prevented them from being successful. The same is done for the multilateral interventions. Finally, common criteria for success for both cases are generalized in a SWOT-like format to highlight strengths, weaknesses, opportunities and threats third parties may face during their interventions and to answer the initial epistemological question – what makes some conflict interventions more successful than others?

Success Factors of Unilateral Interventions

It would utterly be naive to imagine that third parties engage in interventions, which are by definition costly endeavors, entirely with the purpose of saving lives of the people affected by conflicts. It would be equally unfounded to assume that interveners are only concerned with provision of assistance to the belligerent parties they support. In unilateral interventions, perhaps, more than in multilateral ones, the issue of personal benefits and costs for individual states is of key importance. In addition to the considerable domestic and international political risks of interventions, third parties are confronted with economic expenses that might not be even presumed at the deliberation stage of interventions, and the need to have sufficient means to conduct economic and/or military actions, which also have their economic value.

Due to their nature, unilateral interveners have a number of benefits in comparison with the multilateral ones. Unlike third parties acting under the umbrella of multinational organization, single states make decisions on the basis of their own preferences, which they may not be ready to discuss or even agree upon with other states. Hence, they can take decisions and actually intervene in considerably shorter time span that their multilateral counterparts, having the advantages of organizing their operational and tactical decision-making bypassing elaborate and slow process of joint approval of multilateral organization or even obtaining the international mandates for their actions. Sole interveners are also usually free from international scrutiny during their actions on the ground: there are no forces from other countries to monitor their actions. This brings more freedom in movements of troops and equipment to unilateral actors since they do not have to pass through the operational standardization processes of multinational organizations, and can use the means available to accomplish their intervention aims faster and, therefore, more effectively.

At the same time, unilateral interveners have own shortcomings. Their biggest weakness stems from their composition, which is their bias in actions. Even if single actors strife to look neutral and/or impartial to the countries' populations they intervene and to the international community, in very few circumstances are they considered as such. The warring groups usually accuse interveners for supporting their rivals or for not fully punishing them. Operational bias is closely related to the factor of trust to the interveners, which is based on institutionalized legitimacy of the outcomes offered and/or imposed. In comparison with the multilateral third parties, which legitimize the options they offer within institutional settings, trust to the options of sole interveners is grounded on their perceptions and will alone. Following this point is the lower level of acceptability of these options to the local populations: whatever their actions, unilateral interveners will be considered as illegal aggressors by the side they act against.

Within all these general pros and cons of unilateral interventions, there are factors that build-up their potential to succeed or impede implementation of their actions. The factors generated during the case studies of the conflicts in Chad, Georgia, Somalia and Rwanda that contribute to the third parties' ability to reach their goals fall into broader categories of assisting the stronger side in the conflict (which may not always be the government of the target country); operational superiority against their rivals; specific timing of interventions (intervening from the beginning of the conflict); operational externalization of interventions and their institutionalization.

Support to the stronger side

Direction of the third party support to the conflicting parties proved to be insignificant in the statistic analysis of the success of all interventions, even with the value closes to the significant variables in the regression model. The division of support into the categories of unilateral and multilateral interveners was not included in the regression intentionally – the aim was to determine the overall value of this variable in success of all interventions. When viewed separately, however, unilateral and multilateral interventions produce different results in relation to the role support to specific belligerent parties plays in facilitating implementation of intervention agendas.

In most cases, the target country's government appears to be a stronger political actor in the conflict than opposition. Governments are thought to possess more political, military and administrative means to influence the conflict settings than do any other ethnic groups, usually having minority status in the target state. They are also considered to have larger popular support and enjoy a comparative advantage in the areas of human capital and economic resources for sustained combat activities. Military capacities of the majority government are believed to outweigh those of the minority groups, which helps the former conduct warfare more efficiently and to overcome their enemies with lesser costs.

At the same time, it would be erroneous to say that the government equals the majority, which is tantamount to a stronger side in the conflict: there are cases when the governments are, in fact, weaker than the opposition factions. This is because, as it was in pre-1959 Rwanda, governments are ruled by minorities who, while enjoying generally higher presence in key decision-making political positions, are not necessarily stronger than the opposition factions in their comparative belligerent capacities. Such governments appear to be quite vulnerable to clashes with the majority opposition groups and may lose the wars with them. Even if governments do represent majority groups, they may still wars to their rival minority factions due to another reason: as Areguin-Toft (2001) argued that if the minority engages in asymmetric warfare against the government and launches guerilla resistance of attrition, it can actually win the war against a majority.[1] While the differences in the capacities of the warring parties remain the same – the stronger remains stronger after months of conflict – this form of warfare may put the minority in the better position vis-à-vis the majority.

These examples mean that the factor of provision of third party the support to the government does not necessarily mean that it would succeed in its actions if the government is not the strongest of all the warring factions in the target country. This is why the regression model, although placing closely the Support variable (to government or opposition or neutral) to significant variables, still excluded it: direction of support does matter – not to the government but to the stronger side that may as well be opposition.

By adding own resources to the conflict scenery, a unilateral intervener can act at its own discretion, which allows it to quickly deploy forces to be used in the combat. While additional support from a third-party boosts capacities of the stronger side to carry out longer warfare, this, in fact, shortens the conflict duration by bringing the victory to the stronger side earlier than this would happen without such aid. Outside contributions, both in military and economic terms, make the stronger side even stronger, which also decreases its casualties and makes its victory more decisive and, therefore, long-lasting. Whether economic, military or mixed, assistance directed at the stronger side helps it retain its military advantage and elevated the morale of its solders.

Conversely, by putting its interests, capacities, human, military and technical resources to work aiding the weaker side, the third party thus increases belligerent capacities of the former eventually helping it carry on its resistance against the stronger opponent much longer than it otherwise would. Under such circumstances the war is protracted by increased forces of the minority with the third party's help, which leads to additional losses from all the sides involved, more economic devastation and untold human casualties.

When an intervener supports the stronger side, ceteris paribus, the earlier the war ends with its victory, the more chances are for saving human lives and military

1 Areguin-Toft, I. 2001. How the Weak Win Wars: A Theory of Asymmetric Conflict. *International Security*, 26(1), 93-128.

and economic capacities of the both sides. Without such a third party intrusion or its support to the weaker side, an extended warfare is likely to be the result. Such an approach neglects the moral side of victory: it is difficult to judge about success of a party that, with or without third party assistance, has wiped out its rival from the ethnic map of the country. However, the same stands for the victory achieved by a minority groups with the help of an outside actor: equal rules of *jus in bello* apply. The ideal picture after the victory would be ensuring human rights protection through power-sharing mechanisms to be enforced upon the winner (as it was the case with the French interventions in Chad), where third party can actually prevent further resumption of conflicts.

In a line with this argument, successful unilateral interventions in Chad and Rwanda revealed a consistent pattern of success achieved whenever the third parties supported the stronger side. For instance, Libyans managed to reach their intervention goals when they were acting on the side of the GUNT, which was operationally stronger than the rebellion. However, when Libya switched sides and provided assistance to the FROLINAT, being operationally inferior to GUNT, it failed to fulfill its aims of effectively annexing the Aouzou strip. The situation was similar with the French interventions: France never supported the opposition and always acted on the side of the stronger force in the country, which was the acting government (even if this government was formerly in opposition).

In Rwanda France succeeded when assisting Habyarimana's government to buffer the initial attacks of RPF and later in enforcing a buffer zone between the belligerents. While in the first case France acted on behalf of the ruling government, which was stronger than Tutsi opposition, during the second intervention it abstained from acting against the stronger side, now being RPF. The RPF forces, representing the stronger side in the conflict, were potent of inflicting sizable damage on the French troops, the circumstance that France could not neglect. This factor would have reflected negatively on both France and UN, which had authorized the French intervention. Thus, comparative advantage of RPF over escaping Hutu Power operatives prevented France from engaging in direct military clashes against Tutsis had this been necessary. Such a strategy gave France the chance to successfully protect Hutus from the advancing Tutsis, which was the initial goal of the intervention.

Quite close to the question of intervention failure in this respect was the role of Russia in Abkhazia. The Russian troops offered passive support to the Abkhazian rebels, who were in comparative military disadvantage against the Georgian majority. Instead of calming the tensions down and contributing to a quick solution of the conflict for long-lasting benefits for all sides, Russia aided the weaker faction. Its inputs equalized the balance of forces of the opposing sides: neither Georgians could reincorporate Abkhazia into their territory, nor Abkhazians could freely develop their land as an independent state. In this case support to the weaker side prolonged final solution of the conflict until 2008; put Russia in an uneasy international position as an aggressor accused by Georgia; kept ongoing small-scale destabilizing skirmishes in the region; and largely impeded the economic development of Abkhazia and the adjacent Georgian regions.

The second Russian intervention in South Ossetia, however, falsifies the thesis on the positive role of supporting the stronger side in the ability of third parties to reach their goals. In this case a unilateral intervener supported the opposition, which was weaker when compared with the better trained and equipped forces of Georgia. A minor point to mention is that there was no actual military intervention of Russian in Abkhazia: its military forces gained the momentum when the Georgian troops were under attack in South Ossetia and managed to occupy the whole region of Abkhazia. The success of Russian intervention acting on behalf of the weaker side is explained by other factors, which are discussed later, including a superpower factor and decisive intervention strategies.

Institutionalization of intervention

In broad sense institutionalization of interventions means legitimating presence of the third party on the territory of the target country and the options its offers to the belligerent factions. The process of institutionalization of interventions starts with the existence of legal documents justifying deployment of the third party troops and their operational frameworks. Legitimization can be offered by the target government in a form of bilateral agreements with the intervening state and/or (usually with its request) by the international community through adopting relevant resolutions authorizing interventions and their corresponding operationalization in intervention mandates. In this context institutionalization means that an intervention is acquiring additional legal value both to the side they support, the side they act against, as well as domestically in the country of the intervener. Thus, the fact of intervention is additionally strengthened by a legal substance attached to its presence.

As a legal form of interventions, a signed agreement with the side a third party supports brings to the former a number of benefits, which can be viewed on three levels: on the level of the target country's conflict environment (the process of political acceptance and preparation of local political context for the intervention); the third party's own domestic settings (a similar process of endorsing and supporting interventions); and the international system (the process of deliberation and approval of interventions by other countries).

On the target country level, depending on the nature of the agreement with a third party, a host government can structure and regulate its relations with the outside force in various ways. It can more or less strictly define the nature of intervention, be it military, economic or mixed, its composition (unilateral or multilateral), participant military units (their structure, composition, amount), and many more. Through legal frameworks the target government can also have a control over the timing and limit operational presence of third party's troops on its territory. The framework of institutionalized intervention clearly specifies the exit strategy for the intervener: when the intervention will start and, most importantly, for how long it will last. Furthermore, institutionalized intervention brings high popular support to the government seeking outside assistance: it can decrease negative feelings (if any) of its citizens towards the third parties by an open and transparent process of definition of the terms of interventions. Public support is of utmost importance in free and unimpeded operation of the third party troops in the target country, which, in case of hostile communities, would be hindered by unfriendly population. Institutionalization framework help the target government relay its clear and open intentions to own domestic electorate and to the intervener, whose personnel would face less domestic opposition. Finally, such a document will serve as a good "face-saving" exercise for the target government as it can depict the presence of another state's forces within their territory as a legal desire of one country's help to another.

By a virtue of the signed bilateral agreement institutionalizing the intervention the third party will have the air of a statutory supporter of that particular faction. An agreement signed between the intervener and the target government, which is a subject of international law, enjoys the higher degree of institutionalization of intervention than such a document concluded with the opposition: in the former case third parties would not look like as illegal intruders or aggressors to the populations of the country they intervene, their own state and the international community at large. If the document is concluded with the opposition faction, legitimation of third party presence is valid only for the parties to the agreement: usually internationally unrecognized opposition has itself a lower level of legitimacy than the target government, hence the low degree of legitimation of the agreements the opposition has concluded.

With regards to the benefits to the third party, when the intervention is institutionalized, it makes it much easier for the intervener's government to gain legal clearance from a domestic legislator for the activities of the country abroad. This means not only giving a green light to sending soldiers and technical support to the target country, but also authorizing substantial economic resources for keeping them there. Interventions usually put a extensive strain on the intervening countries' budgets, which eventually is translated to additional tax burdens for taxpayers and which can raise uneasy questions locally by constituencies and opposition parties about their cost-efficiency. Institutionalized interventions help leaders of intervening states justify external political obligations to their own electorate, and the process of approval of interventions and budgetary allocations becomes easier, faster and more efficient in comparison with non-institutionalized foreign actions.

As far as the international community is concerned, other states usually tend to endorse institutionalized interventions rather than clandestine actions of their partners. The countries in the region with the target state, as well as other political "stakeholders" – international organizations and NGOs – may have important concerns with regard to third party actions, which they would wish to subject to additional outside scrutiny. This includes alleged human rights abuses and civilian causalities that would be politicized and used for the benefit of other actors. In case of an existing agreement between the target country and an outside actor setting a framework for interventions, when faced with international opposition, the leadership of both states would be able to refer to particular legal documents as setting a baseline for interventions and legitimizing them according to international legal standards, rules and practices, common to majority of states.

Drawbacks of non-institutionalized interventions are numerous. Starting with inability to openly marshal sufficient resources for interventions; preparing favorable public opinion; avoiding negative mass media attention and ending up with covert actions on the ground that may be jeopardized by unavailability of additional back-ups during emergencies, non-institutionalized presence of third party is detrimental to all sides of the conflict deal. For the target country this means less monitoring over actual course of actions and lesser control over third party actions. For the intervener non-institutionalized presence is connected with the task of organizing covert operations, which limit their efficiency due to the difficulty of transparent and efficient allocation of adequate resources. For the international community non-institutionalization is related to inability to oversee fulfillment of universal legal standards of *jus in bello* and protection of the rights and dignities of the local population.

Interventions of Libya and France in Chad and Rwanda were successful whenever they were based on signed agreements with the host countries, which stipulated presence of their troops on the territories of target countries. For instance, on the basis of military cooperation agreements with the AEF countries, France was obliged to support statehood and local order in these states in the times of internal unrest and external threats. In addition to this, there were numerous bilateral cooperation agreements with various Chadian governments, which gave France the right to intervene on behalf of the ruling regimes. From institutionalization viewpoint, presence of French troops on the Chadian territory was viewed as legitimate by the majority of the local Chadian population, which made the French contingent an indispensable part of national security framework of the Chadian state.

Institutionalized intervention also helped Libya in reaching its goals in Chad when the intervention was backed up by a legal agreement with the Chadian state authorities. Since GUNT was an internationally recognized government of Chad, although transitory but created on the basis of the international power-sharing mechanisms of the Lagos Conference, it was easy for Libya to substantiate its presence in the country as legitimate. This brought strong backing from the government troops and large popular support on the territories Libya occupied. Institutionalization also served Libya well domestically and, most importantly, internationally: when referring to Libyan intervention in terms in humanitarian and liberalization content, Quadaffi always alluded to the treaty with GUNT and claimed that Libya would leave as soon as asked by the Chadian government (which it actually did).

Same rule of thumb applied to the French interventions in Rwanda. While the first intervention was based on the official request of Habyarimana, the second had a UN mandated authorization for their operations. Both of these official documents provided for a legal framework of interventions and institutionalized them by delineating structure of their forces, their composition, location, and, most importantly, timing – when to come and when to leave.

Finally, legitimation of interventions can also be beneficial from the point of view of the domestic opposition factions in target countries and their interests since them also become part of the conflict resolution mechanism and sometimes even signatories to the international or bilateral agreements. Much depends on how effectively an intervener demonstrates the legitimacy of the agreement concluded with the legally unrecognized party. This means that signing the agreement with a non-state actor – a break-away region or an opposition political faction – would still require a "stamp of international legitimacy". Hence, the more states support the actions of a third party based on such agreements, the more institutionalized third party actions will be.

Operational superiority/decisive intervention strategies

Unilateral interveners in most cases are driven by their own interests and aspirations and rarely are purely neutral and without bias. For the interveners, thus, success largely depends on their ability to effectively influence the domestic balance of power and the will to use their own capacities so as to produce preferred outcome through their military capacities to overwhelm the strength of the antagonists on the ground. For the recipient of the outside support, foreign military involvement means lower costs, including fewer human casualties, loss of equipment and economic expenditures that must be borne by that party alone. For the side third parties act against, operational superiority and decisive intervention strategies mean vastly greater losses that can be wrought by their externally-leveraged enemy. Notwithstanding the level of engagement (a unilateral intervener may or may not get involved in a direct confrontation with one of the belligerent forces on behalf of another), it should be ready to possess the strength capable of intervening militarily on behalf of the party it supports and the and strong will to use it.

The fact of an ethnic group supported by a superior outside actor, in addition to bringing tangible benefits, is positively related to overall performance of that particular group. Its soldiers seeing the prevailing dominance of their third party patron become more victory-oriented. The presence of a mighty intervener increases own morale of the military of the group they support, and assures them of a forthcoming and easy victory.

In the conflicts in Chad and Rwanda, successful actions of unilateral interveners directly depended on their decisiveness to act quickly and their possession of sufficient military strength to alter the victory-related calculus of the warring factions. One of the key distinguishing features of unilateral interventions is the greater perceived likelihood on the ground that they would become involved in combat operations against the enemies of the groups they supported. In all the instances of their success, the unilateral interveners displayed military and strategic superiority, either in numbers or in technical characteristics and amounts of the weaponry they used or possessed.

During the intervention of France in Rwanda in 1990, its forces played an instrumental role in stymieing the early assault of RPF. 600 French soldiers were involved in combat operations with the Tutsis and, using their military and personnel capacities (high-tech equipment, helicopters, and computer surveillance), managed to rebuff the rebellion and keep Hutus and their president in power for some time. Other good examples of the importance of intervener's operational superiority in the success of intervention were the Chadian operations by France and Libya. Intervention of 2,000 French marines against FROLINAT in support of President Tombalbaye in the very beginning of the conflict; French intervention in Spring 1978 on behalf of another president, Malloum, scattering FROLINAT troops; the successful Libyan intervention against the Chadian political factions – in each of these cases third parties possessed sufficient resources to achieve their goals and political and strategic will to effectively enforce their preferred options upon the antagonists.

To signal their operational superiority and thereby induce the opposing side to retreat, third parties may also resort to a show of force, which sometimes proves quite sufficient for their success. A good case of such "swaggering" was the Operation Turquoise: the huge French military machine was all too much for the lightly armed RPF to confront. RPF, seeing the prevailing superiority of France decided to avoid open military engagement, which allowed Hutus to escape to refugee camps, thus making the intervention successful.

"Swaggering" was also used as a strategy by France in Chad. Calculating that mere presence of more advanced opponents would be sufficient enough for the rival faction to roll back their forces, France frequently employed this tactic. Its actions signaled to the belligerents the imminence of a credible punishment in case of acting against the French soldiers, and served as a credible sign of protection to the side enjoying French support. Show of force is also useful for influencing other actors' decisions to intervene, as it was with the *Manta* and *Epervier*. The former started with a menacing airlift of almost 4,000 French Foreign Legion troops, which created such a military climate in the country – especially around N'Djamena – that the advancing Libyan troops were dissuaded from directly challenging French soldiers, whose military strength and operational superiority was unchallenged. *Epervier* was less numerous and involved only half of the previous French contingent, which was still enough to prevent Libya from further advances.

In contrast to operational and tactical superiority, the ambivalence of the Russian intervention in the conflict in Abkhazia in early 1990s, which was neither backed up by a credible threat of force nor had political will for its decisive use, was an important factor that contributed to the failure of Russia's ability to achieve its vague aims. Unclear goals led to weak operational involvement in the conflict. Russia itself was undergoing dramatic political changes from the Soviet times. The main question was whether to keep the Soviet-style Empire or to move toward a more democratic system.[2] Russian military suffered even more from the collapse of the Soviet Union: it suddenly appeared to be out of demand and completely useless. Under such domestic political climate Russia was quite indecisive as to what it wanted outside of its borders, in this context, in Abkhazia. Clearly, it wishes to use the local disturbances in Georgia for its own benefit, but the benefits themselves were yet unclear. Russia was striving to have a say in the Caucasus region where it had many vital national interests: the Black Sea transport corridor, seaside resorts, and protection of its southern borders, but suffered from chronic lack of political will to enforce its options to the conflicting parties.

In order to be effective, Russia should have been clearer as to what it aimed to achieve in Georgia, which would further define the resources used for fulfillment of specific tasks. On the contrary, its ambiguous intentions specified Russia's low-engagement profile in Abkhazia: to refrain from direct military clashes with the Georgian troops; to support Abkhazian side with only ammunition and some military equipment and, at the same time, to provide the Georgian side with all these; to train occasionally Abkhazian troops; to fly randomly military aircrafts; to refrain from using heavy artillery and to keep the Abkhazian section of the Russian-Georgian border open for the inflow of the mercenaries and volunteers. Completely different was the picture in 2008, when Russia revealed overwhelming political will and insurmountable military superiority and crushed the Georgian troops in less than two full days of military combat. The strength of the Russian 58th army combined with long-distance artillery and air strikes far beyond the immediate conflict territory of South Ossetia were potent enough to persuade Georgia to seek armistice, further surrender to the Russian superpower capacities and to forcefully accept the defeat option imposed by Russia.

Early intervention

The timing of intervention has enormous importance for the ability of third parties to achieve their stated goals. The key point about success of all interventions is to consider whether it is more productive to enter the target country early when the conflict has just started or to intervene after it had reached specific point in its course of development. The time factor is equally important for unilateral and multilateral interveners, however, with completely opposite value.

---

2 Interesting insights concerning Russian failures in peacekeeping operations were given by Andrei Kozirev, the former foreign minister of Russia: "…we [Russia] also have drawbacks from lack of experience and out of former Soviet customs. Even more so, we have to act…under the condition of rapid transformation of the Soviet Army into the Russian one, and diplomacy learns new unknown methods of work in new directions." Cited in Mayorov B.M. 2007. *Mirotvorci: iz Opita Rossiiskoi Diplomatii v Posrednichestve* [Mayorov, M.B. 2007. Peacekeepers. From the mediation experience of the Russian diplomacy]. M.: Moskva: Mejdunarodnie Otnosheniya, 64.

Enlarging and extending Regan's conclusions about the higher probability for success of third parties intervening after the end of warfare and/or following conclusion of ceasefire agreements,[3] current findings show that in order to be successful, unilateral outside actors should be enter the target countries right from the beginning of the conflicts, and not during ongoing hostilities or even after they have de facto ended. To increase odds of success, unilateral interveners should act quickly and should not let the troops of the enemy factions gain momentum in warfare against the groups they support. Any prolongation of conflicts will bring additional damage to all the sides and the chances are good that recipients of the third party support might lose to their rivals. This argument equally covers any direction of external support, notwithstanding the recipient side or whether the interveners are neutral.

In the first case, if the help is provided from the very beginning of the conflict to the majority, its assault on the rebels, supported by a third party, would gain additional force and military strength to crush minority manpower. From a cost-and-benefit point of view, this would spare more lives for the majority and would allow it to put down the rebellion quicker. With the timely external aid, the majority could win its battles more efficiently and decisively, and prevent the minority group from fleeing the country to organize repeat assaults from abroad. Early interventions would prevent the minority from consolidating control over the territories it manages to capture. The minority would not be able to exploit the natural resources and use new recruits from the land they possess during their assault (for instance, to use oil or valuable resources for purchases of military equipment and food for their soldiers) to regain their strength and further prolong the conflict. Third party assistance from the start of the war would also allow the government to better and more effectively block all the chances of the opposition to appeal for any external support on their behalf.

The situation is similar when the third party supports the minority: early presence of an intervener prevents the majority to score a quick victory. The majority would, thus, not have the opportunity to stop the rebellion right from the beginning. Also, resistance of the minority would allow it to better use the resources on the territories it holds. Apart from sparing battle-related casualties from both sides in case of a protracted war (not only the minority's, which it supports, but also the majority's, which would more likely to resort to negotiations seeing that the intervener supports its rival), a third party would thus create a new balance of power in the target country. This would allow for the opposition's physical survival, as well as creation of the conditions under which negotiations between all sides would be more beneficial than a protracted fight.

The cases with successful unilateral interventions all revealed a strong relevance of early interventions and their overall success. In Rwanda and Chad, the French and Libyan troops were more successful when intervening in the conflict right

3 Regan, P.M. 1998. Choosing to Intervene: Outside Interventions in Internal Conflicts, *The Journal of Politics*, 60(3), 754-779.

from the very beginning. For instance, the French military operations in Rwanda against the two assaults of RPF – first in support of Habyarimana and the second to prevent possible ethnic cleansing of Hutus by advancing Tutsis – all were conducted from the beginning of the warfare. In the first instance France prevented the rebels from capitalizing on their initial gains and using the land and human resources to support their future advances, while in the second case intervention prevented massive punitive actions against Hutus. The same held true for Libya's interventions: it was successful when intervened from the very beginning of the warfare, and made the governmental troops unable to crush FROLINAT's numerous attacks in 1983-1987.

The case of the Russian actions in Abkhazia seems to disconfirm the statement of efficiency of early timing of interventions. Although Russia had been present in the region even during Soviet times, before the conflict began, and became involved in the conflict early, the intervention failed to reach its goals. This happened not because it intervened from the beginning of the conflict and lost, but because its actions were not back up by the force decisive enough to bring it victory. Russian involvement in the conflict was limited to small-scale clandestine actions that were too weak to reach their aims no matter when they were taken. Nevertheless, its mere presence and the support to Abkhazia were instrumental in keeping Georgian troops from complete destruction of the rebel military.

The second Russian in intervention in Georgia, however, fully supports the early timing argument. The Georgian military was present on the territory of South Ossetia for only two days when Russia intervened from the North. The regular Georgian army could not manage to make the necessary fortifications for extended confrontation with the enemy, nor could they use the human, economic and communication resources of numerous Georgian villages which were located in South Ossetia to support their advances or to evacuate the Georgian dwellers. Rapid deployment of the Russian 58th army, together with the destruction of the military infrastructure of the Georgian army far beyond the actual war zone, brought them the needed results: Georgians could not withstand advances of the Russian troops and fled the territory they had occupied earlier. Early Russian intervention also helped save the lives of many, including its peacekeepers, and the Georgian and Ossetian civilian population that would otherwise inevitably fall collateral victims.

Externalization of intervention

Another factor crucial to the overall success of third party actions is the actual and perceptual location of the intervener in relation to the target country and its involvement into its domestic affairs. Pros and cons of being based inside or outside the country actually depend on the composition of intervention force, i.e. on its unilateral/multilateral character, and are considered here from several angles: locus (where the intervener is stationed); focus (intervention agendas); resources used for interventions (human and economic); commitment (domestic and foreign responsibility of the intervener). In simple terms, in order to be effective in reaching its goals, a single actor should not only be actively involved in the country throughout the course of the civil war and from the very beginning, but should also minimize its presence in the target country.[4]

This sounds almost oxymoronic, but in reality the less the intervener gets involved in the domestic affairs of the target country, the easier it will carry on its own agendas. The rationale is as follows: lasting presence of foreign troops is connected with considerable expenditures of the third party. Keeping sizable military contingents, military and other support equipment in the conflict zone would be costly to any state, even the most potent. Months of occupation would not only require high commitment of the occupier in human capital and economic means, but would also require regular re-supplies of these recourses. The expected utility of third party presence from the costs-benefit analysis would decrease every month of additional stay in the country with conflicts, taking into account increased expenses and possible losses of the lives of its soldiers that would arise from deep involvement in the conflict-related matters, for instance, by undertaking extensive law and order, public administration and fiscal functions.

The more a third party becomes associated with in the conflict, the more it is susceptible to losses of lives of its troops. Battlefield casualties may happen not only as a result of direct engagement with the opposing side, but also from what von Clausewitz (1873) calls "friction" or "fog of war":[5] pure chance and mishap. The more an intervener engrosses in the country with conflict, the greater the possibility of systematic and sporadic classes with the enemy forces resulting in a greater the propensity for unexpected and unaccounted "fogs". The facts of human losses and high expenses in terms of troops and equipment will be reflected negatively on the internal political arena. Every even miniscule unfortunate incident abroad, every single battle-related death of the interveners' personnel will be seized upon by domestic opposition and magnified at home for the consumption of the domestic audience and putting pressure on their political rivals for own benefits. Domestic power games would challenge the "political durability" of the government of the intervening country and might even lead to abandonment of the intervention agendas, unfulfilled intervention goals and overall unsuccessful intervention.

The situation is completely different when interveners are located outside but in an immediate vicinity of the war zone, which will keep their troops out of pressing danger of military collisions with the antagonists. Third parties will be able to shuttle their personnel in and out the target country when needed and to decrease their war-related expenditures and casualties. Externalization of intervention also

4 An exit strategy for an intervener is discussed in details in Edelstein, D.M. 2004. Occupational Hazards: Why Military Occupations Succeed or Fail, *International Security*, 29(1), 49-91.

5 von Clausewitz, C. 1873. *On War*. The complete translation by Colonel J.J. Graham. N. Trübner, London, 1873 [Online]. Available at: http://www.clausewitz.com/CWZHOME/VomKriege2/ONWARTOC2.HTML [accessed: May 7, 2009].

decreases the problem of external commitment of the third parties. With respect to promises offered and hopes aroused, third party commitment is of dual nature – to its own citizens and to the warring parties. In general, it is hard to persuade domestic electorate to endorse expensive interventions, both in economic and human terms. Usually with democratic countries public opinion closely scrutinizes the actions of their government abroad. It is much influenced by mass media, which portrays interventions in different terms, depending on the actual developments in the target country. Victory be portrayed as a great win; any damage, loss of battle, deaths of soldiers will be reflected, respectfully, as a great loss. In such view, externalization of intervention will help avoid additional losses and make intervener's population largely supportive of its cause.

With regards to commitment to the target country's own government and population, externalization decreased their unsubstantiated excessive expectations (both positive and negative) and hopes placed with the intervener. Notwithstanding what side the interveners support – the majority government or the opposition – they will be considered by the antagonists as actors on the domestic arena. Internalization, thus, expands the third party commitment with additional justification by political, economic and military actions of anticipations of the side it supports and fears of the side its acts against.

The responsibility to support a faction, willingly or not, comes with the mere presence of a third party in the conflict zone. This leads to perceptions of both the recipients of the aid and its opponent that the third party will not only act as a military power against another side, but would also have a say, a role and eventually a significant position in domestic politics. An internalized intervener is perceived by the country population as an additional component of their national political scenery, another player in the game of politics, which is to be taken into account in the battlefield calculus. In order to receive and keep public support for its actions, a third party would undertake additional responsibilities vis-à-vis the side it supports, which may go beyond its initial mandates and goals. The responsibility, which is attached to an internalized intervention, can lock an intervener into a commitment trap and force it to undertake additional functions that had not been initially planned. Such an extended commitment would be quite difficult to fulfill for an intervention that started as purely military. Even if a third party does not wish to have such high stakes in its presence, the more it becomes engrossed in domestic politics, the more its interactions with all the sides, both the government and the opponents, and the higher its unforeseen and unnecessary commitment.

Other factors contributing to the success of externalized foreign actions are limitations in intervention agenda and geographic coverage. When having an externalized modus of action, the interveners minimize their expenses in accordance with the limited goals they plan to achieve. An important thing to consider here is that the goals of the intervention may involve quite distinct and different tasks with separate goals, scopes, range of personnel, economic expenditures, and sometimes even different recipients of their support. The underlying principle behind having externalized interventions is that maintaining a permanent presence in the target country leads one's goals and intervention agendas to become "foggy". With the passage of time, third parties may gradually lose the sense of what their initial goals were and how these goals were reflected in the current operations. For example, an intervention may start with limited agendas (to protect humanitarian personnel or to monitor implementation of a peace deal) and geographic coverage (to deploy forces in a specific important geographic location) and be quite successful in fulfilling this agenda. With the passage of time it may gradually go outside of its area and scope and grow into a multi-dimensional operation that includes other objectives in addition to previously defined ones. This may put the third party in an unknown geographic terrain with unexpected contingencies ranging from unknown climatic conditions to divergent population groups that may not be necessarily supportive to the intervener.

Extension of intervention agendas does not mean failure of the interventions. It would only be detrimental for the third parties' interests if broadening of their involvement is not followed by an increase of inputs and "wholehearted" actions – political, military, and economic will necessary to achieve their expanded goals. Interveners who get internalized in the conflicts would inevitably find themselves in pitfalls of increased pressure to enlarge their intervention actions either by continuous requests from the sides they support or simply by the demands of the situations, requiring additional sources of funding interventions, clearance of all domestic actors, and restructuring of interventions. Eventually interveners would be faced with situations where they would be better-off leaving the scene rather that staying longer.

Quite different is the situation where interventions had from the very start limited goals, the means to achieve these goals, and no situational urge or outside pressure to alter and expand these goals. By fulfilling narrow intervention agendas, third parties remain externalized thus signaling to the recipients of their support that they are not going to play the role of internal actors. This would further make the sides they support feeling increased commitment to their own constituents, conscientiousness in their actions and prevent from transferring the responsibility for the fate of the conflict onto the third parties.

Unilateral interventions in Chad and Rwanda revealed quite a consistent pattern in being successful when they were externalized: based outside of the target country and supporting the parties to the conflict on a *veni-vidi-vici* basis. On the contrary, when they went beyond its initial objectives and included more intervention activities, they were overall less successful in reaching their internalized goals. In Rwanda, for instance, the first French intervention in October 1990 had limited goals that allowed it to stay external to long-term domestic security of the country. The French troops never went beyond buffering RPF attack any further and completely defeating Tutsis outside of Rwanda in Uganda with the purpose of prevention of the Tutsis comeback against Hutus. They certainly had not have in mind keeping the Hutus Power, preserving Habyarimana's regime forever and acting as external patrons of the state. After the French intervention managed to make the Tutsis abandon their initial plans to change the Hutu government, it retreated. The French troops had not stayed in Rwanda long after their successful operation against Tutsis and had not undertaken the functions of domestic policemen and external security providers.

The narrow scope of another French intervention, Operation Turquoise, also contributed to their success in June 1994 with a limited goal – creation of a buffer zone between the antagonists. The French "humanitarian" operation created "safe havens" for Hutus and prevented the large-scale "pay-back" of avenging Tutsis over the fleeing Hutus. With UN mandate, French contingent had no plans to destroy or to thwart RPF advances, which would eventually restore the Hutu regime. A proof of success of this limited intervention was that after a two-month long French action RPF, having previously unwillingly accepted the French presence, continued their attacks, soon occupied Kigali and, eventually, the whole country without considerable human casualties and gross violations of human rights, which was the aim of Operation Turquoise. The intervention also reached its own goal of improving the peacemaker's image of France, after its reputation had been tarnished from supporting the Hutu regime in early 1990s.

Such modus of short-term shuttle interventions also brought plausible results in Chad. All the French interventions there were conducted from outside of the country and had not lasted forever. The French presence was confined to N'Djamena, which they used as a stronghold of their presence. The French troops never went beyond their occupied area to the North that would place them in a hostile surrounding of Muslims sympathetic to Libya and confined sallies only to air raids. Although, after leaving the country, France insisted on conducting administrative reforms with the purpose to improve the domestic political climate in the country through inclusion of the members of the opposition into the governance, as an intervener, it never was the actor in these reforms. France limited itself to giving counsel without commitment to back the advised actions with own resources and force. France had not envisaged any larger and extended agendas of further supervising effectiveness of power-sharing mechanisms and engaging in state-building in the country. In some sense, France had not wanted to play the role of an outside security guarantor – a colonial image it wanted to abandon.

The second French intervention in Chad was also externalized with limited objectives and scope. The French military bombarded the rebel troops; prevented them from taking the northern areas; saved Malloum's regime and retreated. No other additional actions had been undertaken with the purpose of ultimate destruction of FROLINAT. Operation Manta undertaken in 1983 prevented another intervener, Libya, from taking N'Djamena. Libya was unwilling to engage in open confrontations with the French military and soon left the conflict scene. Finally, Operation Epervier, conducted in 1986, was a mere show-of-force and, again, signaled to Libya to keep out of Chad. In all of these actions France had employed externalized *modus operandi* with ad limited operational objectives that made it be viewed both in Chad and at home as an outside actor.

Intervention of the other player, Libya, in Chad was successful only it abstained from permanent and multi-dimensional presence in the country and kept a low operational and military profile. On the basis of the cooperation agreement with GUNT Libya sent in its forces with the task of preventing the former government and current opposition forces FAN from taking N'Djamena. As a result, Libyans successfully managed to help GUNT overcome FAN. However, when Libya signed another agreement – for a merger with Chad – and brought in additional personnel, it soon became clear that it could not sustain such an enlarged objective. To annex the strip of land in Chad was easy, yet to gorge the whole country proved to be an unrealizable and a daunting task.

From the point of view of exit strategy, internalization of interventions also makes it difficult for the third parties to leave the scene. Once the goals have been fulfilled and objectives reached, it is the time for the intervener to leave the conflict scene. The more the third party becomes engrossed in the domestic affairs of the target country the less possible and easy it is to withdraw. By providing extended services to the country's population intervener becomes bogged down in local politics and public administration, which may not be easy to accomplish. This was the case with the Russian intervention in Abkhazia, where Russia was giving out its citizenship and issuing its passports to those Abkhazians who wished to have them. Its officers were acting as military advisors to the Abkhazian government. There were numerous cases of Russian businesses homing in an internationally unrecognized Abkhazia. The more it remained in the region without any decisive actions to de jure institutionalize its presence, the further was its exist. An important point to keep in mind here is that an "exit" does not necessarily mean leaving the conflict environment for the third party – it means end of the intervention and accomplishment of its goals. In doing to an intervener may not even leave physically the target country – it may still keep its physical presence, but in different forms. For Russia the exit would mean de jure recognition of Abkhazia and legitimation of its interests there. For this Russian political will remained latent for more than a decade, which was detrimental for all the parties concerned. Absence of the clear-cut solution of the conflict prevented full recovery of the war-affected territories (according to the Russian scenario); impeded open and larger-scale investments in the region; kept Abkhazia's population on the verge of economic collapse; harmed the Russian image abroad as an annexer and disturbed domestic peace in Georgia by having an unresolved hot-spot.

Multilateral Interventions: Success Factors

Existence of more than one player in interventions has both positive and negative consequences for their successes. On the one hand, the more participants of the coalition there are, the more legitimate (at least, from the point of view of the member-states) their action would be: the increasing number of countries participating in coalitions would mean higher level of institutional "approval" of these operations. Multilateral interventions have common goals uniting several actors, who may engage in actions that go beyond their self-interests. All the results achieved and losses incurred are shared. At the same time, unlike unilateral actors, with multiple interveners we have usually sluggish process of internal bureaucratic decision-making process of approval of deployment of forces; internal rivalry between member-states having their own visions on particular conflicts that may not necessarily coincide and expectations from interventions; disproportionate quality and level of military inputs; sometimes a "say-and-run" behavior of states who pledge to participate in interventions but later provide no contributions; and many more.

The factors, identified during the cases studies, which contribute to the success of the actions of multilateral interveners, in general, confirm and further extend the initial assumptions behind the hypothesis of increased efficiency of multilateral interventions: their institutionalized legitimacy; neutrality/impartiality in their actions; compositional parity between the members of multinational coalitions and specific timing of the intervention (entering the conflict scene after de facto end of hostilities).

Institutionalization of interventions

As with sole third parties, institutionalization of interventions brings a significant value to success of multilateral interventions. The interveners may not be necessarily neutral: they may support one side of the conflict; pursue their own objectives; conduct situational monitoring or provide humanitarian support to the population. In all these activities, in order to be successful, third parties should either be willingly accepted by the belligerents or, at least, not vigorously opposed by them. Here institutionalization of interventions is vital: the ability not only to impose the decision on the combatants but also, more importantly, to make it acceptable to the warring parties. In unilateral interventions institutionalization is a rare occasion and mostly depends on the invitations from the target governments to enter the scene. When single foreign actors support oppositions, institutionalization is practically absent unless oppositions represent former governments in exile on which legitimating of interventions depends (as it was the case with Libya supporting GUNT). On the contrary, interventions are easier institutionalized and legitimized when they are conducted on behalf of international organizations or within non-organizational multilateral coalitions.

In general, all interventions have greater legitimacy when having the consent of the target governments. The invitation to enter the scene may happen as a result of ceasefire agreements that envisage presence of outside external guarantors of peace and security, or even before the announced ceasefire when existence of legal documents stipulating interventions helps authorize and legitimize the interventions. However, an institutional framework for starting an intervention alone is an insufficient guarantee for the eventual success of third party actions. The mere fact that interveners have been invited by the target governments does not mean that their actions will be legitimate in the eyes of all the conflicting parties from the point of view of trusting their interventions and expecting due consequences for their actions. Even more so, what is legitimate and good for the target governments may (and would) be illegitimate and bad for the opposition factions.

Whereas legitimacy of unilateral interventions depends on the image and "weight" of the sole intervener on international arena, for the multilateral interveners it is based on joint consent of the larger community of states. The value of multilateral institutionalization was stressed by Fenwick (1945) at the very birth of the United Nations: "[w]hat would be arbitrary for the individual state would in the case of the whole body of states be no more than the exercise of the higher right of the community to maintain law and order and to see to the observance by separate states of their obligations as members of the community".[6] This means that the more actors are involved in the intervention coalition, or, at best, when the coalition is mandated by an international organization, the more legitimate the interveners' actions would be.

There is difference, through, between the legitimacy of the interventions embarked on by organizations and those carried out by coalitions of like-minded states. When undertaken under the aegis of multinational organizations, such as UN, NATO, OSCE, OAU, and not merely by groups of states with no organizational backing, interventions enjoy higher degree of internationalized arbitrariness in producing and imposing options upon the antagonists. Through their mandates, multinational interventions commit themselves to institutionalize specific outcomes of conflicts, or, as Hartzell (1999) provides, to "provide institutional guarantees for each of the security threats antagonists face..."[7] This proves equally true for unilateral interventions mandated by multilateral organizations, for instance, as in the case of the Operation Turquoise. In non-organizational coalitions, on the other hand, institutionalization of arbitrariness depends on the sheer quantity of states present.

Interventions undertaken by organizations commit their members to legally recognize the end-state of ethnic conflicts: either secession leading to creation of new independent states, like Kosovo, or reintegration with any possible sets of domestic power arrangements. Good examples of such organizational interventions can be the UN peace keeping operations, which, according to Jenne (2003), are "not invested in the outcome of the conflict"[8] and represent the interests of all nation-states and none in particular. The idea of shared stakes is also supported by Diehl et al. (1996), who noted that "...the results of UN intervention [would] carry greater legitimacy than any of the alternatives. That the world community

6 Fenwick, C.G. 1945. Intervention: Individual and Collective. *The American Journal of International Law*, 39(4), 663.

7 Hartzell, C.A. 1999. Explaining the Stability of Negotiated Settlements to Intrastate Wars. *The Journal of Conflict Resolution*, 43(1), 4.

8 Jenne, E.K. 2003. Sri Lanka: a Fragmented State, in *State Failure and State Weakness in a Time of Terror*, edited by R.I. Rotberg. Washington, D.C.: Brooking Institution Press, 234.

supports an action may exert pressure on protagonists to halt hostilities and not renew warfare at some point in the future…"[9]

An important component of success of multilateral interventions from the point of view of legitimacy is not only the ability to unanimously "bless" a specific outcome and to put a seal of approval on the end-results of the conflicts, but, more importantly, to effectively impose a solution upon the belligerents. Institutionalization of third party actions will directly depend very much on how strongly the solutions are offered and/or imposed. If there is indecisiveness to pursue imposition of new solutions, i.e. to overcome the opposition of the warring parties, then the force with which these solutions are put forward will be considered less legitimate. The greater the will and operational strength of imposition, the more the outcomes provided as a result of interventions are viewed as legitimate by the warring factions, who will have fewer incentives to oppose them. Put simply, the more decisive the actions of multilateral interventions and the more the decisions of international community are backed by overwhelming force, the more legitimate these solutions would be viewed by the belligerents. Outcomes can be biased, but in this sense, their bias is legitimized through institutionalization.

Similar to the matter of efficient breach of impartiality, institutionalization of multilateral third parties can endangered through excessive domination of a singe mighty state or groups of states in the intervention coalitions. Decisions made and options offered and imposed will lack multilateral institutionalization if certain powerful members impose their own vision upon other coalition members. Under such "fake" multilateral interventions, bias will no longer be fully legitimized, thus acquiring the cover of unilateral institutionalization. The interventions, even undertaken by organizations, will no longer be considered as truly multilateral by the belligerents who would trust less and have more possibilities for defection. Within their eyes, multilateral interventions will look much like unilateral ones, which are "likely to be given even less justice than community action, quite apart from the fact that it may readily lead to lawlessness."[10]

The fake multilateralism was the cause of the failure of the CIS intervention in Abkhazia. Even though the presence and actions of the CIS peacekeepers were institutionalized by numerous decisions of the Head of CIS states, the legitimacy of the CIS intervention had been eroded from the very start of the intervention because the multilateral intervention was actually a continuation of the unilateral one – by Russia, which was considered as highly biased by the Georgian side. Absence of trust to the pacemaker's image of Russia was transferred to the peacekeeping functions of the CIS PKF. Quite interesting in this respect is the argument of Mullenbach (2005), who claimed that "once a major power has militarily intervened in support of or against the government of the target state, it is likely to oppose the subsequent formation of a peacekeeping mission in the

9 Diehl, P.F., Reifschneider, J. and Hensel, P.R. 1996. UN Intervention and Recurrent Conflict, *International Organization*, 50(4), 687-688.

10 Fenwick, C.G. 1945, 659.

target state by any other third-party actor. The primary goal of the major power in these situations would be to assist one of the parties to the dispute in militarily defeating the other party, and a third-party peacekeeping mission would arguably hinder the achievement of that goal."[11]

What follows from his argument is that Russia, as a major power, would opposed any further foreign interventions in Georgia. There was the other way: to endorse multilateral face-saving intervention where it would become the major and, preferably, the only actor in the multilateral intervention coalition and to try to institutionalize its actions under organizational frameworks, which Russia actually did. By being the only participant in the PKF, Russia reached unilateral legitimacy through unilateral institutionalization of the outcomes of interventions to the antagonists, which was repeatedly rejected by one of them – Georgia.

On the contrary, interventions undertaken by UNAMIR in Rwanda and UNOSOM I in Somalia were successful from institutionalization viewpoint. Both these interveners were invited by the target governments or had consent from the warring factions for initial deployment of their personnel. They were allowed by their mandate to conduct the activities that had been approved by the belligerents, thus avoiding unwelcomed reception and legitimizing those considered to be acceptable or, at least not, harmful to their interests.

When the UN decided to augment the mandate of its intervention by allowing it to use force with the purpose of imposing peace, UNOSOM II failed. This was done under the circumstances of worsening of violence and, especially, the death of the Pakistani peacekeepers. Clearly, these milestones soon came into open conflict with the conflicting groups, since neither Aideed nor Ali Mahdi had agreed upon clearly punitive actions of the UN aimed at their destruction. If previously institutionalized UN options had been acceptable by the belligerents, now the UN failed to successfully enforce their acceptability and fulfill the objectives of its new mandate. This was largely due to the UNOSOM II being heavily influenced by the US who pursued its own objectives directed at increasing its peacemaker's image and prestige on the international arena. Common institutional frameworks of the UN the Security Council were shaken by rigorous US lobby, who was advocating for more decisive actions and ambitious objectives. The UNOSOM's mandate had been enlarged with these tasks; however, the main implementer – the US – failed to effectively impose these institutionalized options on the belligerents, which eventually led to unilateral legitimacy of the UN.

Neutrality versus impartiality

In the context of third party interventions there is connotation difference between the notions of neutrality and impartiality. According to the Cambridge Advanced

11 Mullenbach, M.J. 2005. Deciding to Keep Peace: An Analysis of International Influences on the Establishment of Third-Party Peacekeeping Missions. *International Studies Quarterly*, 49, 537.

Learner's Dictionary, the word "neutral" means "not saying or doing anything that would encourage or help any of the groups involved in an argument or war"[12] while "impartiality" means "not supporting any of the sides involved in an argument"[13] – i.e. preferring no particular and specific beneficiary of the actions. In a general sense, neutrality implies no involvement in actions against any of the belligerent groups. Neutral interveners are merely observing the situation on the ground and refrain from active involvement in conflicts. Impartiality suggests more "intimate" association with the conflicting parties and does mean some reaction against the side that had violated ceasefire agreements or the principles on which the multilateral coalition is based. The main point is that impartial interveners take actions with no preference to particular groups and no prejudice against their rivals. They penalize the defectors not because they think that they are inherently evil, but because what they do is bad. They will, thus, reverse their targets to other groups if they also take same unacceptable moves.

Contrary to the findings of in the statistic analysis on the combined values of the Support variable in success of all interventions, the role neutrality and impartiality play in multilateral interventions is quite noticeable. Their primary inputs in the matter of reaching success is building acceptance and trust from the belligerents, which can be positive, negative and neutral. Positive trust means receiving the benefits from compliance with the options offered by the third parties, such as economic aid, military embargo and increased security to the population on the territories controlled by the antagonists. Negative trust implies credible fear punishment in case of defection from these options. Finally, neutral trust connotes absence of fear of punishment, as well as rewards. In either case, the degree of trust is directly related to the composition of third parties – the more "multiple" the intervention is, the higher the level of trust from the warring factions. The belligerents would, thus, be more willing to accept the party that they trust will guarantee the implementation of mutually acceptable solutions or a party that does not interfere much in their domestic affairs.

In comparison with sole interveners, neutral and impartial third parties reveal more transparency in defining their goals and undertaking actions. Not only is the community of states able to control the course of the developments of troops under joint command in the conflict zone, but also the conflicting parties themselves can monitor actual developments of the situation and check whether there is any defection in the behavior of the interveners in favor of their rivals. Transparency of multilateral interveners helps them build up trust among the warring factions and show credible benefits from compliance with the options offered and credible punishment in case of failure to obey their decisions.

---

12 Cambridge Advanced Learner's Dictionary [Online]. Available at: http://dictionary.cambridge.org/define.asp?key=39269&dict=CALD [accessed: May 7, 2009].

13 Cambridge Advanced Learner's Dictionary [Online]. Available at: http://dictionary.cambridge.org/define.asp?key=39269&dict=CALD [accessed: May 7, 2009].

Because multilateral interveners are composed of more than one state, they take steps towards fulfillment of goals that are generally acceptable to all participants and endorsed by the governments of the coalition members. Although the countries tend to choose like-minded partners as the members of their coalition, who share similar values and viewpoints on international political and legal matters, they would still have their own national or trans-border interests. Coalition members may either directly support no warring faction, or provide assistance to a particular ethnic group based on common blood lineages or out of some other reasons. By serving the interests of all of the coalition members and none in particular, multilateral interventions "neutralize" self-interests of its participants and offer the options to the belligerents out of the shared understanding of the conflict resolution. Coalitions, thus, become "melting pots" for interests of their components, producing joint outcomes out of intra-coalition negotiations and shared goals to be pursued by all their members.

In the process of coalition-building it will be quite difficult to come up with an alternative that would equally satisfy the warring factions. To have an effectively working option in the conflict means to impose it effectively, even if it is about monitoring of ceasefire agreements. Sometimes in imposition of the most neutral decisions of the wider community of states, multilateral interveners cannot escape the pitfalls of acting against some of the belligerents. Every action of third parties against a certain group would always be considered by that group as hostile, and, out of a zero-sum nature of inter-ethnic confrontations, will be viewed as supporting others. The real question is how to impose the options in such a way and without prejudice to any faction so that they would be accepted by all the participants notwithstanding the consequences these options would carry for them. Here, the institutional nature of multilateral initiatives, i.e. their organizational settings, is an important factor determining the acceptability of the interveners' decisions by the belligerents in contrast to unilateral interventions.

While unilateral actors bring own interests and aspirations and may favor particular outcomes from their own perspectives, multilateral nature of intervention, in the words of Diehl et al. (1996), "would allow it to forge a solution that meets the interests of the disputants as well as the international community."[14] An important aspect of multilateral intervention is that it would bring the vision of not only one single party to the intervention, but also "...the interests and views of other actors (e.g., major powers or other states in the same geographic area)...",[15] thus minimizing single party impacts on conflict resolution. In this sense impartiality means not favoring any party in distribution of the rewards and punishments. In multilateral interventions the bias of one state is balanced by the bias of others, which eventually becomes the bias of all.

Neutrality and impartiality of multilateral interventions can be jeopardized internally if the decisions in coalition are taken in a unilateral manner being

14 Diehl, P.F., Reifschneider, J. and Hensel, P.R. 1996, 687-688.

15 Diehl, P.F., Reifschneider, J. and Hensel, P.R. 1996, 687-688.

influenced by certain powerful members of coalition. This was probably the reason why this variable proved to be insignificant in the statistical analysis. The category of multilateral interveners used in the regression included all the types of their composition: under organizational settings and within coalitions, "true" and "fake" multilateral interventions, influenced by a single powerful actor. Disproportionate "weight of say" in decision-making of any separate state(s) acting solely or jointly counter to the spirit of multilateralism can endanger integrity of the interventions. Neutrality and impartiality be also endangered externally if one or several its members can effectively skew the balance for their own favor, thus, faking the true notion of multilateralism by increasing the value of their own operational bias vis-à-vis warring factions.

However, even the most biased and partial multilateral interventions can still reach success if they follow the agendas decisively, i.e. with due political will and sufficient operational capacities and military resources. Failure to effectively enforce biased options on belligerents would mean that multilateral interventions are incapable of reaching their goals. This would also ruin positive, negative and neutral trust of the antagonists who would believe that the interveners lack the capacity to protect them, punish their rivals and penalize them in case of their defection. The problem with biased third parties is that the belligerents might incorrectly perceive their actions and not be able to distinguish between real and perceptional biases. As in a security dilemma situation, when direct military collision becomes imminent, any action, even aimed at assisting the most destitute members of the population, would be viewed as hostile and biased by the groups that were being harmed disproportionately or receive fewer benefits from multilateral actions. "Supporting them" becomes "acting against us" and vice versa.

The lesson for multilateral interveners is either to refrain from using force to maintain the image of their impartiality, or to use such force "wholeheartedly", which would effectively crush the defector side. Multilateral interventions studied in the book, in general, show higher success rates when they managed to retain neutrality in their actions in the conflict environment. The UN interventions in Rwanda and Somalia were successful whenever they kept their impartiality uncompromised. UNAMIR and UNOSOM I were mandated to carry peacekeeping tasks without direct military interaction with the belligerents. Neither of them was allowed to engage in fight against the warring factions; their involvement was minimized to situational monitoring and provision of humanitarian aid. These tasks from the very beginning excluded actions that would have contained any bias against specific groups. For instance, UNAMIR had quite limited operational objectives: to monitor and register the facts of violation of the Arusha agreement and to communicate them to the UN headquarters and the belligerents themselves. The blue helmets were not given the orders to protect Hutus and Tutsis from each other. Nor were they to facilitate peace-building efforts and to restore public administration and war and order in a conflict-torn country. Such an endeavor would have required larger peace-making efforts, for which the international community had neither sufficient economic and military resources at hand, nor the political will to allocate them.

Similarly, the mandate of UNOSOM I ordered no interference in warfare between the Somalian warring factions. The UN mission was tasked with monitoring of the ceasefire agreement and protection for the United Nations personnel and those of other humanitarian organizations. UN peacekeepers were not allowed to impose any decision upon the belligerents. Such "peaceful" interventions with limited goals and resources led the conflicting parties to believe that if UN was not favoring their side, it was also certainly not acting against them. These considerations created neutral trust of non-punishment of UN in the eyes of the conflicting sides and allowed Sahnoun to start negotiating efforts with Aideed and Ali Mahdi. When additional tasks were added to its mandate envisaging peace-enforcement and peace-building efforts requiring substantial resources and their resolute usage, UNOSOM II failed. Its enlarged mandate ordered the peacekeepers to use "enforcement measures to establish throughout Somalia a secure environment for humanitarian assistance."[16] As soon the interveners launched large-scale attacks on Aideed leading to increased own casualties and collateral damage of the civilian population, this positioned UN not only as an actor with its own agenda, but as a supporter of Mahdi. Their subsequent failure to capture Aideed instantly dropped all three types of trust to nil: Aideed was not afraid of credible punishment and neither did Mahdi trust UN's ability to fight with Aideed. Eventually, UNOSOM II failed due to the lack of sufficient power and political will to undertake mandated actions and to effectively impose peace through disarming the belligerents and, in some instances, even targeting their physical presence in the country. Its impartiality was ineffectively breached.

Failure of CIS intervention in Abkhazia shows how impartiality was destroyed by a single actor. From the very deployment of CIS troops, Georgia perceived them as biased towards Abkhazia. Georgians viewed Russia, as the only country in the purportedly multilateral peacekeeping force, as a partial actor. Their beliefs were strengthened whenever Russia opposed changing of the composition of the CIS PRF and inclusion of the military personnel from other CIS member-states. According to the Georgians, Russia, which formerly supported Abkhazia, now, as a inspirer, guarantor and the only keeper of peace agreement in CIS intervention, could not have due credibility as a disinterested actor. With Russian presence as the only member of the CIS peacekeeping force, its unilateral bias was transferred to the multilateral organizational framework. This move violated the whole notion of transparency of multilateral interventions: by mistrusting Russia Georgians started mistrusting CIS as a whole. Instead of accepting the options offered by multilateral intervention as impartial and credible (take the proposition of the Russian side to abolish economic blockade of Abkhazia and to start economic revival of the region),[17] Georgia rejected any options of multilateral intervention as

16 UNOSOM II Official Website [Online]. Available at: http://www.un.org/Depts/dpko/dpko/co_mission/unosom2mandate.html [accessed: May 7, 2009].

17 *Rossiiskii Posol Sovetuet Gruzii Podderjat Reshenie RF po Abkhazii* [The Russian ambassador advises Georgia to support the decision of the Russian Federation on Abkhazia]

illegitimate. The fact that Russia, a former unilateral intervener, now participated in the multilateral intervention, and, even more so, was the sole representative of the "community of states" increased perceptional bias of its actions and was an important factor that limited overall success of CIS intervention.

Compositional parity

Another factor associated with an increased likelihood of success of multilateral interventions and directly related to impartiality and institutionalization of intervention is power parity among the coalition members, i.e. such a composition of multilateral coalitions where partner-states have equal power standings on international arena without a superpower or regional powerful among their ranks. At first glance this may sound counterintuitive: the common logic would dictate that the more combined military power of multilateral interveners, the more effectively they can impose different options onto the belligerents. However, when going into the depth of the compositional peculiarities, misbalance in power parameters of coalition members becomes associated with failures of interventions. Since multilateral interventions represent joint actions of more than one state, it would be important to know what role their internal power games play in their overall success.

Two aspects support the thesis of importance of compositional parity: durability of interventions and trust of the warring factions. The first appeals to the third parties' ability to jointly perform tasks, to pursue common goals, to stay in the coalition and to exit the conflict scene when the goals have been reached. The second relates to the positive reception by the belligerents of the options offered by the interveners.

Generally speaking, composition of multilateral interventions can be of two types: the one with comparative power parity among coalition members with more or less equal power standings and military and economic inputs to their combined intervention power; and the other with power disparity, where a coalition includes states with different levels of economic and military development and participation in the intervention. The level of countries' development and power on international arena in absolute terms does not matter in this particular case since even the most advanced and powerful states can have limited participation in the multilateral coalition. On the other hand, lesser developed countries can put considerable military and economic efforts to make their interventions successful. In the matter of achieving defined targets and objectives, as well as for the overall durability of intervention, the more homogeneous a coalition (i.e. the greater parity there is between the coalition members), the less shaky and unstable the union of states, and the more it is likely to achieve success in its actions.

The RIA Novosti News Agency. 2008 [Online, March 7]. Available at http://www.rian.ru/politics/20080307/100910127.html [accessed: May 8, 2009].

On the contrary, when multilateral intervention in pursuit of its operational objectives depends on a single, even the most powerful state, this means operational overdependence of the coalition on that particular country. Too much reliance on one participant would make multilateral intervention coalition highly vulnerable to external pressure to and domestic disturbances of that particular state. Once this powerful actor decides to exit the conflict scene, every one will follow: the remaining coalition members will no longer be able to carry the intervention burden. Since the durability of the coalition, among other things, is measured by the ability to withhold pressure (both from inside the coalition as well as from outside), if the lead actor for some reason leaves the coalition, this would mean an end to the intervention itself.

Taking into account the factor of trust of the belligerents to the intervention, the stronger actor in coalition does play a more decisive role in the decision-making within the third party. It has more economic resources allocated for the purposes of the intervention; more and better trained personnel and military equipment made available for the intervention's activities; and, naturally, demands more "say" among other members. The more capacities a country brings in, the greater its role in the coalition and the more it can affect the decisions to be followed by other members. Due to its increased inputs, the actor that has higher decision-making power and prevailing advantage in economic and military factors over the remaining coalition members would strife to take a lead role in the final verdict on the coalition's decisions, thus, skewing them in its favor. This is when the impartiality of multilateral coalition is internally jeopardized.

In a coalition with power disparity, the biased vision of distribution of benefits – who shall be winner and loser in the conflict – of a powerful state prevails over the visions of others. Rather than producing a joint outcome, the "melting pot" no longer exists and the product of intra-coalition negotiations reflects the "flavor" of a powerful state making the outcome of the multilateral intervention unilateral in essence. Options of the third party reflect the views and aspirations of the lead actor more than the visions of the others. Instead of equalizing individual biases of coalition partners and producing a joint bias of all, such multilateral interventions suffer from a skewed bias of one lead actor. Bring in a unilateral substance would "fake" multilateral form of intervention. The coalition, thus, will aim for a certain outcome of the conflict that reflects the preferences of the potent state, who may favor one belligerent group over the other. "Fake" multilateral interventions will no longer be considered impartial by the conflicting parties who would have lesser positive, negative or neutral trust towards them.

When there is a general equality between the member-states, the belligerents would trust their actions more since they would know that no one is affecting coalition decisions in a unilateral fashion. The "true" multilateral interventions will be homogenous in their power standings of their individual members; enjoy more consent over the nature of the options presented, offered or imposed on the antagonists; and be more durable under the pressure of different contingencies. In case of exit of one member from the coalition, the others will be able to carry on their mandated tasks since there will be no excessive dependence on a singe actor responsible for overall success of the intervention mission.

In multilateral interventions conducted under the aegis of international organizations, such as the UN or NATO, credibility of equal rewards and punishments for the belligerents is safeguarded by the organization organizations image, as well as separate coalition members. From this prospective, even if the presence of a powerful actor jeopardizes the idea of multilateralism and signals to the warring parties that the intervention is "fake" multilateral, rigid organizational frameworks still equalize operational disparity of its components. However, there are instances when organizational settings are still neglected and a single strong actor decreases the level of credibility of the organization in the eyes of the conflicting parties, who view such interventions as biased by definition.

The issue of compositional parity becomes more important in multilateral interventions organized by the likeminded states without organizational backing. Participants of such coalitions orchestrate interventions; have the initiative and encourage others to join. The "initiators" that are in the hearts of interventions will, thus, have more "say" in coalitions: they are the driving forces behind combined actions; the engines of the interventions, and select the partners that largely meet their visions. Those not necessarily agreeing with such unilateral vision of powerful states will have to accept it or leave the coalitions. Correspondingly, such interveners have low trust of the warring factions.

Going back to the statistical analysis of success of interventions, we can see that presence of a superpower is positively related to overall high probability of intervention success: 48.62 per cent for the unilateral and 87.70 per cent for multilateral interventions. However, the presence of an lead actor is more significant for the success of unilateral interventions. In multilateral actions, a superpower factor has only a 3 per cent effect, raising intervention success from 84.37 per cent to 87.70 per cent, which is quite insignificant.

In Somalia, Rwanda and Abkhazia, the effect of compositional parity over the performance of the multilateral interventions is quite evident. Very significant from this respect is the UN intervention in Somalia, which shows how excessive reliance upon a single actor in a coalition is counterproductive to its success. From the beginning, UNOSOM depended very much on the US presence in the UNITAF. At that time the activities of the UNOSOM I were limited to monitoring the implementation of peace agreement, and the blue helmets were not mandated to enforce peace among the belligerents. The body of UNITAF, as an operational wing of the UN intervention, was composed of 24 nations, among which were such highly developed states as Canada, the United Kingdom, France, Germany, Belgium, New Zealand, Sweden, Turkey, and United Arab Emirates. Within its ranks composition disparity was striking – out of the 37,000 total personnel of UNITAF, the US contribution was 28,000 soldiers, or 75 per cent.[18]

18 UNOSOM I Official Webpage [Online]. Available at: http://www.un.org/Depts/DPKO/Missions/unosomi.htm [accessed: May 8, 2009].

When UNITAF handed over its tasks to UNOSOM II in March 1993, US, thus, became the major player in the multilateral intervention assuming not only the lead role, but also the responsibility for provision of the majority of the intervention's resources. There was a clear gap between US inputs and those of other member countries, which were severely undermanned and underequipped. With its own vision, goals and agenda for the intervention, US created a set of tasks and actions for the multilateral intervention that turned out to be impossible to achieve. The incident of October 3-4, 1993 marked the beginning of the end of US involvement in Somalia. Failure of US to capture Aideed, deaths of its 18 soldiers and destruction of military equipment rendered a severe blow to the Clinton administration's ambitious goals to assert its predominant role in the international arena and was capitalized on by opposition at home.

As soon as the decision for American retreat was made, the remaining states found themselves in capable of continuing the operations within current intervention format. Without excessive contribution of US to the coalition's power, UNOSOM II failed to fulfill its ambitious and large-scale multi-dimensional mandate of peace enforcement and conflict settlement. In less than 3 months after the incident, the UN intervention had actually returned to the tasks that UNOSOM I had succeeded in fulfilling. Former credibility to UN as a potent punisher was already gone and negative trust of the domestic factions toward the UN process had been ruined.

The UN intervention in Rwanda was different in all aspects, including the compositional parity. UNAMIR had the total of 5,442 military staff, international observers, police officers, and local civilians from 21 states, including such advanced countries as Canada, Belgium, and militarily developed Russia. Contributions from majority of states were spread in such a way that made the mission equally dependent on all the participants. For instance, Canada had sent 376 troops, Ethiopia – 805, Ghana – 829, India – 326, Malawi – 170, Mali – 200, Nigeria – 338, Zambia – 455.[19] Even the withdrawal of Belgium from the coalition after assassination of its 10 peacekeepers had not jeopardized the overall mission. While their retreat decreased the total capacities of UNAMIR by 30 per cent, such a downsizing had not undermined the success of the intervention because, unlike in Somalia, its remaining manpower and equipment were enough for pursuit of the limited tasks.

CIS intervention was also different from the multilateral interventions studied in the book in the sense that it was undertaken completely by one state. Russia provided its personnel, equipment and political backing at the Summits of the Heads of the CIS states. The level of trust to CIS PKF from the Georgian side was equal to zero: not only did they remember Russia's actions during the active conflict phase, but also they were suspicious of any processes underway on the territory under control of PKF. The peacekeeping mission represented a relatively easy task since the sides were separated by PKF; however, peace-building efforts

19 UNAMIR Official Webpage [Online]. Available at: http://www.un.org/Depts/DPKO/Missions/unamir_b.htm [accessed: May 8, 2009].

were irreversibly ruined by a single potent state with negative history of interaction with one of the antagonists. Georgians would not entrust to PKF the return of kin-refugees in the region where impartial oversight was absent. Russia, being a lone actor in the "fake" multilateral intervention, was able to exercise its will on the territory it held without proper control from the part of the international community, which had mandated the intervention.

Late interventions

The final factor in the success of multilateral interventions is timing of entry to the conflict scene. Unlike in unilateral interventions, a crucial factor for success of the multilateral intervention is to enter the conflict scene late, when the casualties are insignificant or absent, there are no or low combat activities, and, ideally, there is a ceasefire agreement in place. Key considerations supporting the late intervention variable are the multilateral nature of the composition of the interveners and the inter-coalition settings.

Due to a lengthy process of coalition building, multilateral interventions take place usually only after a conflict has already reached a certain level of severity and casualties. Multilateral coalitions by international organizations are tied up by internal rules and institutional procedures, which would extend intervention deliberations in time. This is especially true for a decision-making process within larger organizational settings, such as the UN Security Council, which is further slowed down by possible blocking from states with veto power. Non-organizational interventions also take some time to negotiate with states to bring them into coalitions and to arrange for gathering of troops and equipment.

Intervening during the heat of hostilities is connected with a high risk of casualties of the interveners. A country, participating in an intervention coalition, apart from its vital national interests, has to project third party image on international arena – as a peacemaker and a strong punitive force – as well as domestically as a potent state. Decisions on interventions are usually made after careful cost-and-benefit calculation of coalition members at home. In addition to the high level of casualties, intervening from the very beginning usually requires using one's domestic economic resources. In multilateral interventions, the length of this process is multiplied by the number of coalition members. Multilateral interventions, hence, tend to be "clumsier" than single states both in pre-intervention decision-making process and in operational deployment. The possible way to act quickly is to issue an organizational mandate to a state willing to intervene alone but waiting for organizational blessing.

When the multilateral actor decides to intervene after the end of hostilities, it has higher chances to build a coalition for the intervention due to that fact that the resources needed for intervention and expected casualties will be much lower than when the intervention comes at the beginning or middle of hostilities. Furthermore, countries would be much more willing to join the coalition and bring in their own inputs – manpower, equipment, airlift, supplies – when they see the limited inputs that would not be endangered. This would assist the coalition-building process and would be a facilitating factor for their ultimate success.

Late interventions have other rationales as well. After a period of high heat of war, the parties that failed to achieve a decisive victory over their rivals would be more inclined to use a third party to help them conclude agreements. This could happen partly due to domestic pressures from people fearing increased rate of casualties and devastation. Also, the belligerents might need some respite from warfare and consequently would be more willing to accept an outsider's help: as Doyle and Sambanis (2000) put it, "the parties grow tired of fighting, and any prewar uncertainty about the probability of military victory or the parties' relative resolve is removed. Longer wars offer a chance for the parties to learn by reflecting on the benefits of peace and by controlling war-related hostility."[20] The sides might be more willing to accept a third party intervention as a face-saving exercise while conducting talks with their enemies or regrouping for a renewed offensive.

The relevance of late interventions for multilateral coalitions is a matter of considerable interest to both policy-makers and scholars. Diehl et al. (1996), who examined third party actions statistically, are overall pessimistic about their success, but claim that multilateral operations intervening after the end of hostilities "tend to freeze the status quo and inhibit change as well as remove some of the pressure on the disputants to make concessions and settle the dispute."[21] Regan (2002) also concluded that the probability of success of interventions decreases with the increase of the number of casualties.[22] The fewer casualties the coalition suffers, the longer its members will be willing to remain in the coalition, which is generally a positive factor for its durability. This means that the member-states are willing to stay together to carry out common tasks, which would strengthen the intervention actions.

Interventions studied in the book revealed a higher level of success when conducted after the actual end of war, when the coalition personnel was less likely be direct or unintended targets of the warring factions. In Rwanda, UN intervened after conclusion of the Arusha Agreement when the war level was low, and, therefore, was not involved in active peace-enforcement associated with high rate of fatalities for interveners. UN casualties in this case were very limited due to no active fight between the antagonists and only included collaterals to the conflict (the Belgians blue helmets had not participated in the fights and were lightly-armed and had not shown any resistance to the *Interahamwe* who had captured them).

---

20 Doyle, M.W. and Sambanis, N. 2000. International Peacebuilding: A Theoretical and Quantitative Analysis. *American Political Science Review*, 94(4), 785.

21 Diehl P.F., Reifchneider J. and Hensel P.R. 1996. United Nations Intervention and Recurring Conflict. *International Organization*, 50(4), 687.

22 Regan, P.M. 2002. *Civil Wars and Foreign Powers – Outside Intervention in Intrastate Conflict*. University of Michigan Press.

Conflict in Somalia was different with respect to the UN involvement. Initially UN was quite successful in monitoring the ceasefire agreement between Aideed and Ali Mahdi and to provide humanitarian assistance, the tasks performed by light or non-armed UN security personnel not participating in inter-faction fights. When, due to the worsening of the situation, UN enlarged its activities and extended its mandate to "preventing any resumption of violence and, if necessary, taking appropriate action…maintaining control of the heavy weapons of the organized factions…[and] seizing the small arms of all unauthorized armed elements…"[23] this brought it into direct conflict with Aideed. The fatalities of the coalition members increased dramatically, the first to be hit was Pakistan and later US. The factor of casualties of the coalition members had a serious impact on the its ability to fulfill its tasks and their durability when the US abandoned it.

The experiences of the CIS PKF in Abkhazia stand as exceptions to these rules. In this conflict, the intervention variable of "timing" was insignificant from the point of view of success. There, the multilateral intervention was an extension of the unilateral actions of Russia, which was present from the very beginning of the conflict. Although established after the actual cessation of hostilities and the signing of the corresponding agreement in 1993, the CIS peacekeeping mission was nothing but the continuation of the Russian presence in the region.

23 UNOSOM II Official webpage [Online]. Available at: http://www.un.org/Depts/dpko/dpko/co_mission/unosom2mandate.html [accessed: May 8, 2009].

Conclusion

States alone and in coalitions intervene in the matters of other states for various reasons. Some want to use this opportunity for their own benefits, to spread their influence over the conflict territories, for example, while others seem to be purely altruistic. Interveners may have their own rationale while intervening or may be genuinely interested in acting as neutral and impartial arbiters and to undertake peacekeeping responsibility. States may still want to help stop bloodshed and assist countries in their post-conflict recovery or may be interested in extending the conflicts.

Notwithstanding the multiplicity of rationales for state interventions and their case-specific differences, the decision of one state to intervene in internal affairs of another is usually based on two considerations: positive cost-and-benefit calculation of the intervener to enter the conflict and its felt moral commitment vis-à-vis the belligerents. In both cases, outside actors are assessing the conflict situation in a target country from the point of view of the likelihood of success of their actions and, correspondingly, make decisions to intervene or to not.

In the first case, states evaluate the expected utility from intervention and the possible losses they could suffer. If the country leadership thinks it stands to benefit more that it stands to lose, it decides to intervene. This, however, does not mean that the state conducting rational situation assessment intervenes for purely mercantile reasons. State interests may also include deliberations of other actors: governments of the target countries, warring ethnic groups, neighboring states and international organizations.

With regard to the second set of motives, states also assess the situation – not through weighing hypothetical benefits or costs but in accordance with the norms, rules, morality and ideational settings they are themselves governed by. Here, states intervene if they view a particular situation in the target country as violating the principles on the basis of which their own domestic society or the institutional arrangements of which they are a part operate. They might intervene even if their cost-benefit calculus turns out to be negative: intervention will be conducted no matter what because the situation in a target country is morally intolerable to outside actors. Similarly, states might abstain from intervention in domestic affairs of other countries if they believe that the situation is within the realm of moral and ideational acceptability.

Interventions studies in the book had the following factors that contributed to their success and made possible their failures:

Table C.1 Success factors of intervention

Intervention	Success	Failure
Unilateral	Support to the stronger Operational superiority Early Intervention Externalization of intervention Institutionalization of intervention	Support to the weaker Operational parity or inferiority Late intervention Internalization of intervention
Multilateral	Impartial and neutral Late Intervention Institutionalization of interventions Compositional parity	Bias Early intervention Direct involvement in conflict Compositional disparity

The table above gives a roadmap for successful interventions. To sum up the findings: in order to be successful, unilateral actors should be effectively biased in their actions and use their operational superiority decisively for fulfillment of their agendas. Successful unilateral interventions provide support to the stronger side of the ethnic conflicts, which are usually but not always the governments of the target countries, thus minimizing operational costs and losses for themselves. Early interventions are more successful because they indicate to the warring parties the strong commitment of the outside actor to win by all means, even if casualties are expected. Unlike multilateral interveners who usually wait to be invited by the target state or deliberate until the conflict reaches a certain level of atrocities, unilateral actors may be hitting early, when the casualties are still not high and their inputs are more efficient because the opponents have not yet gained momentum in their attacks.

Support to the government increases the chances for success for the interveners and makes their actions more legitimate on the domestic and also international level. From the point of view of legitimacy of their actions, solitary interveners should seek institutionalized frameworks (agreements) that would allow for their official involvement and, like the mandate of multilateral interventions, delineate their further involvement in the conflicts. Agreements for outside support may include a description of cases requiring foreign aid and define the operational involvement of third parties. With the help of legal documents defining their actions sole interveners would justify their involvement to the people in the target countries, their own constituents and the larger international community and would "wrap up" their interventions into a veil of institutional support to their partner-governments.

A very important factor for success of unilateral interventions is their distancing from the belligerents and pursuing their own agendas without getting too much involved in domestic matters that might become a long-term engagement. Non-permanent presence of foreign troops on the territory of the target state would tie their actions to a specific situation rather than a specific actor. It will allow interveners to use their resources efficiently and to undertake actions where they believe they are more likely to succeed, while to refrain from those where they are likely to fail.

Unlike unilateral interveners, to succeed, the multilateral third parties should be impartial and neutral so as to gain acceptance from all the parties involved in the conflict; be conducted late in the course of the conflict in order to avoid direct military clashes with the belligerents and to save its personnel; its presence in the target country should be permanent and visible to the population; the legitimacy of its actions should be clearly stipulated in its international mandate; and operational longevity of the intervention should not depend overly on the actions of any of its members.

In multilateral intervention, commitment of the belligerents is diffused in a coalition of states, thus decreasing the possibility of hidden and biased commitment of any of its member to any conflicting side. Multilateral intervention become more impartial in their actions: the belligerents rest reassured that if they violate moral and legal principles, norms and rules of the institution (conventions, charters, statutes, etc.), they would be punished.

In the case of UN, its actions directed to restoring peace and stopping security threats are embedded in three articles of its Charter: Article 51 (collective self-defense), and Article 52 (peacekeeping) and Article 53 (enforcement of peace by regional organizations). The decision-making body is the Security Council, which determines "…the existence of any threat to the peace, breach of the peace, or act of aggression and shall make recommendations, or decide[s] what measures shall be taken…to maintain or restore international peace and security."[1] Organizational normative field of action sets the standards for enforcement, which do not depend on the nature of the violator, are neutral and impartial from the viewpoint of collective action, and make third party actions legitimate in the context of international law.

Compositional parity among the members of multilateral intervention also helps to overcome the problems of neutrality and impartiality of the members of multilateral coalitions and contributes to their acceptability by local communities. Since the coalition members bring along their own interests to the coalition, the stronger they are, the more likely they are to influence the organizational decision-making process and to put their own bias to the operations of the coalitions. Such players will bring their affective ties to the coalition: they are there because of the particular situational settings (own vital interests, neighbors, ethnic kinship, etc.). Lobbying of a strong coalition member would erode the notion of impartiality and jeopardize the main principles, norms and standards by which the organizations undertaking interventions have been created and operate, making it more situation-oriented. This would further undermine the main characteristic

1 Article 39, Chapter VII of the Charter of the United Nations. Available at http://www.un.org/aboutun/charter/ [accessed: April 24, 2008].

of a successful intervention – credible trust. On the contrary, compositional party among the intervening states, however, strengthens impartiality of the coalition: when the participants of multilateral coalitions are equal players, the functional impartiality of the intervention balances out the interests of the states of which it is composed.

Bibliography

Africa Confidential 28(8). 1987, April 15.

Anderson, E., Ross, W.T. Jr. and Weitz, B. 1996. *Commitment and Its Consequences*. American Agency System of Selling Insurance, INSEAD working paper, 96/42/MKT.

Areguin-Toft, I. 2001. How the Weak Win Wars: A Theory of Asymmetric Conflict. *International Security*, 26(1), 93-128.

Atkinson, R. 1994. The Raid That Went Wrong: How an Elite U.S. Force Failed in Somalia. *The Washington Post*, January 30, A1.

Azevedo, M. and Nnadozie, E.U. 1998. *Chad: A Nation In Search Of Its Future*. Westview Press.

Barth, F. 1969. *Ethnic Groups and Boundaries: the Social Organization of Culture Difference*. Bergen/Oslo: Universitetsforlaget.

Bates, B. 1984. *Encounter in the Nile: The Fashoda Incident on 1898*. London: Oxford University Press.

Bloomfield, D. 1995. Towards Complementarity in Conflict Management: Resolution and Settlement in Northern Ireland. *Journal of Peace Research*, 32(2), 151-164.

Bogaturov, A.D. (ed.) 2006. *Sistemnaya Istoriya Mejdunarodnix Otnoshenii* [The System History of International Relations]. M.: Kulturnaya Revoluciya, 278-279.

Bolton, J. 1994. Wrong Turn in Somalia, *Foreign Affairs*, 73(1).

Bowden, M. 1999. *Black Hawk Down: A Story of Modern War*. Atlantic Monthly Press. Berkeley, California, US.

Brecher, M. and Wilkenfeld, J. 2000. *A Study of Crisis Data Project*. University of Michigan Press.

Brubaker, R. 1994. Nationhood and National Question in the Soviet Union and Post-Soviet Eurasia: An Institutional Account. *Theory and Society*, 23(1), 47-78.

Carment, D. and Harvey, F. 2001. *Using Force to Prevent Ethnic Violence: An Evaluation of Theory and Evidence*. Westport, Connecticut, London: Preager Studies on Ethnic and National Identities in Politics. Praeger.

Carment, D. and Rowlands, D. 1998. Three's Company: Evaluating Third-Party Intervention in Intrastate Conflict, *The Journal of Conflict Resolution*, 42(5), 572-599.

Chaigneau, P. 1984. *La Politique militaire de la France en Afrique*. Paris, 1984.

Chapelle, J. 1980. *Le Peuple Tchadien*. Paris: Hartman, 1980, reprint in *World Almanac* (1993). New York: Press Publication Company.

Chopra, J., Eknes, A. and Nordboe, T. 1995. *Fighting for Hope in Somalia*. Oslo: Norsk Utenrikspolitisk Institutt.

Collier, P. and Hoeffler, A. 2000. Greed and Grievance in Civil War. *CSAE WPS/2002-01.*

Contini, P. 1969. *The Somali Republic: An Experiment in Legal Integration*. London: Frank Cass.

Cornell, S.E. 1999. The Devaluation of The Concept of Autonomy: National Minorities in The Former Soviet Union. *Central Asian* Survey, 18(2), 185-196.

Cornell, S.E. 2001. *Small Nations and Great Powers: A Study of Ethnopolitical Conflict in the Caucasus*. Curzon Press.

Cornell, S.E. 2002. Autonomy as a Source of Conflict: Caucasian Conflicts in Theoretical Perspective. *World Politics*, 54(2), 245-276.

Destexhe, A. 1995. *Rwanda and Genocide in the Twentieth Century*. New York: New York University Press.

Diehl, P.F. 1993. *International Peacekeeping*. Johns Hopkins University Press.

Diehl, P.F., Reifchneider, J. and Hensel P.R. 1996. United Nations Intervention and Recurring Conflict. *International Organization*, 50(4), 683-700.

Doyle, M. and Sambanis, N. 2000. International Peacebuilding: A Theoretical and Quantitative Analysis. *The American Political Science Review*, 94 (4), 779-801.

Drysdale, J. 1997. Foreign Military Intervention in Somalia: The Root Cause of the Shift from UN Peacekeeping to Peacemaking and its Consequences, in *Learning from Somalia: The Lessons of Armed Humanitarian Intervention*, edited by W. Clarke and J. Herbst. Westview Press.

Dubey, A. 2002. *Domestic Institutions and the Duration of Civil War Settlements*. Paper to the Annual Meeting of the International Studies Association, New Orleans.

Eckerson, W.W. 2006. *Performance Dashboards: Measuring, Monitoring, and Managing Your Business*. Hoboken, New Jersey: John Wiley and Sons, Inc.

Edelstein, D.M. 2004. Occupational Hazards: Why Military Occupations Succeed or Fail, *International Security*, 29(1), 49-91.

Elbadawi, I. and Sambanis, N. 2001. How Much War Will We See? Estimating the Incidence of Civil War in 161 Countries. *World Bank Policy Research Working Paper*.

Fearon, J.D. 1998. Commitment Problems and the Spread of Ethnic Conflict, in *The International Spread of Ethnic Conflict*, edited by D.A. Lake and D. Rotchild. Princeton: Princeton University Press.

Fenwick, C.G. 1945. Intervention: Individual and Collective. *The American Journal of International Law*, 39(4), 645-663.

Field, A. 2000. *Discovering Statistics using SPSS for Windows: Advanced Techniques for the Beginner*. London: Sage Publications.

Fortna, V.P. 2004. Does Peacekeeping Keep Peace? International Intervention and the Duration of Peace After Civil War. *International Studies Quarterly*, 48, 269-292.

Franceschini, F. 2007. *Management by Measurement: Designing Key Indicators and Performance Measurement Systems*. Springer-Verlag Berlin, Heidelberg.

Franche, D. 1996. There's Only One Ethnic Group in Rwanda: Rwandan. *Le Monde Diplomatique/Guardian Weekly*, November 24.

Galtung, J. 1965. Institutionalized Conflict Resolution: A Theoretical Paradigm. *Journal of Peace Research*, 2(4), 348-397.

George, A. 1979. Case Studies and Theory Development: The Method of Structured, Focused Comparison, in *Diplomacy: New Approaches in History, Theory and Policy*, edited by P.G. Lauren. New York: Free Press, 43-68.

Gilkes, P. 1993. From Peace-Keeping to Peace Enforcement: The Somalia Precedent. *Middle East Reporter, Despots and Democrats Political Change in Arabia*, 185, 21-24.

Goldberg, S. 1994. *Pride of Small Nations: The Caucasus and Post-Soviet Disorder*. London and New Jersey: Zed Books Ltd.

Gourevitch, P. 2000. *We Wish To Inform You That Tomorrow We Will Be Killed With Our Families*. Picador: Macmillan Publishers Ltd.

Hall, M.J.H. 1989. *Handbook of Banking Regulation and Supervision*. New York and London: Woodhead Faulkner.

Hartzell, C.A. 1999. Explaining the Stability of Negotiated Settlements to Intrastate Wars. *The Journal of Conflict Resolution*, 43(1), 3-22.

Hartzell, C.A., Hoddie, M. and Rothchild, D. 2001. Stabilizing the Peace After Civil War. *International Organization*, 55(1), 183-208.

Henderson, E.A. and Singer, D.J. 2000. Civil War in the Post-Colonial World, 1946-92. *Journal of Peace Research*, 37(3), 275-299.

Hertzig, E. 1999. *The New Caucasus: Armenia, Azerbaijan and Georgia*. London: Pinter Publishers.

Hiernaux, J. 1974. *The People of Africa*. New York: Charles Scribner's Sons.

Horowitz, S. 2004. Identities Unbound: Escalating Ethnic Conflict in post-Soviet Azerbaijan, Georgia, Moldova, and Tajikistan, in *Ethnic Conflict and International Politics*, edited by S.E. Lobell and P. Mauceri. Palgrave Macmillan.

Issa-Salwe, A.M. 1994. *The Collapse of the Somali State*. Monograph. Published by the Author in association with HAAN Associated. London.

Jenne, E.K. 1990. A Bargaining Theory of Minority Demands: Explaining the Dog that Didn't Bite in 1990 Yugoslavia, *International Studies Quarterly*, 48(4), 729-754.

Jenne, E.K. 2003. Sri Lanka: a Fragmented State, in *State Failure and State Weakness in a Time of Terror*, edited by R.I. Rotberg. Washington, D.C.: Brooking Institution Press.

Jenne, E.K., Saideman, S.M. and Lowe, W. 2007. Separatism as a Bargaining Posture: The Role of Leverage in Minority Radicalization. *Journal of Peace Research*, 44(5), 539-558.

Jost, J.T. and Banaji, M.R. 1994. The Role of Stereotyping in System-justification and the Production of False Consciousness. *British Journal of Social Psychology*, 33, 1-27.

Kagame, P. Interview. *The Newsweek,* International edition, April 1, 1996 CXXVII/12:54.

Kakwenzire, J. and Kamukama, D. 2000. The Development and Consolidation of Extremist Forces in Rwanda 1990-1994, in *The Path of a Genocide: The Rwanda Crisis from Uganda to* Zaire, edited by A. Howard and S. Astri. Transactions Publishing.

Kaufman, C. 1996. Possible and Impossible Solutions to Ethnic Civil War. *International Security*, 20(4), 136-175.

Kaufman, S. 1996. Spiraling to Ethnic War: Elites, Masses, and Moscow in Moldova's Civil War. *International Security*, 21(2), 108-138.

Keohane, R.O. and Nye, J. 1977. *Power and Interdependence: World Politics in Transition*. Boston, Little and Brown.

Klinghoffer, A.J. 1998. *The International Dimensions of Genocide in Rwanda.* New York: New York University Press.

Kuperman, A.J. 2001. *The Limits of Humanitarian Intervention. Genocide in Rwanda*. Washington, D.C.: The Brookings Institution Press.

Laitin, D.D. and Samatar, S.S. 1987. *Somalia: Nation in Search of a State.* Boulder, Colorado: Westview Press.

Lake, D. A. and Rothchild, D. 1996. Containing Fear: The Origins and Management of Ethnic Conflict. *International Security*, 21(2), 41-75.

Lawler, E.J., Ford, R. and Large, M.D. 1999. Unilateral Initiatives as a Conflict Resolution Strategy. *Social Psychology Quarterly*, 62(3), 240-256.

Lederach, J.P. and Stork, J. 1993. The Intervention in Somalia: What Should Have Happened: An Interview with John Paul Lederach. *Middle East Report, Radical Movements: Migrants, Workers and Refugees*, 181.

Lemarchand, R. 1970. *Rwanda and Burundi*. New York: Preager.

Levin, S., Sidanius, J., Rabinowitz, J.L. and Federico, C. 1998. Ethnic Identity, Legitimizing Ideologies, and Social Status: A Matter of Ideological Asymmetry. *Political Psychology*, 19(2), 373-404.

Lezhava, G. (ed.) 1997. Mejdu Gruziei i Rossiei: Istoricheskie Korni I Sovremennie Faktori Abkhazsko-Gruzinskogo Konflikta (XIX-XX gg.) [Between Georgia and Russia: Historic Roots and Modern Factors of the Abkhazian-Georgian Conflict (XIX-XX)]. Moskva: UNMO.

Licklider, R. 1995. The Consequences of Negotiated Settlements in Civil Wards, 1945-1993. *The American Political Science Review*, 89(3), 681-690.

Lijphart, A. 2004. Constitutional Design for Divided Societies, *Journal of Democracy*, 15(2), 96-109.

Mack, A. 1975. Why Big Nations Lose Small Wars: The Politics of Asymmetric Conflict. *World Politics*, 27(2), 175-200.

Mamdani, M. 2001. *When Victims Become Killers: Colonialism, Nativism, and the Genocide in Rwanda*. Princeton University Press.

Mayorov, B.M. 2007. *Mirotvorci: iz Opita Rossiiskoi Diplomatii v Posrednichestve* [Peacekeepers. From the mediation experience of the Russian diplomacy]. M.: Moskva: Mejdunarodnie Otnosheniya.

Melady, T.P. 1974. *Burundi: The Tragic Years*. Maryknoll, N.Y.: Orbis.

Melvern, L. 2000. *A People Betrayed. The Role of the West in Rwanda's Genocide*. London: Zed Books.

Menkhaus, K. 1997. International Peacebuilding and the Dynamics of Local and National Reconciliation in Somalia, in *Learning from Somalia: The Lessons of Armed Humanitarian Intervention*, edited by W. Clarke and J. Herbst. Westview Press.

Miller, B. 1992. Explaining Great Power Cooperation in Conflict Management. *World Politics*, 45(1), 1-46.

Morrison, D.G., Mitchell, R.C. and Paden, J.N. 1989. *Understanding Black Africa: Data and Analysis of Social Change and Nation-Building*. New York: Paragon House and Irvington.

Mullenbach, M.J. 2005. Deciding to Keep Peace: An Analysis of International Influences on the Establishment of Third-Party Peacekeeping Missions. *International Studies Quarterly*, 49, 529-555.

Nolutshungu, S.C. 1996. *Limits of Anarchy: Intervention and State Formation in Chad*. University Press of Virginia.

Omar, R. and de Waal, A. 1995. *Rwanda: Death, Despair and Defiance*. London: African Rights.

O'Neill, J.T. and Rees, N. 2005. *United National Peacekeeping in the Post-Cold War Era*. New York: Routledge.

Ottaway, D. 1987. The US May Send Chad Some Stingers. *The Washington Post*, September 17, A36.

Pampel, F.C. 2000. *Logistic Regression: A Primer*, Sage Publications; Series: Quantitative Applications in the Social Sciences, 7-132.

Parmenter, D. 2007. *Key Performance Indicators (KPI): Developing, Implementing, and Using Winning KPIs*. Hoboken, New Jersey: John Wiley and Sons, Inc.

Perlez, J. 1992. Witnesses Report a Somali Massacre before U.S. Arrival. *The New York Times*, December 29, A1.

Posen, B.R. 1993. The Security Dilemma and Ethnic Conflict, in *Ethnic Conflict and International* Security, edited by M.E. Brown, Princeton University Press.

Pottier, J. 2002. *Re-Imaging Rwanda: Conflict, Survival and Disinformation in the Late Twentieth Century*. London: Cambridge University Press.

Prunier, G. 1995. *The Rwanda Crisis: History of a Genocide, 1959-1994*. London: Hurst and Co.

Pryaxin, V.F. 2002. *Regionalnie Konflikti na Post-Sovetskm Prostranstve. Abkhazia, Yujnaya Osetia, Nagornii Karabakh, Pridnestrov'e, Tajikistan* [Regional Conflicts on the Post-Soviet Space. Abkahzia, South Ossetia, Mountainous Karabakh, Transdniestia, Tajikistan], Moscow: Publishing House GNOM and D.

Putnam, R.D. 1998. Diplomacy and Domestic Politics: The Logic of Two-Level Game. *International Organization*, 42(3), 427-460.

Regan, P.M. 1996. Conditions of Successful Third-party Interventions in Intrastate Conflicts. *The Journal of Conflict Resolution*, 40(2), 336-359.

Regan, P.M. 1998. Choosing to Intervene: Outside Interventions in Internal Conflicts. *The Journal of Politics*, 60(3), 754-779.

Regan, P.M. 2002. *Civil Wars and Foreign Powers – Outside Intervention in Intrastate Conflict*. University of Michigan Press.

Robbins, R.H. (1999, 2002). *Global Problems and the Culture of Capitalism.* Allyn and Bacon.

Roe, P. 1999. The Intrastate Security Dilemma: Ethnic Conflict as a Tragedy? *The Journal of Peace Research*, 36(2), 183-202.

Rosenau, J.N. 1969. Intervention as a Scientific Concept. *The Journal of Conflict Resolution*, 13(2), 149-171.

Ross, M.H. 2001. Psychocultural Interpretations and Dramas: Identity Dynamics in Ethnic Conflict. *Political Psychology*, 22(1), 157-178.

Ross, M. 2006. Mineral Wealth and Equitable Development, *Equity and Development*, World Bank Development Report, Background Papers.

Rwanda: Who is Killing, Who is Dying, What is to be Done. African Rights Report. 1994. London.

Sanders, E.R. 1969. The Hamitic Hypothesis: Its Origin and Functions in Time Perspective. *Journal of African History*, 10(4).

Segal, A. 1964. Rwanda: The Underlying Causes, *Africa Report*, 9(4).

Sellstom, T. and Wohlgemuth, L. 1997. *The International Response to Conflict and Genocide: Lessons from Rwanda Experience. Study 1, Historical Perspective: Some Explanatory Factors*. Uppsala, Sweden: The Nordic Africa Institute.

Shoumatoff, A. 1992. Rwanda's Aristocratic Guerrillas. *New York Times Magazine*, December 13.

Smith, J. 2001. *The K.P.I. Book: The Ultimate Guide to Understanding the Key Performance Indicators of Your Business.* Insight Training and Development Limited.

Snyder, J. and Jarvis, R. 1999. Civil War and the Security Dilemma, in *Civil Wars, Insecurity, and Intervention*, edited by B. Walter and J. Snyder. New York: Columbia University Press.

Sokolov, A.V. 1997. *Mirotvorcheskaya Aktivnost I Mirotvorcheskie Sili Rossii v SNG* [Peacekeeping and Peacekeeping forces of Russia in CIS], in *Restructuring the Global Military Sector, Volume 1: New Wars*, edited by M. Kaldor and B. Vashee. London and Washington: Pinter [Online].

Somalia. Human Rights Abuses by the UN Forces. 1993. African Rights Report. London.

Suny, R.G. 1989. *The Making of the Georgian Nation*. London: I.B. Tauris.

Suny, R.G. 1993. *The Revenge of the Past: Nationalism Revolution, and the Collapse of the Soviet Union*. Stanford University Press.

van Beurden, J. 2000. *Somalia: From Permanent Conflict to More Peacefulness? Searching the Peace in Africa*. European Center for Conflict Prevention. European Center for Conflict Prevention.

Theiler, T. 2003. Societal Security and Social Psychology. *Review of International Studies*, 29, 249-268.

Thompson, V. and Adloff, R. 1981. *Conflict in Chad, Research Series – Institute of International Studies, #45* (University of California, Berkeley).

Varshney, A. 2003. Nationalism, Ethnic Conflict, and Rationality. *Perspectives on Politics*, 1(1), 85-99.

von Clausewitz, C. 1873. *On War*. The complete translation by Colonel J.J. Graham. N. Trübner, London, 1873.

Walter, B.F. 1997. The Critical Barrier to Civil War Settlement. *International Organization*, 51(3), 335-364.

Wolfers, A. 1962. *Discord and Collaboration: Essays on International Politics*. Baltimore: The Johns Hopkins Press, 3-35.

World Bank 2005. *Conflict In Somalia: Drivers and Dynamics*. (http://siteresources.worldbank.org/INTSOMALIA/Resources/conflictinsomalia.pdf).

Zdravomislov, A.G. 1997. *Mejnacionalnie Konflikti v Post-Sovetskom Prostranstve* [Inter-ethnic Conflicts in Post-Soviet Space] Moskva: Aspekt Press.

Zverev, A. 1996. Ethnic Conflicts in the Caucasus 1988-1994, in *Contested Borders in The Caucasus*, edited by B. Coppieters. Brussels: Vubpress.

Organizational/Governmental Sources

Cambridge Advanced Learner's Dictionary (http://dictionary.cambridge.org).

Failed States Index, Fund for Peace (http://www.fundforpeace.org/).

Human Rights Watch (http://www.hrw.org).

Information Agency "Gazeta.Ru" (http://www.gazeta.ru).

Information Agency Ria Novosti (http://www.rian.ru).

Information Bulletin "Demoscop", Institute of Demography, State University – High School of Economics (http://demoscope.ru).

International Commission on Intervention and State Sovereignty (http://www.iciss.ca).

International Court of Justice (http://www.icj-cij.org/).

Library of Congress, Federal Research Division, Country Studies (http://www.country-data.com).

Ministry of Foreign Affairs of Russia (http://www.mid.ru).

UCDP/PRIO Armed Conflict dataset v.4-2008 (http://www.pcr.uu.se/research/UCDP/data_and_publications/datasets.htm).

UN Department of Peacekeeping Operations (http://www.un.org/Depts/dpko/dpko/home.shtml).

UNAMIR, United Nations Assistance Mission in Rwanda, 1996, Department of Public Information, United Nations (http://www.un.org/Depts/DPKO/Missions/unamir_b.htm).

UNOMIG, United Nations Observer Mission in Georgia, 1996, Department of Public Information, United Nations (http://www.un.org/Depts/dpko/missions/unomig/background.html).

UNOSOM I, United Nations Operation in Somalia I, 1997, Department of Public Information, United Nations (http://www.un.org/Depts/DPKO/Missions/unosomi.htm).

UNOSOM II, United Nations Operation in Somalia II, 1997, Department of Public Information, United Nations (http://www.un.org/Depts/DPKO/Missions/unosom2b.htm).

University of Southern California, School of International Relations (http://www.usc.edu/dept/LAS/ir/cews/database/Rwanda/rwanda.doc).

List of Documents

Accords et Conventions de Maintien de l'Ordre dans les etats Africains et Malgashes [Agreement and Conventions to Maintain Order in African Malagasy States] 1966-1967. United Nations Treaty Collection.

Agreement of Ceasefire and Separation of Forces, Abkhazia. May 14, 1994, UNOMIG.

Agreement Concerning Technical Military Assistance between the French Republic and the Republic of Chad. 1960. United Nations Treaty Collection.

Agreement on Cultural Co-Operation between the Government of the French Republic and the Government of the Republic of Chad. 1976. United Nations Treaty Collection.

Agreement on Technical Military Cooperation between the Government of the French Republic and the Government of the Republic of Chad. 1976. United Nations Treaty Collection.

Assistance Agreement between the French Republic and the Republic of Chad, 1960. United Nations Treaty Collection.

Decision on Adoption of the Statute of Collective Peacekeeping Forces in the Commonwealth of Independent States. January 19, 1996. Uniform Registry of Legal Acts and Other Documents of the Commonwealth of Independent States.

Decision of The Council of The CIS Heads of States on Usage of Collective Forces to Maintain Peace in The Conflict Zone of Georgian-Abkhaz Conflict. August 22, 1994. Office of the State Minister of Georgia for Reintegration.

Defence Agreement between the French Republic, the Central African Republic, the Republic Of The Congo And the Republic Of Chad. 1960. United Nations Treaty Collection.

Rossiya-Gruziya Itogovii Dokument Moskovskoi Vstrechi 3 Sentyabrya 1992 Goda [Russia-Georgia. Final Document of the Moscow Meeting on 3 September 1992].

Soglashenie Mejdu Pravitelstvom Rossiiskoi Federacii i Pravitelstvom Respubliki Gruziya o Regulirovanii Processa Pereseleniyha I Zashite Prav Pereselencev (Zaklucheno v g. Tbilisi 03.02.1994) [Agreement Between the Government of the Russian Federation and the Government of the Republic of Georgia on Regulating the Process of Re-settlement and Protection of the Rights of Displaced Persons (Concluded in Tbilisi, 03.02.1994)].

Treaty of Friendship and Alliance between the Socialist People's Libyan Arab Jamahiriya and the Republic of Chad. 1980. United Nations Treaty Collection.

The UN Security Council Resolutions #733, 751, 775, 794. 1992, New York, United Nations (http://www.un.org/documents/sc/res/1992/scres92.htm).

The UN Security Council Resolutions #814, 846, 872. 1993, New York, United Nations (http://www.un.org/Docs/scres/1993/scres93.htm).

The UN Security Council Resolutions #912, 918, 929. 1994, New York, United Nations (http://www.un.org/Docs/scres/1994/scres94.htm).

The United Nations, Charter of, 1945, New York, United Nations (http://www.un.org/aboutun/charter/).

Index